THE HENRY L. STIMSON LECTURES SERIES

# The Chessboard and the Web

## Strategies of Connection in a Networked World

ANNE-MARIE SLAUGHTER

### Yale
UNIVERSITY PRESS
*New Haven and London*

The Henry L. Stimson Lectures at the Whitney and Betty MacMillan Center for International and Area Studies at Yale.

Yale University Press books may be purchased in quantity for educational, business, or promotional use.For information, please e-mail sales.press@ yale.edu (U.S. office) or sales@yaleup.co.uk (U.K. office).

Set in Janson and Van Dijck types by IDS Infotech Ltd.
Printed in the United States of America.

Library of Congress Control Number: 2016951588
ISBN 978-0-300-21564-9 (hardcover: alk. paper)

A catalogue record for this book is available from the British Library.

This paper meets the requirements of ANSI/NISO Z39.48-1992 (Permanence of Paper).

10 9 8 7 6 5 4 3 2 1

*To my parents, Ned and Anne Slaughter*

# Contents

CONTENTS

# Introduction

IN June 2015, China and forty-nine other nations created the Asian Infrastructure Investment Bank, or AIIB. The United States had urged all its allies not to participate because it saw the AIIB as competition for the Asian Development Bank, which it had created in 1966 along with a cluster of European nations, Australia, New Zealand, Taiwan, Japan, India, and others. That the AIIB got off the ground was widely seen as a diplomatic fiasco for the United States.

The bank was an effort by the Chinese government to create its own international financial institutions as alternatives to the Bretton Woods institutions—the International Monetary Fund and the World Bank—set up by the United States and Western European nations after World War II. Ironically, President Obama fought hard to increase China's share of the vote in the IMF and World Bank, only to be blocked by his own Congress.

The same Western European nations that participated in the Bretton Woods agreements were the first to defect from the U.S. position on the AIIB. British Prime Minister David Cameron announced in March 2015 that Great Britain had important trading relations with China and would subscribe as one of AIIB's founding members. Germany, France, and Italy followed suit, as did Australia, New Zealand, and South Korea. Only Japan and Canada held back.

In the traditional terms of geopolitical competition, China 1, United States 0. Unfortunately, that frame of reference is what led the U.S. government to the wrong stance toward the AIIB in the first place. What if it had taken a different perspective from the outset? What if it had started from the proposition that more investment in infrastructure, wherever it comes from, is a positive development for the people affected and for regional and ultimately global economic growth? The starting point here is not competition between states but the well-being of citizens globally. The United States should still have been concerned that AIIB funds might be invested in ways that would benefit corrupt governments much more than their citizens, something the World Bank has plenty of experience with. The United States might rightly want to influence the development of the AIIB's rules and practices.

If the goal were having the most influence over the AIIB's development to benefit the people of Asia, the United States would have pursued a very different strategy. Influence requires connection; the denser the web of relationships, the greater the influence. From this perspective, the United States should have *encouraged* its allies and friends to sign up for the AIIB. We would then have had more insight into the bank's workings and much more ability to influence our friends to influence its development. This kind of indirect influence is often more effective than if we had joined the bank ourselves as a counterbalance to China.

The same blinders were at work, far more tragically, in our policy toward the Syrian civil war. From a state-centered geopolitical perspective, President Obama was perfectly justified back in 2011 when he concluded, as Secretary of State James Baker said of the war in the Balkans in 1992, "We don't have a dog in that fight." Following the short-lived Arab Spring, when the shooting started after six months of peaceful protests by Syrian civilians, and through the winter and spring of 2012, when the Syrian government under Bashar al-Assad sought to crush its opposition by the most brutal methods, the United States could reasonably conclude that the situation did not imperil Israel, Saudi Arabia, or Turkey, our principal allies in the region, and so did not directly affect U.S. geopolitical interests.

So the administration undertook a series of half-hearted and ultimately ineffectual measures aimed at trying to identify, unify, and bolster the Syrian opposition, although not in a way that gave them any chance against the Syrian army, or against the much better-financed and -equipped radical Islamist groups that ultimately became Jabhat al-Nusra and ISIS. The threat of ISIS, once it emerged, finally justified the use of air power in a way that even Assad's use of chemical weapons and barrel bombs on his own people had not. But we directed this weaponry only against ISIS itself, not against the Syrian army. As of this writing, Russia and Iran are emerging as the clear geopolitical winners in Syria; U.S. allies in the region, other than Israel, are troubled by what they see as American weakness. Still, in strict geopolitical terms, the United States could reasonably conclude that its political, diplomatic, and military resources were better deployed elsewhere.

Yet from another perspective, the stakes of the Arab Spring for the millions of people who took to the streets across the Middle East and North Africa could not have been higher. This region, which has given us endless war and global terrorism of a kind that intrudes ever more insidiously into our daily lives, suffers from slow, repressive, unresponsive government that cannot deliver hope and opportunity to its young, restive populations. Its people are historically connected by a common language, history, culture, and religion—and connected today via cell phones and social media, instantly galvanized by pictures of demonstrations and decapitations, and collectively moved by endless narratives of human suffering. The atrocities of the Assad regime, which to date has killed half a million of its own people and created the greatest refugee crisis since the Second World War, are an open wound in the middle of the Arab world.

Taking this connected human factor into account, the massacre of Syrian civilians with barrel bombs, chemical weapons, and starvation is not just a humanitarian issue but a strategic one as well. People subjected to such horrors have only two options: to fight or to flee. Those who have chosen to fight are watching American planes take to the air only to bomb ISIS installations, not to protect their family members from barrel bombs. They and the millions watching across the Middle East will conclude that our fine words about democracy and human rights are just that. They will turn their allegiance to whoever claims to offer protection and vengeance—precisely the fanatics we seek to defeat.

Those who have chosen to flee include an estimated eleven million people—more than half the Syrian population—who are now either refugees or internally displaced. At least a million have fled to Europe, and more will follow. Those rivers of humanity are now roiling European politics, fueling the rise of right-wing parties across Europe and a vote in Britain to leave the European Union. The coming apart of Great Britain and the EU, and possibly of the United Kingdom itself, *is* an issue of geopolitical concern. The United States does have a dog in that fight.

The answers in Syria are not easy. We cannot fight other people's wars or stop all the world's atrocities. In a deeply interconnected world, however, the people themselves—not just their governments—are actors on the world stage. Their fate must become part of the strategic calculus that foreign policy makers consider. Hindsight is always clearer than the blurry and murky landscape of actual decision. But what foreign policy makers today lack is not simple foresight. It is an entire way of seeing and understanding the real world we live in.

## THE CHESSBOARD AND THE WEB

Statesmen and foreign policy experts have long been taught to view the world as a chessboard, analyzing the decisions of powerful states and anticipating rival states' reactions in an endless game of strategic advantage. Nineteenth-century British and Russian statesmen openly embraced this metaphor, calling their rivalry in central Asia "the Great Game."[1] The theoretical basis for interstate bargaining, spelled out in 1960 by Thomas Schelling in *The Strategy of Conflict*, is game theory. Half a century later, *Game of Thrones* offers us a particularly gory and irresistible version of geopolitics as a deadly, subtle, and endless competition among contending kingdoms.

Henry Kissinger is the reigning grandmaster of this game—the Metternich or Bismarck of the twentieth century, who executed bold, transformative moves such as the 1972 opening to China.[2] Kissinger himself has broadened the metaphor, distinguishing between American and Chinese foreign policy strategists by pointing out that Americans play chess and the Chinese play *wei qi*, or Go. Wei qi "implies a concept of strategic encirclement" and "generates strategic flexibility," whereas chess "is about total victory" and "produces single-mindedness."[3]

The chessboard is such a dominant metaphor for seeing and understanding the world of states that Joseph Nye has described the more complicated world of post–Cold War global politics as a "complex three-dimensional chess game."[4] The top board is the U.S.-dominated game of military power; the middle is the multipolar world of economic power; and the bottom is the diffuse realm of nonstate actors. Diplomats and foreign policy decision makers now play multiple games at once, and as we shall see, not all of those games are chess. Still, the players remain locked in a competition to advance their nation's interests, sometimes alongside those of other nations, but more often at their expense.

The chessboard view of 190-odd competing states—as well as the much smaller numbers that are players in any given bilateral, regional, or global game—remains accurate and relevant much of the time. But it is not the only view, and seeing the world only through a chessboard lens obscures another equally important and relevant landscape.

Think of a standard map of the world, such as might have hung in your fifth-grade classroom, showing the borders and capitals of all the countries. That is a chessboard view. Now think of a map of the world at night, with the lit-up bursts of cities and highly concentrated regions and the dark swaths of rural areas and wilderness. Those corridors of light mark roads, cars, houses, and offices; they mark the networks of human relationships where families and workers and travelers come together.

That is the web view. It is a map not of separation, marking off boundaries of sovereign power, but of connection, of the density and intensity of ties across boundaries. To see the international system as a web is to see a world not of states but of networks, intersecting and closely overlapping in some places and more strung out in others. It is the world not only of terrorists but of global trade, both licit and illicit; of drugs, arms, and human trafficking; of climate change and declining biodiversity; of water wars and food insecurity; of corruption, money-laundering, and tax evasion; of pandemic disease carried by air, sea, and land. In short, it is the world of many of the most pressing twenty-first-century global threats. That ever-changing map is the frontier of our age.

In 1996, the sociologist Manuel Castells published *The Rise of the Network Society*, the first of what became a three-volume series entitled *The Information Age: Economy, Society, and Culture*.[5] Still in the early days of the Internet, Castells saw already that almost every traditionally vertically integrated domain of human activity was being reorganized along horizontal lines. Digital technology was shrinking the world in ways that allowed anyone to communicate information to and from anywhere instantaneously, bypassing traditional hierarchies and channels of authority. Just as the technology of mass production reshaped the social organization of the agricultural age, Castells argued, information technology will reshape every domain of society.

Networks ignore national borders. Castells saw the network society constituting itself "as a global system" that would enable globalization.[6] A year after Castells began his exploration, in 1997, Geoff Mulgan, then a top adviser to British Prime Minister Tony Blair, published *Connexity: How to Live in a Connected World*. Mulgan argued that the growing connectedness of the world was "the most important social and economic fact of our times" and that it rendered woefully inadequate the traditional analysis of the world as composed of discrete and separate entities.[7]

The second half of the 1990s was a time of great optimism about both globalization and networks. Nearly two decades on, another prophet has entered the lists, with an equally sweeping but decidedly more pessimistic view. Joshua Cooper Ramo, co-CEO and vice chairman of Kissinger Associates, takes the title of his brilliant book *The Seventh Sense: Power, Fortune, and Survival in the Age of Networks* from Friedrich Nietzsche. Nietzsche thought humans needed, as a "sixth sense," a feeling for the rhythms of history in order to appreciate the full scope of the changes the Industrial Age was bringing to every aspect of life. Today, Ramo argues, we need a "seventh sense" to navigate "our new age of constant connection . . . to the whole world of networks that surrounds and defines us everywhere." The seventh sense "is the ability to look at any object and see the way in which it is changed by connection." *Everything* will be connected—"our bodies, our cities, our ideas"—in ways that are already compressing time and space, empowering a "new caste" of network masters, and creating new topologies of virtual space that shape our lives every bit as much as the physical topologies we now inhabit.[8] If we fail to grasp the magnitude and consequences of connection, Ramo writes, we risk not seeing and preparing for a coming apocalypse, just as the industrial titans of the first Gilded Age failed to imagine the horrors of industrialized warfare.

It is undoubtedly true that the connections we see around us now are only the beginning of the Networked Age. When all humanity is connected beneath the surface like the giant colonies of aspen trees in Colorado that are actually all one organism, and when we can create neural networks that whirl far faster than our own brains can comprehend, much less match, many very bad things could happen. But I begin from the simple observation that foreign policy makers, at least, are still looking through the lenses of the seventeenth-century world, when the Peace of Westphalia created the framework of sovereign and equal states that forms the basis of international law, international politics, international business and trade—and even the very word "international." Whatever the future brings, we need the ability and the tools to operate effectively in a very different world, where states still exist and exercise power, but side by side with corporate, civic, and criminal actors enmeshed in a web of networks.

## A TWENTY-FIRST-CENTURY TOOLBOX

Thomas Schelling published *The Strategy of Conflict* in 1960, at the most dangerous point of the Cold War. The United States and the Soviet Union were fighting over Cuba, where Fidel Castro had just won his revolution; the failed U.S. invasion at the Bay of Pigs in April 1961 would be followed by the Cuban Missile Crisis a year and a half later, in which the world came terrifyingly close to a nuclear holocaust. Schelling's great contribution, for which he later won the Nobel Prize in economics, was to transform what appeared to be perpetual conflict between the United States and the Soviet Union into a series of bargaining games in which a common interest could often be identified and achieved.

*The Strategy of Conflict* showed scholars and policy makers that the apparent zero-sum, battle-to-the-death frozen war with the Soviet Union was actually a field of competition in which some positive-sum outcomes were possible. The trick was to figure out, across many issues and events, which game the two superpowers were playing at any particular moment. Schelling laid out three basic games: the deterrence game of chicken, the coordination game of stag hunt, and the cooperation game of prisoner's dilemma.[9] Though surprisingly complicated to play, these games are simple to describe.

- Chicken: two drivers head straight at each other, each trying to deter the other from staying the course.

- Stag hunt: two hunters choose to go after either a hare on their own or a stag together. The best outcome for both players is to get a stag, but if one defects and hunts a hare, the other goes hungry. Each player chooses without knowing the choice of the other.
- Prisoner's dilemma: two prisoners are jointly accused of a crime and interrogated in separate rooms; each can either implicate the other or stay silent. The best outcome is for both to stay silent—then they will get the lightest sentence—but the dominant strategy for each player is to implicate the other.

Once the game was identified, policy makers could then pursue the strategy most likely to advance their interests.

Following in Schelling's footsteps, Robert Axelrod published *The Evolution of Cooperation*, testing different strategies for transforming a prisoner's dilemma from a game both players were likely to lose to one in which they could reach a cooperative outcome. Tit-for-tat, the winning entry in a contest among computer algorithms for the best strategy, was a fairly simple entry: in a game of multiple rounds, a player cooperated on the first round and from then on did whatever its opponent had done on the previous round. It never beat its opponent but never lost by more than one move. The strategy allowed two players to reach an outcome that was second-best for each of them but better than what either was likely to obtain from any other strategy.[10] These kinds of games and strategies have formed the basis of our thinking about international relations for decades.

But for many of our most pressing problems today, none of these games fits. The web world, the world of networks, has plenty of conflict and competition. But the modal web relationship—the most common and defining relationship—is connection. Problems and threats arise because we are too connected, not connected enough, or connected in the wrong ways to the wrong people or things. ISIS can motivate lone-wolf individuals to massacre their officemates. A deadly virus can spread across the globe in a week through airline hubs. A demand for ever cheaper goods manufactured across large and complex global supply chains feeds a demand for slave labor. On the other hand, the disconnection of millions of young people from the possibility of a decent education, a job, and a fulfilling life fuels rage and violence that spill across borders. Without positive connections to schools, jobs, families, and visions of their future, they connect to destructive causes that make them feel like part of a larger whole.

When the problem is connection, where are our strategies? These are not bargaining games. Networked threats require networked responses. More broadly, threats arising from people and patterns of behavior need responses that directly engage people and patterns of behavior. This means responses below the level of state action. In the chessboard world, the assumption is that statesmen can negotiate agreements that require states to exert control over their populations—to vaccinate their citizens, say, or to break up global criminal networks by arresting members on their territory. But often the problem is precisely that the government in question is corrupt, incompetent, or barely existent. Even well-intentioned and effective governments are often not close enough to the problem to solve it. This is why global cities, from New York to Jakarta, engage with one another after terrorist attacks to share information and develop protective strategies.

In all these cases, building a network—connecting people or institutions in specific ways for specific purposes—is a far better starting point than a strategy of deterrence, cooperation, or coordination with another government. It is also a much more systematic strategy than what government officials typically do today when they realize they must engage people, businesses, or institutions directly, which is to call a meeting. Conferences and summits are the tools of choice for everything from spurring global entrepreneurship to securing the rights of women. The hope is that one-time or annual meetings will spur attendees to action and will generate networks by fostering useful connections. Enormous effort goes into organizing and holding these meetings, far less into curating the attendees and nurturing the connections among them for specific action.

We have no playbook for strategies of connection, or for crafting the tools we need to implement them. To create it, we must turn to network theory as Schelling once turned to game theory. Different networks have different structures and properties for different purposes.

India, in 2012, suffered the worst blackout in history, leaving 670 million people without power. The root of the failure was inadequate supply to meet demand; but the reason it spread so widely across the country was that India's transmission grid was highly centralized. The entire network was dependent on a few key power generation stations. Taking out just a few crippled the entire system. A decentralized mesh would have performed much better.

Alternatively, consider the way a virus spreads, through a random but dense assortment of contacts that can be tracked and mapped as a network only after the fact. In the case of a rapidly spreading disease we use isolation and quarantines to disrupt the network. But when a meme "goes viral," we marvel that the same kinds of decentralized, ad hoc networks have the power to spread information swiftly and broadly. Knowing where the choke points or central hubs are in those networks *before* death or delight spreads across them is critical to strategies for both promoting and preventing dissemination.

Digital technology means we can map human networks in real time. Human connections via voice, keyboard, and face-to-face interactions, whether virtual or real, all leave digital signatures. If we make a time-lapse photograph of cars on city streets, we create trails of light that will quickly fill a metropolis, creating nodes and edges, brighter paths and dimmer ones. In theory—and subject to a new generation of privacy and security regulation—we can track all human activity, local to global, the same way, mapping who is connected to whom, when, and how. We simply need the strategies and tools to act on that knowledge once we have it.

## Network Pioneers

I do not mean to say that governments are ignorant of networks. As we will see throughout this book, a few farsighted people and departments are already implementing network strategies. Among the fastest-growing areas of global governance, as I wrote in *A New World Order* in 2004, are networks of ministers operating at the regional and global level, and networks of judges and occasionally legislators.[11] The United States is thinking about networks at the country level as well; to take one recent example, in June 2016 U.S. Defense Secretary Ash Carter called for the formation of a "principled security network" in the Asia-Pacific, aimed at building an inclusive, stable, rules-based order in the region.[12] The United States is encouraging Asia-Pacific militaries to train, exercise, plan, and eventually operate together, with the goal of connecting Southeast Asia and East Asia, from Australia to Japan, into a self-reliant, regional network not dependent on American power—turning what is right now a star network into a distributed mesh. Six years earlier, former U.S. SOUTHCOM commander Admiral James Stavridis argued for a similar approach in our own hemisphere, laying out a strategy for deepening and developing linkages among the Americas to improve security and prosperity.[13]

Below the level of the state, the U.S. military, the intelligence community, the homeland security community, and the global health community are all building networks of various kinds; I will draw on their examples throughout this book. National security officials are directly building counternetworks to combat terrorist and criminal networks; homeland security officials in particular work with thousands of state and local officials and must think in terms of how to connect large numbers of actors to get necessary information quickly but also to increase resilience. Indeed, Christopher Fussell, a fifteen-year veteran of Navy SEAL teams and an expert on networked warfare, observes: "The vast majority of our current system for considering and engaging in conflict is based on and biased by a nation state-centric optic. As these systems fail, the vacuum will continue to be filled by distributed networks with little recognition of the traditional rules of the game. It is our system, not theirs, that will need to adapt."[14]

Some diplomats are also working hard to master this new world. Matthew Barzun, who served as ambassador to Sweden during President Obama's first term and to the United Kingdom during his second term, came to government after a career as a technology executive. When I met with him in the U.S. embassy in London, I was delighted to see, right next to his grand ambassadorial office, a small office with the sign next to the door: "Office of Network Engagement." The office is dedicated to building sustained, meaningful connections with British citizens, industries, and groups in order to strengthen the special relationship. It is also a matchmaker, constantly identifying new contacts and partnership opportunities. Barzun has pioneered network building and engagement as core diplomatic work.

These are promising shoots of a new foreign policy. They offer early lessons, however, regarding what works and what doesn't. The United States—and other nations, such as China and those in Europe—are responding to the imperatives of an ever-more interconnected world. But no state is systematically adopting the strategies of connection I have in mind. What we see are ad hoc responses to the inexorable logic of the web not grounded in any deeper or more systematic strategic thinking.

## Grand Strategy

The imperative of thinking through strategies of connection and developing a toolbox to implement them is all the greater when we look at grand strategy. Grand strategy refers to how a state harnesses all its instruments of power—military, political, economic, cultural, technological, even moral—in harmony to further its prosperity and security.[15] Grand strategists on multiple continents are thinking in network terms, even if they have not thought systematically and scientifically about how to match their broad visions with their actual capabilities.

China has an explicitly networked grand strategy. My family lived in Shanghai for a year in 2007–2008, and I vividly remember the first time I saw airline maps depicted with China as the hub rather than the United States, with routes fanning out east and west to the Americas, Europe, the Middle East, and Africa. It was a striking representation of China's historic view of itself as the "Middle Kingdom" at the center of a vast web of tributary relations, the center of the universe in much the same way that medieval Western kingdoms imagined the Earth to be the center of our solar system.

Today China sees itself returning to its rightful place in the world. Its strategy is once again to weave a global web of commercial and political relations, described in terms of a new Silk Road of economic activity running through countries to its west and a "Maritime Silk Road" to South and Southeast Asia. As U.S. Naval Academy Professor Yong Deng describes it, China's "Silk Road strategy is based on open networks in Euro-Asia and maritime Asia strung together through Chinese-financed infrastructure and transportation projects, as well as trade and financial ties."[16] In other words, a world of networks in which all roads lead to Beijing.

The European Union is in many ways a collection of networks; its governing councils are networks of different ministers—transportation, finance, agriculture, justice, homeland security, and many more. Thus it is not surprising to see that the EU's new strategy focuses on how it can advance its interests in a networked world. In its 2016 Global Strategy for Foreign and Security Policy, the EU declares it "will act as an agenda-shaper, a connector, a coordinator and facilitator within a networked world." It calls for deepening partnerships with civil society, the private sector, regional orders, and global governance structures. It will pursue its priorities "by mobilizing [its] unparalleled networks."[17]

Similarly, the Liberal Party of Canada, now in government under Prime Minister Justin Trudeau, calls its foreign affairs approach the Global Networks Strategy and explicitly recognizes that "influence is gained through connectedness" because "networks define how the world works today."[18] The strategy's cornerstone is collaboration with other governments, nongovernmental organizations (NGOs), the private sector, and demographic niches ranging from Canada's youth and academia to faith-based groups and artists.

President Obama also articulated a web grand strategy in his first term, even if he didn't know it. In his first inaugural address, he spoke to nations that the United States had shunned for decades: "We will extend a hand, if you are willing to unclench your fist."[19] By the end of his presidency he had persuaded Myanmar, Cuba, and Iran to do just that, to varying degrees. He used traditional diplomatic means, sending small teams of diplomats to open secret talks, putting together the complicated agreements necessary to remove the deep historic impasses that had led to a severing or freezing of relations in the first place. In the case of Iran, that work is only partially done. Reaching an agreement to stop Iran's nuclear weapons program has at least opened the door to ending commercial and other sanctions the United States imposed decades ago, but the road to full relations is still long and difficult.

Those diplomatic agreements and the negotiations that precede them are core chessboard strategy and tactics. They are essential; it is impossible to weave a web of commercial, educational, cultural, and human relations without opening the door at the highest levels. But once that door is open, we need midrange strategies of connection to achieve those grander goals, as well as more sophisticated and systematic integration of both the chessboard and the web.

## FOREIGN POLICY INTERRUPTED

I belong to perhaps the last generation to do foreign policy the old-fashioned way.[20] I knew what I wanted for my career from high school onward. My mother is Belgian, my father American—I've always said I'm the product of an international affair—and I chose to attend law school thinking I would go to work for a big New York or DC law firm and then move in and out of government, as generations of top State Department appointees had traditionally done.

The fly in the ointment of my grand plan was that I really didn't *like* big-firm law practice. I became a law professor instead, teaching international law and international relations to generations of young men and women who also sought foreign policy careers. Unfortunately, as I tried to provide career advice, I would continually dampen my students' aspirations by telling them that although they could find plenty of legal work that would send them to foreign countries and require them to immerse themselves in foreign cultures, the actual practice of foreign policy—working with or against other nations to solve global problems—was limited to a small handful of government jobs.

Not anymore. One of the most exciting features of the web world is that the group of people making a real impact in discovering, formulating, and implementing solutions to global problems has expanded dramatically. Within the U.S. government alone, the Treasury Department, the Securities and Exchange Commission, the Justice Department, Homeland Security, the Centers for Disease Control, the Environmental Protection Agency, and many other agencies are all involved in foreign policy. Governors now lead trade and investment delegations to foreign countries. And many city officials are essentially practicing urban foreign policy, working with their counterparts in other cities across borders to address problems ranging from climate change to terrorism.

Out of government, many participants in the web world are also shaping it. Large foundations, universities, and civic organizations of all kinds are on the ground trying to tackle what used to be known as "development issues" or international problems such as climate change and global health.[21] MIT's D-Lab, for instance, stewards the Practical Impact Alliance, a network of private and public organizations such as Mercy Corps and Siemens that develop and implement business and technological solutions to global poverty.[22]

Bloomberg Philanthropies has played a leading role in creating and funding international climate change networks, most notably the Global Covenant of Mayors for Climate and Energy, which connects and mobilizes government and non-government actors in more than 7,100 cities across the world to reduce carbon emissions and mitigate the effects of climate change.[23] From the web perspective, these issues are foreign policy issues just as much as war and peace are. They involve people and institutions that are either disconnected from networks of opportunity and resources or are interconnected in ways that mean their behavior has negative global impact.

The private sector is also catching up. Mastercard's Center for Inclusive Growth believes the key to equitable and sustainable growth worldwide is to connect microenterprise entrepreneurs to "vital networks," such as financial service networks, peer networks, social networks, and human capital development networks.[24] When Jared Cohen, now president of Google Jigsaw, a geopolitical technology incubator, worked for me in the State Department, he used to reflect on how great it would be if corporations around the world all had policy planning staffs who could look at the big issues and trends in the world and think through strategies the same way governments do. Jigsaw was Google's way of implementing that idea and has created various products, such as a cyberattack shield for election monitors, human rights organizations, and independent news websites. Other corporations are following suit.

Many multinationals are also taking responsibility for environmental and human rights conditions in their global supply chains, signing on to a growing network of private-public partnerships and multilateral standards organizations that are adopting the U.N. Guiding Principles on Business and Human Rights.²⁵ Corporations ranging from Apple to Nike to Walmart now publish and, to varying degrees, enforce supplier codes of conduct. More and more businesses understand that in the web world, the state of health, education, opportunity, environmental conservation, and physical security in the communities and regions where they work is as much their problem as the government's problem.

In straight power terms, many large global corporations have greater market capitalization than the GDP of many small countries. Of the world's 175 largest nation-states and private firms, 112 are corporations.²⁶ Their CEOs are more important global players than most prime ministers and foreign ministers, at least for purposes that do not require a vote in the United Nations or other international or regional organizations. For example, ExxonMobil, the world's largest oil company, finances private armies, retains an elite foreign policy team of former diplomats and National Security Council officials, and in some nations wields as much influence as any government.²⁷ Even in situations where solving a problem does require a vote, governments of weaker nations rarely go against the position of concentrated business interests. And they often seek the support and help of developed country civic organizations in drafting resolutions and supporting their positions in international organizations.²⁸

Organizations like Care, Doctors Without Borders, and Amnesty International wield similar power on the global stage; they *are* much of the global humanitarian infrastructure. The meetings between leading public, corporate, and civic leaders that take place in New York at the Clinton Global Initiative, in parallel with the U.N. General Assembly meeting, or at the World Economic Forum meetings around the world, map the reality of power and influence of global actors. That map looks very different from the United Nations roster.

But the more this new world of international relations evolves, the greater the disconnect. Students and practitioners of foreign policy are not blind to its growth, but they have no formal way of integrating these actors into frameworks that are theoretically and legally structured only for states.[29] In universities and at the State Department, the web world's participants are called "non-state actors," which as Clay Shirky has pointed out is like calling a car a "horseless carriage."[30] Looking backward, we know what they are not. But looking forward, we have no affirmative vocabulary for what they *are*.

In the web world, they are foreign policy actors, full stop. They have the same identities they do in the domestic realm, as individuals, businesses, charities, civic organizations, criminal syndicates, universities, and all the other actors we recognize in our national space. In the web world, they are all, like government officials and agencies, equally capable of creating networks and operating as nodes within those networks.

## BOTH/AND

Hillary Clinton is a "both/and" politician. When I worked for her in the State Department, my staff and I would often write memoranda setting forth a choice of policy options. Often she would reject the choice, saying that the issue was not "either/or" but "both/and." Problems have multiple sources and multiple solutions; complex problems often need solutions from the right *and* the left, more government *and* more family and community, regulation *and* innovation.

In this book I present a both/and way of seeing and understanding the world. "The international system" and "global politics" are abstract conceptions, mental maps of what we imagine to be out there. The chessboard and the web are different options for constructing those maps, and they are not mutually exclusive. We can simultaneously engage in chessboard deterrence or bargaining with states like Russia, China, and Iran, and build networks engaging Russians, Chinese, and Iranian people and institutions.

We must learn to see in stereo. Humans and other primates have binocular vision: two eyes facing forward as opposed to one eye on either side of our head, like many mammals, which provides a much wider panorama of vision. With two eyes facing forward, each eye registers a slightly different version of the same object; the brain processes those differences and creates a three-dimensional image. Each eye perceives a different reality; together they create a richer and more accurate picture of the whole.[31] If we combine the chessboard and the web perspectives, we can see states as unitary actors competing and cooperating with other states and also as sites of many different networks spreading beyond their border but incorporating their citizens, corporations, civic, and criminal organizations.

We must learn to see all global events in terms of both the chessboard and the web. If you mention the year 1949, a chessboard-trained foreign policy expert will immediately know that that was the year the Washington Treaty was signed creating NATO, a Western alliance to counter the Soviet Union. A web-trained expert will more likely think of the Universal Declaration of Human Rights, the anchor for spreading webs of human dignity. Eleanor Roosevelt chaired the committee responsible for the Universal Declaration; in his film *The Roosevelts*, Ken Burns captures her response to Soviet U.N. delegate Andrey Vyshinsky, who demanded that more than one million asylum seekers from Eastern Europe be forced to return to states now under Soviet rule. She said, "The United Nations was created to safeguard the rights of individual human beings, not the prerogatives of governments."[32] A few frames earlier, author Jon Meacham is quoted describing Franklin Roosevelt at Yalta in perfect chess terms: Roosevelt, he says, "was always a practical politician" who "never believed in making the first move."

Both things happened; each captures an important part of international reality. The chessboard and the web: we must learn to integrate both perspectives into our vision, seeing states and people, nations and networks at the same time. We must understand, for instance, that when the United States proclaims its desire to stand up for universal values but then acts on strictly self-interested power calculations, we are likely to generate different reactions in the chessboard and web worlds. Government officials typically understand that hypocrisy is part of the currency of diplomacy. Most citizens do not; they register the gap between American words and deeds and often hate us for it, more than if we simply proclaimed an adherence to realpolitik.

When we can see a richer, more accurate, more three-dimensional world, we are able to develop strategies of connection as well as of conflict and competition. We will come to understand the rich variety of network structures and designs; we will learn to tailor network solutions to specific web problems. We will proceed by trial and error, of course, but at least we will have a starting point, a framework of analysis and a set of tools. That is what this book is for.

# PART I

## The World of the Web

CHAPTER ONE

# Of Great Powers and Globalization

M Y first encounter with the academic discipline of international relations was as a Princeton sophomore in the fall of 1977, enrolled in Politics 240, "An Introduction to International Relations" (a course my husband now teaches!). The professor teaching it then, the late Fouad Ajami, assigned a new book by two rising stars in the field, Joseph S. Nye and Robert O. Keohane, entitled *Power and Interdependence*. Like many undergraduates, I had no idea their theories were new; I took the book as eternal truth. It in fact became a classic, with a fourth edition published in 2011. Rereading it now, I can see that it describes precisely the worlds of the chessboard and the web.

Nye and Keohane juxtaposed two ideal types of world politics: the traditional realist world of power politics—"a struggle dominated by organized violence"—with the world of "complex interdependence."[1] In the realist (chessboard) vision of the international system, states are the "dominant actors" in world politics and act as "coherent units" or unitary actors; force is both usable and effective as a policy instrument; and military issues trump economic, social, and environmental issues in a strict foreign policy hierarchy. In the world of complex interdependence, by contrast, states share the global stage with transgovernmental and transnational actors; international politics comprises many kinds of issues with no clear hierarchy; and force is not a realistic option.

Complex interdependence does not describe the globalized world as a whole, only the most interconnected portion of it: relations among what today are the advanced industrial-digital democracies. In other words, "the West" plus Japan, South Korea, and a few islands of globalization such as Singapore, Hong Kong, and Bangalore. British diplomat Robert Cooper describes this deeply interconnected zone as a "postmodern system." Writing in 2003, he was referring primarily to the European Union but extended his framework to include Japan and the United States. Cooper also focused on the absence of force as a viable policy option among European states. He pushed farther than Keohane and Nye in emphasizing that Europe was witnessing a "breaking of nations," the emergence of an order in which "state sovereignty is no longer seen as an absolute," national "borders are increasingly irrelevant," and nations permit outside interference in their foreign and domestic affairs.[2] Challenges to the decades-long march of European integration emerged in the mid-2010s, with a resurgence of nationalism and border controls in some European countries and the United Kingdom's vote to leave the EU, but the European experiment is still the most ambitious effort to pool sovereignty the world has ever seen.

Complex interdependence is the extreme case of the web world. Keohane and Nye observed the density of networks among different government officials across Europe and the United States. Thirty years later, in *A New World Order,* I focused on the explosion of those networks—among regulators, judges, and to a lesser extent legislators—not only within the EU and between the EU and other mature liberal democracies, but more generally around the world. I argued that the complex of government networks—from the Basel Committee of Central Bankers to a global network of antitrust regulators to a listserv of supreme court judges worldwide—was laying the foundation for a complementary world order alongside official global institutions like the United Nations, the International Monetary Fund, and the World Trade Organization.

But if Keohane and Nye described the chessboard and the web forty years ago and generated an ongoing body of scholarship, why reintroduce those two basic models today? Because even though we know that states share the global stage with lots of other actors, foreign policy makers still focus primarily on state-based foreign policy tools. Robert Keohane in particular went on to lead an entire body of scholarship focused on how to design international institutions to bring about cooperative international solutions. Complex interdependence describes the web world, but it does not give us web strategies.

Other scholars have focused on networks as actors in their own right, but more from a descriptive than prescriptive point of view.[3] This literature comes from a wide range of fields: international relations scholars, political scientists, and international lawyers; scientists; and norm entrepreneurs. All have grown interested in the advantages and impact of networks relative to other kinds of international organization. A parallel body of work applies complexity theory to global politics, which we will visit at the end of this chapter.

## BEYOND THE CHESSBOARD

When Keohane and Nye wrote *Power and Interdependence,* they were taking on the dominant paradigm in international relations in the 1970s: structural realism. Their goal was to make a rigorous theoretical case for a world that was not condemned to endless rounds of zero-sum state conflict, but could instead support sustained cooperation among states with common interests in improving the lot of their citizens and solving global problems. They wanted to show that "military security" would not automatically be "the dominant goal" in these states' political interactions and that "military force" would not necessarily be the most effective instrument of state policy.[4] Writing in the midst of the Cold War, they needed to make the case that the world of complex interdependence could be a world of interstate cooperation rather than relentless conflict.

Political scientists are in the business of trying to figure out the underlying drivers of political behavior, which in international relations has traditionally meant state behavior. If states are black boxes seeking military security above all, they will be locked in permanent competition and conflict with other states. But if states are collections of different government actors, each embedded in a network of relations with their counterparts in other governments and subject to pressure by networked actors in their own societies, then they will have multiple goals in different issue areas and cooperation will be possible at least some of the time. The key question then, for Keohane and Nye, was what tools we needed to *get* to cooperative solutions. Their answer was international institutions, which would "set agendas, induce coalition-formation, and act as arenas for political action by weak states."[5]

In the 1980s and 1990s a debate raged between realists, whether "structural" or not, and a group of scholars, drawn more from political economy than international security, who came to be known as liberal institutionalists.[6] They tussled over the conditions under which states could be trusted to seek and stick with cooperative solutions in which everyone benefited and the conditions under which they would be more concerned with relative gains over one another.[7] The two camps also developed various models to take account of the impact of domestic politics on international outcomes.[8]

Andrew Moravcsik took liberal institutionalism one step deeper and developed a liberal theory of international relations that effectively merged the chessboard and the web. He argued that "state-society relations—the relationship of states to the domestic and transnational social context in which they are embedded—have a fundamental impact on state behavior in world politics."[9] Translated into lay terms, Moravcsik's point of departure is individuals and groups in domestic society who connect to their counterparts in other societies:

exactly the picture of the web. Moreover, he assumes that the "universal condition of world politics is *globalization*."[10] It is the web of globalized economic, social, and political relationships that determines the living conditions of individual citizens, corporations, and civic groups and shapes what they want and thus what their governments want.[11] (All governments, democracies and dictatorships alike, respond to the preferences of *some* interest groups.)

Let's not pretend, then, that the web is new. It is the lens through which many social scientists, businesses, and civic groups—not to mention criminals—already see the world. We will return to some of their work later in the book. That lens, however, still focuses on web actors as determinants of state behavior, not as global actors in their own right.

## NETWORKS TAKING CENTER STAGE

A small coterie of international lawyers and political scientists has begun to integrate network science and international politics. Political economist Miles Kahler collected some of this work in a 2009 edited volume entitled *Networked Politics*. In his words, "networks have become the intellectual centerpiece of our era" but are too often "a metaphor rather than an instrument of analysis."[12]

The volume's contributors study both "networks as structures," looking at how the structure of a network affects the nodes or actors within it, and "networks as actors," examining whether networked organizations are more effective than hierarchies or markets or simply have a different impact in the international system. They use social network analysis to map al Qaeda, explore the structure of Colombian drug trafficking networks, and examine the evolution and effectiveness of transnational advocacy networks like the debt cancellation movement Jubilee 2000. Other chapters in the book identify the informal networks that arise when states sign preferential trade agreements, and compare networked organizations like Amnesty International to their more hierarchical peers.[13]

The most important contribution of this work lies in the insights it provides into the nature of power within networks and exercised by networks, a subject I will return to in Chapter 7. Given that political scientists are students of power, this emphasis is not surprising, and it adds a healthy corrective to network studies by scholars in disciplines less attentive to power dynamics—work that I will describe in the next chapter. It also allows international relations scholars to test findings about individuals in networks—such as the enmity members of a clique typically express against nonmembers, or the likelihood that more centrally located members of a network are likely to be more aggressive—to see whether they hold up as predictors of state behavior.[14]

Scholars who have mastered the concepts and tools of social network analysis are just beginning to apply their methods to global politics. But work done to date already yields a number of insights. These include:

1. Network position and degree of connectedness can give participants bargaining power and social power that can offset inequalities of material power.[15] Small but highly connected nations, for instance, can maximize their power by brokering

their connections to nations that large nations are less connected to. Switzerland has exploited this advantage for centuries.

2. Some networks exhibit a "rich get richer" pattern, in which new nodes tend to attach to the hubs that already have the most connections. This tendency enhances the power of central norm entrepreneurs, enabling them to set advocacy agendas.[16]

3. Actors that can provide information about a network can enhance their position within the network.

4. Participation in some networks can influence participation in other networks. For instance, trade between two countries increases if they are members of the same intergovernmental organizations.[17]

5. Many successful networks, from al Qaeda to Amnesty International, are actually hybrids of hierarchy and network.

6. Networks with a strong central hub are more efficient than less centralized networks but less resilient and harder to scale.[18]

For scholars studying networks as actors in global governance, the central question is whether and when networked international organizations, regimes, or informal initiatives are more effective at solving international problems or achieving members' objectives than traditional international organizations. In *A New World Order* I argued that for global problem solving, transgovernmental networks of central bankers, government ministers, judges, and legislators were an essential complement to more traditional organizations like the United

Nations, the World Bank, or the IMF. The proliferation of these networks is a result of what I called "the disaggregation of the state," meaning that different parts of government were peeling away from the chessboard model of foreign policy directed by the head of state and the foreign ministry, and instead creating networks of both private and civic actors.

More fine-grained work in international law and international relations has parsed the value of transgovernmental networks in different issue areas.[19] Much of this work has concentrated on global regulatory processes. States neither want nor expect global government. Yet actors—from corporations to criminals to professionals of every description—increasingly act globally, crossing borders and regulatory jurisdictions with the click of a mouse. Unless agencies and judges, and increasingly legislators, cooperate or are at least aware of one another, they can create and enforce rules of behavior only for a piece of a much larger whole.[20] Understanding the way national governments and private organizations are actually making and trying to enforce rules will ultimately change the ways in which national and global policy makers approach public problem solving and will feed the evolution of a body of formal and informal global administrative law.

The work I will describe in this book ventures beyond the chessboard to look at web actors, global actors other than states. Relatively few studies have pushed beyond state networks to look at global networks of individuals, groups, and institutions. Part of the problem is the tension between "structure" and "agency." When we study the international system, we have to start somewhere, and it is easiest to analyze and predict the behavior of states as a function of some kind of international structure—whether that is the distribution of power as in a unipolar, bipolar, or multipolar system, a set of alliances, or membership in an international organization. Once you assume or identify the structure of the system, you can analyze and ultimately predict how agents—states—will act within that structure.

It's actually a chicken-and-egg problem. Agents create structures and structures shape the behavior of agents. Network analysis provides a number of tools for examining how agents behave, even when those agents are numerous. Starting with agents in networks opened up another set of possibilities for trying to explain global politics.

### GLOBAL EMERGENCE

Chaos theory seeks to describe deterministic, usually closed nonlinear systems in which very small changes can have very big effects. The example most commonly used is the "butterfly effect," the idea that the flap of a butterfly's wing can affect the course of a hurricane. This property and other insights from chaos have informed the burgeoning study of complexity and complex adaptive systems.[21] These systems have "a large number of mutually interacting parts, often open to their environment, [which] self-organize their internal structure and their dynamics with novel and sometimes surprising macroscopic ('emergent') properties."[22] Financial markets, the earth's climate, and the human brain are all complex adaptive systems.

A number of international relations scholars have been taken with the possibilities of understanding such systems using "agent-based modeling": essentially the idea that computer simulations make it possible to stipulate initial conditions for a set of agents—whether individuals, corporations, states, or other actors—and then to simulate what happens when these agents interact with one another over time. As the great theorist of cooperation Robert Axelrod puts it, "agent-based modeling is a way of doing thought experiments," changing the decision rules according to which large numbers of actors interact and adapt to one another, and then seeing what state of the world emerges.[23]

Zeev Maoz uses this methodology to model international relations as a "network of international networks."[24] The networks themselves are "emergent structures," meaning that they evolve and crystallize from the interactions of states adapting to one another's behavior over time. Other scholars who use this approach, however, do not focus on networks specifically. Axelrod has pioneered fascinating studies of how corporations set standards, how norms evolve and stabilize, how states choose sides, and how new political actors emerge.[25] Lars-Erik Cederman uses agent-based modeling to break apart states and nations, countering the tendency of international relations theorists to assume that nation-states are the default condition of the international system.[26] How did those states get there? Why have some nations succeeded in becoming states when others, like the Kurds, have not?

Understanding global politics as a complex adaptive system gives us a world of states as a system of moving parts, rather than as a (temporarily) static equilibrium like the Congress of Europe or the bipolar stalemate of the Cold War. Simulations can allow us to see how those equilibria emerge, just as complexity theory allows us to see how the interaction of many elements of an ecosystem, all influencing and adapting to one another, produces a result that could not have been predicted by tracking only one or a few of those elements.

This work intersects network science in several ways. The computer models used to analyze complex adaptive systems are often the same ones used to generate hypotheses about how networks form and grow; indeed, the systems themselves in complex adaptive systems are often referred to as complex networks. Alternatively, scholars who focus on networks in global politics define them as "emergent properties of persistent patterns of relations among agents that can define, enable, and constrain those agents."[27]

We need not focus on emergence in this book. It is more relevant to understand how different actors—whether states or individuals—are connected to other actors, how different patterns of connections form different types of networks, and how the position of specific actors within a network, together with the quantity and quality of their ties to other actors, determines power, influence, and the fragility of nodes within a network and of the network as a whole. Still, as policy makers actually begin to create networks as tools to accomplish various foreign policy goals, being able to model the growth and evolution of those networks as complex adaptive systems may be valuable for scenario planning.

### A POLICY TOOLBOX

We have established that the chessboard and the web are familiar models of the international system in the academy, even if I am giving them new names. Web actors, typically called nonstate actors—or sometimes, when they involve parts of governments, transgovernmental actors—are well recognized as drivers of state action, even if scholars disagree on precisely what the transmission belts are between what these actors want and what states actually do. And a small but growing number of scholars are researching different kinds of networks as global actors in their own right.

None of this literature, however, provides foreign policy makers with network tools to help them do their jobs, which is to say respond to a global crisis, affirmatively advance U.S. diplomatic, military, or commercial interests, or work with other global actors to solve common problems ranging from climate change to terrorism. Advice abounds on how to set up a global institution; literature on the intersection of domestic and international politics offers pointers on when and sometimes even how to try to build domestic political coalitions in support of international goals. But networks are never addressed as potential tools, to be designed, activated, and managed to achieve specific policy goals.

To create those tools, we need a different kind of science: the systematic study of networks themselves. The insights listed above are a start, but a far richer trove of scholarship on networks exists in multiple disciplines, from biology to physics to industrial organization. It is time to get granular about networks.

# CHAPTER TWO

# Networks Everywhere

UMAN networks are as old as human relationships: kinship networks, tribal networks, friend and family networks. The study of networks in the natural and social sciences has roughly accompanied the rise of the computer, a technology that derives most of its power from being connected to other computers, and that allows mathematicians, physicists, and economists to simulate, analyze, and predict network interactions.[1] Before they had the power to crunch massive amounts of data and perform vast numbers of computations, scholars could not study the connections among more than a small group of people. Today, the very technology that allows us to study networks—the global network of computers that we know as the Internet—has become the metaphor and emblem of the network age.

Network theory extends across a wide range of fields. It informs weighty tomes on mathematical graph theory and advanced game theory, neural maps of the human brain, and business books analyzing innovation and supply. In this chapter I survey the landscape, focusing on what the scholarship tells us about networks in the world around us, how they form, and how they behave. Most important, at the end of the chapter I talk about how immersion in networks leads us to a different view of human nature and a different understanding of motivations and incentives. Changing those embedded assumptions about how the world works, many of which we are not aware that we even hold, is critical to policy making.

## A DISCIPLINARY CORNUCOPIA

Most of us understand networks primarily as a way that humans organize themselves. When I try to think of an example of a network, the first one that always comes to my mind is "the old boys' network," the invisible club of powerful men that allows them to extend their power by influencing one another to hire and promote their respective protégés, donate to their respective causes, and build a web of reciprocal favors and debts that allows them collectively to rule an organization, an industry, or a society. At least, that is the way many women see it! The network is a pattern of social relations.

Given that we have this intuitive understanding of social networks—among friends, acquaintances, neighbors, coworkers—it is not surprising that the study of networks arose first among psychologists, anthropologists, and sociologists.[2] It grew out of the study of how people connect to other people. Society can be mapped as an overlapping set of human networks, some of which are more densely connected than others.

In recent decades, the world has more and more resembled these maps. Think of the Internet: the name itself means a network of networks. They are networks of computers, all attached to people. These computers have the ability to amass enormous quantities of data and to find patterns and connections that allow us to map almost anything in terms of a set of nodes and links. A link, after all, is an ongoing connection between two things, or nodes.

Before the Internet, the word "link" meant both a physical object—a circle of metal connecting two other circles of metal—and an abstract concept describing the same kind of tie between two people or organizations or ideas. A human link was a relationship that could be identified as a function of interaction: whether two people knew each other, how often they met or contacted each other, how many and what kind of activities they engaged in together. Paradoxically, as these links became virtual, transforming into a set of ongoing electronic interactions, they became physical. We can actually *see* connections in real time. The digital trails that people (and increasingly things) create are visible links to other people and things.

Think about your Facebook page. All of us could have described our group or network of family, friends, and acquaintances based on our mental assessment of the people we are closest to and interact with the most. But now that network is visible as a set of tiny faces, avatars, and names on an electronic page that we have on our desks, carry around in our pockets, and spend a great deal of time on. We can now see and measure how much we actually interact. The sociologist's abstract representation of our relationships has sprung to electronic life in a virtual world that is increasingly the world we actually live in. Moreover, it has never been easier to connect with new people or organizations. Tap, click, connect.

Next time someone says that the world is more interconnected than ever before, imagine a map of the night sky, with lines drawn between stars and planets to show the shapes that humans long ago labeled constellations. Now imagine each of those stars and planets connected to others, all across the universe, with new connections appearing all the time. For natural and social scientists, the growth and nature of those networks offer a whole new constellation of interesting problems to solve. "Network science" is thus emerging as its own scientific subdiscipline, bringing together the insights of mathematicians, physicists, biologists, computer scientists, sociologists, and economists. It is related to but distinct from complexity theory, the study of how self-organized networks emerge from complex adaptive systems.

It is impossible to summarize or even survey all these bodies of work. But we can draw on them for principles and insights that will help us think about how to *create* networks for specific purposes. We can learn not only how to see the world in terms of networks but also how to operate more effectively within it.

## Friends and Acquaintances

Drawing on psychology, physics, and mathematics, sociologists have pioneered the use of "social network analysis" or SNA: a set of concepts and methods that allow us to identify who is connected to whom within a specific network, the density of their ties, the positive or negative nature of their relationships, their positions relative to one another and to the network as a whole, and the structures and properties of the networks themselves.[3] SNA is increasingly used by social media companies to measure influence, by businesses to map the structure of human relations in their companies not captured by the organization chart, and by scholars interested in how networks form, emerge, and evolve.[4] It maps the relationships between one individual and all his or her friends and acquaintances, or a complete set of relationships among a designated group of individuals.

The most basic concept of network analysis is the way of measuring who is connected to whom (or what to what), described by network theorists as a matter of "degree."[5] The degree of a particular node, Node A, is the number of direct connections it has to other nodes. Nodes that are directly connected to Node A are referred to as being in Node A's neighborhood. Node A's neighbors, however, typically have additional neighbors, which are connected to Node A as a matter not of first but of second degree. Node A's neighbors' neighbors then have neighbors of their own, which are Node A's third-degree connections, and so on. (This science inspired the Kevin Bacon parlor game Six Degrees of Separation, in which movie buffs try to connect any given actor to Bacon: Actor A was in Movie X with Actor B, who was in Movie Y with Actor C . . . and so on until they reach someone who acted alongside Bacon.) As sociologist-physician Nicholas Christakis and his coauthor political scientist James Fowler demonstrate, influence flows across networks up to three degrees away.[6] What your friends' friends' friends eat or do or think will influence what you eat or do or think—but further connections will not.

It is not just how many connections you have that matters, however, but also whether your connections are connected to one another. The most famous contribution of social network analysis to our daily lives came from an article written by sociologist Mark Granovetter long before SNA started relying on complex software packages and computer simulations. In "The Strength of Weak Ties," published in 1973, Granovetter showed that job seekers were more likely to find employment through people they knew only slightly than through the people they interacted with much more closely.[7]

The logic is that you and your friends are already connected to one another and to a larger group who probably possess the same general knowledge as you, including knowledge of job opportunities. People you know only slightly, however, belong to different social networks and are more likely to have information you do not. The strength of ties correlates with "network density," a property describing the connectedness and cohesiveness of a network.[8] A dense subnetwork within a larger network is called a cluster.

One branch of sociology measures the strength of ties across a society in terms of social capital, a concept that political scientist Robert Putnam made famous in his book *Bowling Alone.* He refers to "bridging capital" (weak, sparse ties) and "bonding capital" (strong, dense ties), observing that a strong society needs both kinds.[9] Weak ties can shorten intergroup "path length," the number of steps it takes to get from one node to another in the network, and bridge information gaps between different groups—what sociologist Ronald Burt dubbed structural holes.[10] Bonding capital can exist when groups exhibit "closure"—when each person is connected to every other, allowing for shared norms, effective monitoring, and mutual trust to take hold.[11]

In addition to the concepts of degree and density, another key insight emerging from the sociological study of networks is that of centrality, which measures how well connected and important a given node is in a network. There are four main types of centrality.

- Degree centrality is the most basic, which simply tells how many links a node has.
- Closeness centrality describes the average distance between a given node and all the other nodes in the network.
- Betweenness centrality measures a node's position between other nodes; a node with high between- ness centrality sits at the intersection of the shortest paths between other nodes, like a trading post at the confluence of two rivers or highways that everyone has to travel through to get somewhere else. Functionally, betweenness centrality "reflects the amount of control that [a] node exerts over the interactions" and flow of information among of other nodes in the network.[12]
- Eigenvector centrality measures the average degree of a node's neighbors. By this measure, the importance of a node hinges not on how many friends it has, but rather on how well connected those friends are.

We will return to these different concepts of centrality when we talk about power in networks in Chapter 7.

## Global Markets, Global Networks

Another branch of sociology, the sociology of organizations, blurs into industrial management and industrial relations. These scholars see networks as an organizational form. Over the past two decades this literature has been focused on the attributes and advantages of networks as compared with markets and hierarchies. Much of this work is descriptive, identifying and categorizing the properties of each form. For our purposes, the insights from this literature are valuable less in deciding how to design a network for a specific purpose than in figuring out when constructing a network is the most appropriate foreign policy tool in the first place.

In a famous 1990 paper, sociologist Walter Powell identified networks as an organizational form distinct from markets and hierarchies. Markets, Powell wrote, are characterized by "discrete" (one-off) transactions among independent, "disinterested" actors (who don't know each other). Hierarchies arise when transactions recur and require substantial investment. The transactions become routinized, governed by a central authority and dictated by rules. Networks, however, defy both categories: they are based on mutually beneficial, recurrent exchanges among flexible yet interdependent actors. Unlike markets, they enable long-term relationships, but they are also nimble enough to adapt to environmental ambiguity in a way that hierarchies cannot.[13]

The sociologist Manuel Castells, the chronicler of the Digital Age whom we met in the Introduction, built on Powell's theoretical analysis of the virtues of networks by applying it to the corporate world.[14] In his 1996 book *The Rise of the Network Society* he described how businesses were reacting to the demands of their new environment: intensely competitive global markets that required both massive scale and fast, flexible adaptation to rapid change. Their solution was to transform themselves from "vertical bureaucracies" into "horizontal corporations." Silos of top-down control became networks of "multifunctional decision-making centers": different units or indeed different businesses within the same corporation operating and interacting as equals in a decentralized structure but under a common strategic framework. Alongside this organizational transformation came new ways of collaborative production: cocreation, or what Don Tapscott and Anthony Williams call "peering."[15]

Consider Boeing, which shifted in the late 1990s and early 2000s from airplane manufacturer to "systems integrator," relying on a "broad horizontal network of partners who are collaborating in real-time, sharing risk and knowledge to achieve a higher level of performance."[16] Cisco Systems, by contrast, came of age in the digital world and organized itself from the beginning on a "global networked business model," meaning that every part of the organization is a network and the organization as a whole is a network of networks. For Castells, Cisco exemplifies an age in which "*networks are the fundamental stuff of which new organizations are and will be made*," just as hierarchies were the fundamental building blocks of Industrial Age organizations.[17]

Fifteen years later, the network-versus-hierarchy question has become standard fare in the business literature. The accounting and consulting firm PWC, for instance, proclaims that "the network business model is a system for the digital age."[18] Table 1 provides an excellent descriptive summary of

TABLE 1

Characteristics of Hierarchical Versus Networked
Organizations

| Hierarchies | Networks |
| --- | --- |
| • Centralized | • Distributed |
| • Fordism: workers perform specialized tasks over and over as part of defined sequence | • Flexible specialization: small-scale production teams simultaneously work on complementary projects |
| • Employee traits: deference to authority, obedience, conformity | • Employee traits: autonomy, adaptability, problem solving, collaboration |
| • Ties are strong but few | • Ties are loose but many |
| • Tasks, managers, and departments are organized by function | • Tasks, managers, and departments are organized by project |
| • Communication is vertical command through defined channels | • Communication is lateral as well as vertical consultation |
| • Management derives authority from title, rank, and seniority | • Management derives authority from expertise and contribution |
| • Job descriptions and areas of control are narrowly defined | • Job descriptions are broad and boundaries are permeable |
| • Transaction and payment are the glue of relationships | • Trust and reputation sustain relationships |

*(Continued)*

TABLE 1

*(Continued)*

| Hierarchies | Networks |
|---|---|
| • Slow to adapt, difficult to change | • Quick to adapt, easier to change |
| • Key decisions are centralized so coordination costs are low | • Decentralized decision making, so higher employee satisfaction and loyalty |
| • Performs well in stable, predictable environments | • Performs well in ambiguous environments that require efficiency and flexibility |

*Sources:* Walter Powell, "Neither Market nor Hierarchy: Network Forms of Organization," *Research in Organizational Behavior* 12 (1990): 295–336; Bruce Pietrykowski, "Beyond the Fordist/Post-Fordist Dichotomy: Working through *The Second Industrial Divide,*" *Review of Social Economy* 57, no. 2 (1999): 177–198; Duncan J. Watts, *Six Degrees: The Science of a Connected Age* (New York: Norton, 2003); Marshall Van Alstyne, "The State of Network Organization: A Survey in Three Frameworks," *Journal of Organizational Computing* (1997), available at http://ccs.mit.edu/papers/CCSWP192/CCSWP192.html; and PWC, "Hierarchy vs. Network—A New Business Model for Success?" 2014, http://www.digitalinnovation.pwc.com.au/hierarchy-vs-network-business-models/.

the differences between hierarchies and networks in terms of structure, properties, and employee attributes and relationships.

Some scholars see markets, networks, and hierarchies arrayed on a continuum, with markets and hierarchies at either pole and networks in between. An alternative version focuses not on how well people know each other but on the type and depth of their interaction. Market transactions take place on a one-time basis among strangers and are governed by law; network transactions are repetitive among individuals bound by the "alchemy of mutual give and take over time."[19] On this spectrum it is hierarchies that are in between: exchanges are repetitive and routine, as in a network, but depend on a "governing authority," as a market does.

Networks, at the far end of this spectrum, depend on the trust born of reciprocity. Corporate anthropologist Karen Stephenson argues that though trust is the natural glue of human connection since prehistoric times, it is mostly absent in modern hierarchies—especially in government, where vertical silos compete with and undermine one another, often within the same bureaucracy. Stephenson also argues that measures of an employee's social capital should be included in performance reviews, particularly across organizational silos, which would in turn allow managers to evaluate employees' willingness to "run to, rather than away from, problems," to try to solve a challenge as a team rather than protecting their turf. This kind of incentive structure could combat "the myopic exclusivity of the silo mentality." At best, it could unlock network capacities within and across government bureaucracies that could combat global criminal, fraud, and terrorist networks.[20]

### Mapping the World in Nodes and Edges

Network theory relies heavily on what mathematicians call graph theory, the ability to transform a three-dimensional problem into a two-dimensional graph of nodes and edges (the links between the nodes). Graph theory allows mathematicians and physicists to quantify relationships between objects or people and to formalize their properties mathematically. A high school social network, for instance, becomes the abstraction you see in Figure 1.

Computers give us the ability to crunch the massive amounts of data and perform the thousands, even millions of calculations needed to represent and quantify much larger networks. It is thus not surprising that many of the contributions to our understanding of networks come from physicists and applied mathematicians. Duncan Watts, a physicist and sociologist who studied under the mathematician Steven Strogatz, has specialized in the study of "small worlds," the

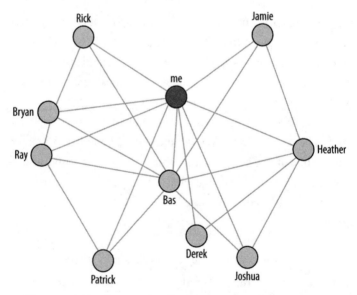

Figure 1. Friend network: a high school social network with
ten students

phenomenon captured by the Kevin Bacon game: everyone in the world is connected by only six degrees of separation. The formal properties of a small-world network demonstrate that even in a world in which everyone knows only her two nearest neighbors, it requires only a few "shortcuts," or links between widely separated clusters, to connect everyone very quickly, whether to discover mutual friends or acquaintances or disseminate information—or viruses.[21]

Physicist Albert-Laszlo Barabasi, working on the structure and evolution of networks at the same time as Watts, added another important piece to the puzzle with his discovery of scale-free networks. By graphing actual networks that had evolved organically, Barabasi realized that the distribution of links among nodes was far from linear. Normally, we would expect that most nodes would have an average number of links, with those having more and fewer links falling to either side in a bell-curve distribution. But that is not what he observed. In many networks—such as the World Wide Web—a small number of nodes have an enormous number of links (we call them hubs) and the vast majority have very few.[22] This kind of distribution is called a "power law." Barabasi's finding has particular implications for the resilience of scale-free networks. It is possible to destroy most nodes with no effect on the greater network. But the targeted destruction of a few of the biggest nodes can bring down the entire network.

Both of these bodies of work tell us the same thing: small changes—the right small changes—can have a big impact. That is also a principal lesson of complexity theory, as we saw in the last chapter. But complex adaptive systems are far less predictable and manipulable than deliberately designed networks. Targeting only a few specific nodes, for either positive or negative purposes, can dramatically strengthen or destroy a network. And power, wealth, opportunity, and vulnerability are often distributed very unevenly across self-organized networks.

## The Web of Life

Still another physicist, Fritjof Capra, reminds us that everyone, from biologists to philosophers, has long talked about the "web of life," the countless interdependencies of all living organisms. Capra relates the networks that make up individual organisms and cells to social networks, providing an organic lens that, in contrast to the formal representations of graph theory, focuses on very different properties.[23]

Biologists have come to see organisms as networks of cells and cells as networks of molecules. The links that create these networks, however, are not physical ties but processes, flows of "energy and matter through a network of chemical reactions."[24] Unlike a static set of nodes and edges, a biological network is continually repairing and renewing itself through these dynamic flows. Social networks can be similarly understood, Capra argues, as networks of communication through which ideas and meaning flow and change.

This perspective yields several valuable insights for understanding and designing networks. First, the network itself exists only as long as exchanges are happening across it. In graph theory, we draw lines between the nodes to indicate what is connected to what, thereby rendering a group of people, say, who know each other and communicate regularly as a network. But Capra reminds us that the network is a network only as long as those communications are actually flowing. Dead organisms have DNA, genes, proteins, and molecules just as live ones do; what makes a living organism a network is the flow of energy and matter within it. The consulting firm McKinsey and Company has recently adopted this perspective in looking at global networks; it now has a Connectedness Index that measures global flows of goods, services, finance, people, and data. The index ranks countries in terms of how connected they are to other countries, both in terms of the absolute value of these flows and that value as a share of the country's GDP. The United States and China rank highest in absolute value, but Singapore and the Netherlands rank first and second in the global chart because the total value of flows in and out is many multiples of their GDP, versus 39 percent for the United States and 63 percent for China.[25]

Second, in a biological network, where cells have semipermeable membranes that admit some flows and shut out others, the boundaries are "not boundaries of separation but boundaries of identity."[26] They keep the cell distinct but nevertheless connect it to other cells as much as they separate it from them. In the same way, the nodes in social networks—meaning the people—are both distinct from and connected to other people by their communications and common action with them. Separate and connected are not opposites but complementary and coexisting states.

Third, the biological metaphor helps us see that every organization features "a continuous interplay between its informal networks and its formal structures." A biological network is self-generating: it creates, maintains, and repairs the structure in which it lives. As Capra describes it, "in a cell . . . the proteins, enzymes, the DNA, the cell membrane . . . are continually produced, repaired and regenerated by the cellular network."[27] At the level of a complex multicellular organism like a human being, chemical reactions among the different parts of our body are constantly renewing our skin, hair, circulatory systems, and internal organs. The external structure is created by the internal networks, which in turn depend on that structure to survive.

Just so with a human organization. Imagine the standard org chart of any business, setting forth the formal structure of who reports to whom. Now imagine how that business really works: who gossips with whom, who is the troubleshooter, who is the problem solver, who is the router who always knows what is going on. The McChrystal Group, a consulting firm that specializes in transforming hierarchies into networks, performs a network analysis on each new client shortly after it is hired, to discover the veins and arteries through which the lifeblood of the organization actually flows. They typically find that relatively few people, or nodes, convey most of the information to their peers. The formal structure can clearly shape the informal networks by hiring or firing people—adding or removing potential nodes. But the informal network also shapes the org chart, by influencing how well individual nodes are able to perform and determining the productivity and health of the organization as a whole.

A final insight from biology is the role of modularity in complex systems. "Modularity" refers to the interactions of partially independent, separable parts. A group led by cell biologist Leland H. Hartwell answered the question of how cells are organized by proposing that a cell is a network of modules, each responsible for a different function. This structure enables the cell to perform many diverse tasks at once.[28]

Modularity has important implications for a network's resilience. Evolutionary biologist Simon Levin and marine biologist Jane Lubchenco study ecosystem-based management of natural resources, building on Levin's work on complex adaptive systems.[29] The relationship between modularity and resilience, they write, is best understood through "Herbert Simon's parable of the two watchmakers." One watchmaker builds watches by first constructing the separate components of a watch—modules—and then putting them all together to create the whole watch. The other builds one whole watch at a time. If their work is disrupted, the first watchmaker has only to repair the module being assembled at the time, whereas the second has to start from scratch. Modularity "confers robustness by locking in gains and compartmentalizing disturbances."[30] In both man-made organizations and natural systems, modular structures provide "buffering against cascades of disaster."[31]

## Networks and Human Incentives

Economists came to the network party relatively late, but the introduction of *homo economicus*, that fabulously rational agent who makes all decisions according to a careful analysis of personal costs and benefits, has led to the study of the networks that result from deliberate human choices. Members of other academic disciplines often joke that "homo economicus" describes no real-world person except economists themselves;

nevertheless, the assumption of rational choice allows them to model complicated systems of human interaction based on simulated games.

When an economist looks at a network, she sees (as the economist Sanjeev Goyal puts it) a "pattern of connections between persons in a society."[32] She does not see a random distribution such as a mathematician might graph, or a pattern dictated by social norms and structures, as a sociologist would assume. The economist's pattern "reflect[s] rational decision making of individuals."[33] Friends choose their friends, business associates choose their suppliers, and buyers choose sellers according to their self-interest. The traditional economist says that it is necessary to manipulate human incentives to change those patterns, by changing the amount and quality of information people receive or by rewarding some choices and punishing others.[34]

Human beings in a network reach out to one another to obtain information; the amount and quality of the information they get depend on whom each is connected to. As we have seen, their incentives—the desirability of specific choices over other choices—are also affected by the people they are connected to. Economists thus study how different types of networks—variations in structure, size, and density—affect the incentives of individual members and the quality and quantity of information available to them. Their distinctive contribution is that they use game theory to model how individual decisions are affected by these different properties of networks. Using computer simulations to alter and extend these properties, they can run experiments that are impossible in the real world. The results tell us that different network architectures are better for certain purposes, such as diffusing information or encouraging cooperation.

In addition to systematizing our knowledge of network effects on the individuals within them, economists also focus on networks and public policy. Goyal reminds us that governments are continually trying to improve the information available to citizens to help them make better choices. Suppose, he writes, a government wants its citizens to make better choices about information technology. Policy makers might assume that the existence of dense social networks means that any information they provide will spread quickly throughout the network and thus they need not invest much in advertising. In fact, however, the economic study of network effects shows that sometimes, more is less: more connections (a very dense network) may actually decrease the amount of information available to each individual. They will cut back on gathering information themselves since it's available via their connections for less cost. Policy makers should thus increase their advertising budget.[35]

Economists also focus on the gap between "socially desirable outcomes and the outcomes that actually arise out of the purposeful activity of individuals." Their assumptions allow them to model what pattern of connections would arise if all individuals made perfectly rational decisions based on perfect information about the costs and benefits of the choices available to them. This leads the economists to study network formation: what leads rational individuals to choose the connections they do, and whether the result—among businesses seeking strategic partners, buyers and sellers, job seekers, or any group trying to build a network to maximize flows of valuable information—is as good as it could or should be. And if not, can government do anything to make it better?[36]

## Social Physics

Alex Pentland, director of the Human Dynamics Group at the MIT Media Lab, has been pioneering a discipline called social physics to tackle just those questions. Using big data, this approach examines and tweaks patterns of idea flow in networks. By "tuning" the structure of social networks and the specific exchanges taking place within them, policy makers can shape processes of social learning and social pressure to increase collective intelligence and generate cooperative norms.[37]

Pentland argues that a process he calls "engagement" can foster behavioral coordination and cooperation. Engagement begins with regular and frequent interaction among relatively small numbers of individuals in an organization; it focuses on coownership of processes and outcomes, consensus building, and trust building through direct cooperative interactions. It is essentially team building backed by complex mathematics. The equations permit the modeling of social influence; big data makes it possible to adapt and refine the models by, for example, combining performance data with team member behavior during meetings, such as conversational turn taking, tone of voice, body language, and other social signals.[38] As like-minded researcher Paul Adams writes, "For the first time in humanity, we can accurately map and measure human-to-human interaction."[39]

This work is all still at an early stage. It may ring of Orwellian privacy invasion and dangerously optimistic social engineering. Yet the entire science of behavioral psychology—

the use of a psychological "nudge" to push us toward desired behaviors—is social engineering. And as Pentland points out, although social physics assumes that "learning from examples of other people's behavior . . . is a major and likely dominant mechanism of behavioral change," it accepts "an irreducible kernel of uncertainty" resulting from conscious thought.[40]

## THE CHEAT SHEET

The wealth of scholarship on networks offers a continuing and expanding resource for network designers. For current purposes, I have distilled a set of insights that provide a starting point for thinking about how to create and sustain networks to advance specific foreign policy goals. In Chapters 4 through 7, I will use these insights to address particular foreign policy problems.

### Hierarchy or Network?

1. Networked organizations are more flexible, creative, adaptable, autonomous, and resilient relative to hierarchies; hierarchies are more efficient and easier to manage in clear and predictable conditions. Networks can be faster or slower for specific purposes than hierarchies, depending on the circumstances and how they are designed and led.
2. Networks depend on trust and reciprocity.
3. Networks do not require a governing authority.
4. Every organization features a continuous interplay between its informal networks and its formal structures. All formal hierarchies contain informal

networks; all networks will develop informal hierarchies based on experience or expertise.

### Select Your Structure

5. The density of networks matters for different purposes: weak ties bridge different groups, strong
ties reinforce existing groups.[41] Weak ties work
best for input, strong ties for output.

6. Nodes can be "central" in different ways and for
different purposes, including information diffu-
sion, control over other nodes, vulnerability, and
community building.

7. Two densely clustered networks that are geo-
graphically far apart can become connected with
the addition of only a few "shortcut" links between
clusters, creating "small worlds."

8. Some networks develop unevenly, with a small
number of nodes having a large number of links.
The distribution of whatever flows across them
thus follows a power law rather than a bell curve.
Targeting the big nodes in these networks can
have dramatic positive or negative effects.

9. Organizations composed of modular networks
may be more resilient and able to multitask, as
each module can carry out a different function.

### Assess Your Impact

10. The structure of a network affects the behavior of
individuals within it; impact is thus always both
internal and external. Impact can result from

changes in incentives or information, or through processes of social learning and social pressure.

11. Individuals in a network make choices that are affected not only by their friends but by their friends' friends and their friends' friends' friends.

12. Small changes in complex networks can have big impacts, as with the creation of small-world networks.

13. Networks generate emergent effects and outputs greater than the sum capacity of the individuals involved.[42] Well-managed networks can thus be force multipliers, but these effects and outputs can also be negative.

## The Network Mindset

14. A living network exists only when information, communication, or material of some kind is actually flowing among its nodes. The flows create the network.

15. The boundaries in a network are best understood as boundaries of identity rather than separation. The flows between nodes that give the network life connect them as part of a larger whole; thus nodes, clusters, and larger structures are distinct but not separate entities.

We are almost ready to apply these principles to the design of actual networks. Let us pause for a moment, however, to catalogue all the differences between the chessboard and the web views of the world, and to exercise the mental muscles that will allow us to put both views together.

# CHAPTER THREE

# Seeing in Stereo

WHEN you look at the picture in Figure 2, what do you see? Most people, at first glance, see an old woman with a great hooked nose and a narrow black slash of a mouth. Viewed another way, however, her mouth becomes a necklace on the neck of a lovely young woman with her face turned away from the viewer. The old woman's nose becomes the outline of her jaw. This picture is a famous perceptual illusion; the trick is to learn how to move easily between the different images in the same picture.

So, too, with the chessboard and the web. When I was in graduate school, the word "ontology" was a weapon we students deployed against one another in an effort to sound sophisticated. Like "epistemology," it's a scary metaphysical word that can be hard to wrap your mind around. In fact,

Figure 2. Old or Young? The famous perceptual illusion "My Wife and My Mother-In-Law," by cartoonist W. E. Hill in 1915, adapted from an anonymous German postcard circa 1888

neither word is that hard: "epistemology" just means your method for getting knowledge, and "ontology" means what exists for you.

What is the world you see? Do you see states balancing against one another and periodically fighting in an endless game of power politics? Do you see international organizations and institutions as having a power of their own? Do you see global corporations, terrorists, drug and arms traffickers, and human rights, environmental, and religious groups pursuing their interests and shaping a world of their liking? Different theories of international relations posit different ontologies. Scholars, experts, and policy makers look out at the "world" or the "international system" and see different things.

The ontological shift from seeing a world of states to seeing a world of networks is the shift from separation to connection. During the Cold War, the dominant relationship in the international system was a frozen conflict between two very different states. The natural condition of a state was to be a separate sovereign in the world, free to make alliances with other states or to exist in splendid isolation.

The globalization of the 1990s built on the globalization of the 1960s and 1970s, the weaving of global webs that led Keohane and Nye to publish *Power and Interdependence*. Growing webs of relationships among states and peoples created a new map of the international system, in which connection was the dominant relationship for most states and most peoples. Abram and Antonia Chayes even redefined sovereignty itself to mean not the right to be left alone but the right to participate in international organizations and networks.[1]

Before we can learn to design and deploy networks as foreign policy tools, we have to make sure we can move back and forth between the chessboard and the web, seeing them as the "both/and" halves of the world we actually inhabit. But those twin images go deeper than mental models of what is outside of us; they make different assumptions about human nature itself.

Many network theorists note that human beings differ dramatically from the rational profit maximizer of social science theory. Neuroscientists exploring different regions of the brain, sociologists mapping an increasingly networked society, and entrepreneurial enthusiasts of the sharing economy challenge the highly individualist conception of the individual that many economists embrace. Instead of homo economicus, let us consider *homo sociologicus*, a person driven as much by the desire to belong and connect as by her individual goals.

## THE CHESS PLAYER AND THE NETWORKER

For the sake of simplicity, let us assume that practitioners of traditional geopolitics—chess players—are most at home with homo economicus. They assume a world of rational profit maximizers and transpose that image onto states. The British mastermind Lord Palmerston captured this sentiment with a line statesmen have quoted ever since: "Nations have no permanent friends or allies, they only have permanent interests."

Weavers of global webs—networkers—focus on people much more than on states. They have different expectations about how those people will behave. The social psychologist Susan Fiske captures the essence of homo sociologicus when she describes humans as "social beings," people who "are motivated to belong to groups, to develop socially shared understanding, to control their interpersonal outcomes effectively, to enhance (esteem or at least improve) themselves, and to trust others by default."[2] Self-interest, in this view, lies beyond the self. Indeed, social psychologists, neuroscientists, evolutionary biologists, and anthropologists have come to the conclusion that "evolutionary adaptation apparently favors the group-oriented person."[3] Seeking society and opening ourselves to the emotions and impact of connection may have increased our genes' reproductive chances.

Yet whatever the evolutionary origins of his or her behavior, homo sociologicus is motivated by a primary desire, not an instrumental desire, to belong and connect.[4] Connection, in this view, is as important and as life-sustaining as a full belly. It is an end in itself, not just a means to an end. Engaging human beings in ways that connect them to other human beings in a common endeavor thus increases an individual's sense of personal well-being regardless of what that endeavor is. In a 1995 review of Francis Fukuyama's book *Trust*, Fareed Zakaria noted that connectivity is not necessarily positive, pointing out that the mastermind of the horrific bombing of the federal building in Oklahoma City had been in a bowling league with like-minded conspiracy theorists.[5] Still, networkers may actually be different animals from chess players, subject to different influences and motivations.

Humans pursuing deep, complete connections respond to quite different incentives from those that influence self-interested utility maximizers.[6] Rewards, monitoring, and punishments are less likely to be effective than engagement, communication, norms, socialization, identity, and common purpose.[7] They share not out of a calculation of reciprocity but from a psychological pleasure in sharing.[8] Those seeking connections make decisions from their hearts as well as their heads, influenced by emotion, fairness, empathy, and intuition.[9] Their behavior, thoughts, feelings, and even personal attributes are highly socially contingent.[10]

The range of humanity includes individuals who display every possible combination of selfishness and sociability. Moreover, Susan Fiske explains that social psychologists themselves attribute "prosocial behavior" to a wide range of motives: "egoism, altruism, collectivism, and principlism." Collectivism is the motive to improve group welfare; principlism is "upholding moral standards" in conformity with a set of abstract values." In addition to differences among individuals, different societies and cultures vary in reinforcing more prosocial or pro-self behaviors. The point here is not to choose but to push back against an insistence on one narrow view of human nature.

Proponents of rational choice models of human behavior know that they are abstracting from and simplifying actual human behavior; the entire discipline of behavioral economics seeks to modify economic models based on insights into actual human behavior and motivation. Still, all of us, perhaps especially foreign policy makers in moments of crisis, are prisoners of our mental models. Foreign policy practitioners in the web world must address policies to individuals as well as states. It is thus critical that we operate from a full set of assumptions about human interests, motivations, incentives, and constraints.

## PUTTING IT ALL TOGETHER

Political scientists often disdain typologies, but contrasting what we see when we look at the chessboard world versus the web world makes it easier to see what the chessboard view overlooks. It is important that we see power *and* interdependence, states *and* people, structure *and* agency, stasis *and* dynamism, all at the same time.[12]

Table 2 shows what the world looks like, in terms of the actors we see—the assumptions we make about them alone and in relation to one another, and about human nature—if we put the twin optics of the chessboard and the web together.[13]

It is a necessarily cryptic table; each cell summarizes and simplifies ongoing scholarly debates. But it captures two quite different points of departure in looking at the world and making sense of what we think we see. As in the old woman/young

TABLE 2

The Chessboard and the Web

|  | Chessboard | Web |
| --- | --- | --- |
| **Units** | States | People |
| **State of nature** | Separation | Connection |
| **Focus of analysis** | Static equilibria | Dynamic flows |
| **Source of power** | Individual attributes | Relationships |
| **Sovereignty** | Autonomy | Participation |
| **Human nature** | Self-interest | Sociability |
| **Modal behavior** | Bargaining | Sharing |
| **Behavioral mechanism** | Calculation | Adaptation |
| **Motivation** | Incentives | Social identity |
| **Identity** | Fixed | Fluid |
| **Means of influence** | Coercion | Engagement |

woman illusion, both pictures exist simultaneously. It is just that for centuries now, ever since the emergence and crystallization of the modern state system, the majority of men and women who study global politics and are charged with steering their countries through the turbulent currents of the world have focused on one picture much more than the other. Going forward, we must learn to see in stereo, understanding how to operate effectively in both worlds to achieve the outcomes we need.

## STATECRAFT AND WEBCRAFT

Statesmen have played chess for centuries; indeed, their strategies define statecraft. Distinguished diplomat Dennis Ross characterizes statecraft as "the use of the assets or the resources and tools (economic, military, intelligence, media) that a state has to pursue its interests and to affect the behavior of others."[14] These strategies are by and large strategies of conflict, or at least of competition: the objective in chess is to win.

Not victory at any cost, however. *The Strategy of Conflict* taught U.S. policy makers how to play the game with the Soviet Union so as to advance American interests without blowing up the world. In a nuclear world, limited and confined conflict is acceptable, but all-out war is not. Inverting Clausewitz, diplomacy among great powers is war by other means.

The strategies of conflict remain highly relevant among great powers. More broadly, the 194 states in the world continue to compete with each other in many ways, seeking to advance their interests as autonomous, separate units in a world defined by a particular distribution of material and cultural power. Traditional statecraft certainly has its place.

But when we turn to the web world, the portfolio of strategies to advance national interests and achieve global goals is almost empty. We know how to assemble a coalition of nations to impose sanctions on Iran and to negotiate with the Iranian government to ensure that it does not build an atomic bomb. We don't know how to build commercial, educational, and social networks with the Iranian people, networks that would provide resilience against government propaganda, or to build webs of collaborative scholarship and research, and jump-start new enterprises in both our countries.

The standard foreign policy approach to the world of people is "connecting and convening": holding a conference, hosting exchanges, creating working groups or task forces, or, more recently, catalyzing public-private partnerships. But we do not have strategies of connection in the sense of knowing whom to connect how, where, and when to advance specific foreign policy goals. These network strategies can be just as nuanced and sophisticated as any chessboard gambit. They need to be developed, studied, tested, and refined. Foreign policy practitioners need to become equally proficient at webcraft.

These web strategies tend to be longer-term tools than many chessboard strategies. Building networks takes time. But the patience and care put into their creation can pay off.

Consider our own decades-long strategy of containing the Soviet Union. In addition to building alliances of nations, the American government and many U.S. civil society groups built support and resilience networks for movements like

Solidarity in Poland, the Czech underground, and East German church groups. These networks emerged over years, even decades, and actively inserted themselves into national politics only when the opportunity arose. Still, they were there, underground, sustaining opposition activists and quietly expanding their operations all along. Supporting them with money, information, and material assistance is not nearly as flashy as imposing sanctions or threatening force against another government. But over time, it may be much more effective.

What if we could help create those networks with much more understanding of how to structure and support them in ways that would maximize their resilience, capacity for action, ability to scale? Instead of letting them emerge or hoping they would, we could actively seed them and help them grow. Not by stirring up opposition or funneling cash under the table to insurgent groups, as intelligence agencies around the world have long done. But rather as a set of foreign policy tools aimed at advancing interests and solving collective outcomes in a world of people shaped and motivated by specific patterns of connections. In the rest of this book we shall see how those tools might develop.

# PART II
## Strategies of Connection

TO DEVELOP A set of tools that foreign policy makers—a category that includes not only government officials but also civic, philanthropic, and corporate leaders—will actually use, it is critical to start with a set of problems that they currently find difficult to solve. The range of problems seems nearly infinite; as defense expert Julianne Smith put it, the United States now faces "an interconnected web of global and regional threats, whose sheer volume and complexity are overwhelming."[1] But it is helpful to group the hardest problems into three broad categories: resilience problems, execution problems, and scale problems.

Resilience problems involve avoiding and responding to crises, whether man-made, natural, or both, ranging from a direct military attack to an earthquake to a famine. Execution problems require the implementation of a specific task or set of tasks by identifiable individuals or organizations to accomplish a concrete goal such as addressing a financial crisis, implementing a peace treaty, or finding new ways to reduce carbon emissions. Finally, scale problems arise when challenges are being overcome at the micro level but not at the macro level.

A typology necessarily stylizes and simplifies: any important global issue is likely to have resilience, execution, and scale dimensions. Making categories inevitably means drawing somewhat arbitrary lines. Creating a scale network of nongovernmental organizations, government agencies, and corporations all working on education of girls, for instance, could also be described as executing a long-term task. Building a resilience network could include linking together a number of small networks into a larger one, which makes it also a scale network. Still, we have to start somewhere!

The core of my argument is that we can identify specific types of networks—resilience networks, task networks, and scale networks—that can be created, shaped, and supported to address each type of problem. Before exploring these categories, let me say something about method. The phrase "can be created, shaped, and supported" reflects my vantage point as a doer as much as a thinker. We will draw on the work of the scholars described in Chapters 1 and 2—researchers, analysts, and theorists who are using quantitative and qualitative methods to explain and predict the natural and social worlds. But we will be applying that work to solve public problems, much as an engineer applies physics, chemistry, and mathematics to solve engineering problems.

That means we will move back and forth between network theory and actual examples of networks that work in the world. I will match theories of what should work to increase resilience, execute tasks, and scale microsolutions to problems with examples of networks that are actually working in each of these categories. The result will be neither fully deductive nor fully inductive, but a blend of both.

I hope that over time, the study of networked solutions to public problems will generate what political scientist Donald Stokes, inspired by Louis Pasteur, called "use-inspired basic research," in which the study of concrete problems motivates advances in fundamental knowledge.[2] Network experts will work with foreign policy practitioners and other problem solvers to design and create networks that they will then learn from, modifying both theory and practice. If that aspiration is too grand, I hope that the typology and structure of networks described here will at least serve as a starting point for further refinement and research.

## CHAPTER FOUR

# Resilience Networks

I N a world facing increasing natural disasters caused by climate change, from hurricanes to floods to droughts, "resilience" is very much in vogue. Simon Levin and Jane Lubchenco merge resilience with robustness for purposes of ecosystem management. They define this broader concept of resilience as having "two key aspects: 1) resistance to change (as well as flexibility, the amount a system can be perturbed from its reference state without that change being essentially irreversible); and more generally, 2) the ability of the system to recover."[1] Andrew Zolli, in his book *Resilience*, focuses on people as well as systems, offering a definition that draws on both ecology and sociology: "the capacity of a system, enterprise, or a person to maintain its core purpose and integrity in the face of dramatically changed circumstances."[2]

The notion of resilience as *capacity*—the capacity of individuals, a community, a system, or a population to survive and thrive in the face of threats and challenges—is particularly helpful in foreign policy. Many governments and NGOs have struggled with "capacity building" as the answer to the myriad problems that result from weak and ineffective government. Strengthening a regime's ability to administer a region, from collecting taxes to delivering services, will also enhance its ability to withstand popular protest or external efforts to destabilize it. Rockefeller Foundation President Judith Rodin has written about the "resilience dividend," a virtuous circle through which communities, cities, and organizations build the capacity to both prevent predictable crises and bounce back from unpredicted ones. She argues that social cohesion and immediate citizen response are key foundations of resilience.[3]

The basic elements of resilience for natural systems are diversity, modularity, and redundancy. No surprises here: think of a pathogen spreading through a population. Diversity helps ensure that some will survive even as others succumb. Modularity creates the possibility of a firebreak, so that infecting one does not automatically mean infecting all. And redundancy means that even if large numbers of one species die out, more remain, just as if many rivets on an airplane wing fail, others remain to hold it together.

Networks are the common currency of resilience studies: the theory and vocabulary of networks provide a universal framework "for describing how information, resources, and behaviors flow through many complex systems," including "biological, economic, and ecological systems."[4] A network is also more resistant than a hierarchy, in the sense that it is harder to decapitate. Building resilience thus starts with basic network structures.

In 1964, a RAND Corporation researcher named Paul Baran was asked to design a communications system for the U.S. government that could withstand a nuclear attack. As network theorist Albert-Laszlo Barabasi tells the story, Baran came up with "three possible architectures for such a network—centralized, decentralized, and distributed" (Figure 3).[5] We can call these the star, the hub, and the mesh.[6]

At first glance, it seems obvious that the star is the least resilient structure, and the mesh the most resilient. Baran argued that only the mesh—the distributed network—could survive a nuclear attack, as it is the only structure with no center that can be taken out. He was ignored, although

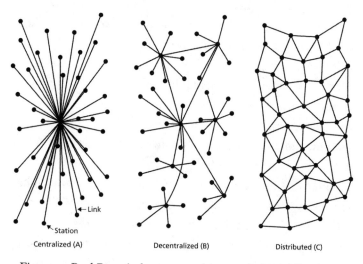

Centralized (A)        Decentralized (B)        Distributed (C)

Figure 3. Paul Baran's three network types: the centralized star network, the decentralized hub network, and the distributed mesh network. Of the three, the mesh network is most resilient to failures and attacks.

ultimately the wires, routers, and servers that we now call the Internet did indeed evolve as a mesh network. As we shall see, the mesh is the most resilient for some purposes—but it cannot be sealed off against a virus or an electronic pulse the way the other two types can.

Moreover, the mesh lacks the "power of clusters," of the "densely packed distributed diversity" that has helped both cities and coral reefs survive through continual innovation and change.[7] Not all modules are created equal: clusters ideally combine density and diversity, allowing individuals, groups, and organizations to change friends and functions as necessary to adapt to changing circumstances. In a healthy reef system, various species of fish and other marine life play different roles at different points in the reef's life cycle. A healthy city combines and recombines neighborhood groups, businesses, political constituencies, arts and cultural communities, and developers as the tides of space and time ebb and flow.

In the human environment, trust has proved critical in resilient systems.[8] Resilience demands cooperation during a crisis; cooperation requires a basic level of trust. Trust, in turn, requires repeated human interaction, building a reservoir of social capital that supports the propensity of human beings who know and like one another to self-organize into groups and associations.[9] Generations of political theorists and social scientists, from Alexis de Tocqueville to Robert Putnam, have reflected on the relationship between social capital and healthy societies.[10]

Patterns of human connection contribute to or detract from resilience in countless ways; it is impossible to explore them all. But let us begin with three broad subcategories of resilient networks that are particularly relevant to foreign policy challenges: defense networks, response networks, and stabilization networks. In each subcategory we can identify a basic structure that offers a promising starting point for policy makers.

## DEFENSE NETWORKS

In the conflict in eastern Ukraine, Russia has been accused of perpetrating a new form of hybrid warfare, infiltrating soldiers who cannot be identified as Russian troops but who fight alongside Ukrainian separatists in an effort to destabilize the country. Russian tactics in Syria's civil war have been similar: President Putin denied sending Russian ground troops but did announce that thousands of "volunteers" were heading to Syria to support President Bashar al-Assad's government. War is normally a chessboard issue, but fighting terrorist networks and other nonstate actors—the Russian "volunteers" are not formally state actors—requires the national security establishment to think in network terms. How to build a defense network that will be resilient against persistent armed destabilization?

Alternatively, consider the need to build defense networks against the spread of pandemics, either actual or virtual. Computer viruses spread in the same way biological viruses do. In both cases, the connectivity that creates robustness under some circumstances can bring down an entire network. Many health systems, as well as the Internet, are "scale-free networks," characterized not by a rising symmetry of connections in which nodes and links are distributed randomly, but rather by a pattern of relatively few major nodes, or hubs, and thousands or millions of smaller nodes. Barabasi uses the analogies of the U.S. interstate map versus the airline map: the highway system is a random network, where every major city (node) is linked to two or three major highways, and the airline system is a scale-free network, in which some cities are major hubs serving many routes but others have only a few routes (Figure 4).[11]

The scale-free hub structure is remarkably robust against a random failure in any part of the system, as it is almost always possible to find another route to a particular destination. If a road is blocked to one city in a region, a clinic is closed in

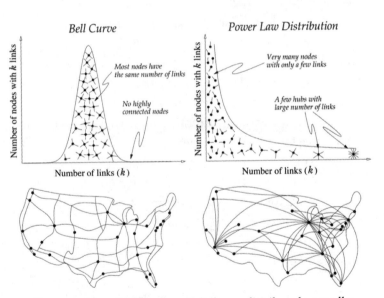

*Bell Curve*   *Power Law Distribution*

Number of nodes with $k$ links

Most nodes have the same number of links

No highly connected nodes

Number of links ($k$)

Number of nodes with $k$ links

Very many nodes with only a few links

A few hubs with large number of links

Number of links ($k$)

Figure 4. In a random network, links are distributed normally among the nodes. In a scale-free network, a few hubs have many links, and the rest have only a few.

one village or town, or one router goes down, another road, clinic, or circuit will be available and will be connected to and through a hub city, hospital, or portal. On the other hand, deliberate attacks against major hubs can quickly bring down the entire network.[12]

A true defensive network must thus look like a mesh. That may be cold comfort in eastern Ukraine, where the network of cities, towns, villages, and the roads connecting them has grown up over centuries in a hub rather than a distributed form. Warfare has always been about capturing major hubs. But to prepare for hybrid warfare, in which armies no longer march across borders but use small bands of special forces to infiltrate territory, resilience requires altering the objects of attack rather than countering the invaders directly. Transportation, manufacturing, and garrison networks must be distributed as evenly and as widely as possible, with airstrips and bases downscaled and spaced apart. Knowledge industries are already heading in this direction, as workers can be located wherever their computers are, often in small clusters but without the need for large central headquarters.

Such prescriptions fly in the face of the megaurbanization that futurists routinely predict.[13] It is not possible to resist the economic forces propelling urban growth, or to stop central planners in countries like China from creating megalopolises. Distributing defense assets is also more expensive than creating hubs. But as New York businesses discovered after Hurricane Sandy, firms that had made provision for a more distributed workforce, allowing flexible work-from-home arrangements, were more resilient and productive through the crisis.

Mesh defense need not be universal. But for Ukraine and other countries next to powerful and aggressive neighbors, such networks should be constructed in border areas. Existing cities cannot be dismantled, but a distributed transport, military, and manufacturing net can be effectively laid over them. Hybrid enemies can take over small nodes, but it will be much harder for them to control an entire region or subregion. Think of it as keeping the network of medium and smaller roads in good shape even while most people are using airports.

The same strategy applies to viruses. A typical health system, with its major hospitals, smaller hospitals, and clinics, looks much like an airline routing system. The most routine care is done locally; the smaller hospitals take care of major illnesses and common surgeries; the major urban teaching hospitals handle what doctors call "zebra cases," the hard and rare diseases that require sophisticated diagnosis and specialized research.[14] Patients come from all over the country and the world to these hub hospitals, funneled through to them by local and regional physicians. That system works well in normal times, ensuring both broad access for a population and the development of specialized medical expertise that is practicable only in a large teaching hospital. But the Achilles' heel of such a system is evident the minute a deadly virus like Ebola is introduced. The big hospital hubs become transmission points, just like major city airports.

Effective defense against an epidemic requires a distributed network of clinics and hospitals specifically designed for fighting infectious disease that can be transmitted from human to human via bodily fluids or in aerosol form. It is essential to isolate infectious patients and to provide protective equipment in order to ensure the safety of caregivers. Even within cities, infectious disease hospitals can be isolated, either as completely separate wings with their own emergency facilities or as separate establishments. Viruses or bacteria with the potential for mass injury or death, such as the respiratory syndromes that have emerged in East Asia (SARS) or the Middle East (MERS), H1N1 or any other deadly bird flu, or Ebola, AIDS, or other tropical viruses, must be treated through this parallel distributed system, which can be active all the time or can be activated as soon as such a virus emerges. Protection against cyberviruses is already evolving in the same way.[15]

Constructing a distributed health system alongside our current hub systems may again seem impossible or at least impossibly expensive. But pandemics are among our gravest security challenges in the twenty-first century precisely *because* the world has become an interlocking set of networks connected by a perilously small number of major hubs. The great strength of the system for spreading knowledge, economic growth, and positive innovation becomes, in the face of communicable diseases, its greatest weakness. Just as a building has a backup electrical system in case of blackouts, so must cities, regions, and nations develop backup systems to build the resilience we need. And those systems must take a very different networked form.

The U.S. Department of Homeland Security (DHS) has been exploring the value of creating a distributed information grid to improve cybersecurity. For more than a year, the federal government's Office of Personnel Management (OPM) failed to detect Chinese hackers stealing the personal information of nearly twenty-two million Americans. OPM's cyber defenses were antiquated, but the breach underscored a larger problem, identified by DHS Undersecretary Suzanne Spaulding: "Today our adversaries exploit a fundamental asymmetry in our network infrastructure: while nearly all of our systems and networks are globally interconnected, our defensive capabilities are not."[16] To fix this, DHS is building an automated cyberdefense network that shares threat information and countermeasures in real time. It is a "network of networks," connecting federal, state, and local agencies and law enforcement as well as private companies, which own much of the nation's critical infrastructure.

The brain of this system is the National Cybersecurity Communications Integration Center, or NCCIC. Its mission is to limit the likelihood and severity of cyberattacks to the nation's critical digital and communications infrastructure.[17] It does this by gathering and sharing information about incidents and vulnerabilities in public and private systems. This threat information generates a visual, constantly updating "cyber weather map." The NCCIC also disseminates information products, services, and updated protective software, called Einstein 3A, to federal government agencies, building a cyber "immunity system."[18]

The physiological metaphor is interesting. From an information point of view, the more sensors and the more connected they are to one another, the better. More links mean better resilience, because more alternative pathways are available in case of a local failure. But from a pathological point of view, fewer connections are often better. As with sepsis or poison spreading through the bloodstream, it may be essential to cut off an affected limb. The trick is to find the optimum balance between distributed and modular, between more connections and fewer, to meet the needs of a particular system.

Consider the Iranian blogosphere, a vibrant and diverse discussion space with much political commentary that persists in the face of a determined state effort to shut it down. Two Harvard researchers mapped a network of sixty thousand blogs constituting twenty subcommunities with no central hubs; they suggested that the decentralized structure is the key to its survival. The "peer-to-peer architecture of the blogosphere is more resistant to capture or control by the state," they wrote, than the "hub and spoke" structure of traditional mass media.[19]

In another repressive society, the 2011 Egyptian revolution succeeded in overthrowing the Mubarak regime because the activists' networks were both distributed and parallel. Protesters occupied the virtual space of online social media and the physical space of Tahrir Square. In the early days of the uprising, the regime tried to knock out the activists' communication networks by blacking out mobile phone coverage and blocking 93 percent of all Internet traffic in the country. So activists communicated through more traditional networks: landlines, ham radio, and dial-up. This diversity gave the movement the resilience to withstand the regime's attacks.[20]

Thus far I have used "defense" to mean defense against direct attack over short periods. Slower threats, such as climate change, resource scarcity, or dramatic demographic shifts, also require increased resilience. Here, effective response and recovery require different kinds of networks.

RESPONSE NETWORKS

Resilience in the face of mass emergencies and disasters is as much about response as about preparation. The creation of distributed defense networks, parallel networks that can be activated when a threat materializes, is itself a response to anticipated dangers. But in a moment of acute crisis, particularly a relatively localized one like an earthquake or hurricane, immediate response networks are equally essential to minimizing the loss of life and providing assistance to those in need.[21]

The most immediate need in a natural disaster, or an attack like the destruction of the World Trade Center in New York on 9/11 or recent terrorism in Paris, Bamako, Jakarta, Brussels, Istanbul, and elsewhere, is for information. People in the strike zone need to know what is happening, where to go, and how to summon or get to help. First responders need to know where to go to rescue victims and how to avoid danger to themselves. People both inside and outside the zone want to know what may have happened to family members and other loved ones. Disaster assistance organizations, both governmental and nongovernmental, need to know the areas of greatest need and the best ways to get there.[22] The central government needs information with which to calm a frightened and distressed public and to communicate to other governments and international organizations. Ordinary citizens want to know how they can help.

What would a speedy, accurate, and effective information network look like? It requires a combination of scouts, aggregators, and curators. A scout is essentially anyone in the area with a cell phone. Aggregators are the people and machines that can assemble streams of information from multiple sources and integrate the content in real time, thereby filtering for accuracy. They take crowd-sourced information and layer reports on top of one another to create a topography of the disaster. If two conflicting reports about a fire or collapsed building or washed-out bridge come in, both are suspect. But if ten reports come in, perhaps with pictures of the affected site, an accurate map emerges.

Curators determine what information should be disseminated outward, to responders, victims, families, and the public at large. They must be experienced both in disaster response and in the kinds of curation tools afforded by new types of social media. Storify offers one such example, Twitter Moments another, where editors put together stories based on curating thousands of Tweets or other social media posts that themselves link to other sources of information. Curation demands a critical ability to sift out hyperbole and insist on multiple sources, as well as awareness of what kind of information different audiences need and how best to present that information. None of this sounds like a typical government job description, even for FEMA employees, but these functions are essential in a crisis.

Such a network must include as many tiny nodes as the affected area has citizens, who serve as the initial scouts. It must also have one central node, one clearinghouse for all information received. A simple star model, however, is too inefficient. Imagine, for instance, if all information about the World Trade Center attacks on 9/11 had to be routed through a command center in Washington. That center would be simultaneously fielding information and inquiries from the attack on the Pentagon and from observers of the crash of Flight 93 in a Pennsylvania field, as well as from frightened citizens all over the country. New York needed its own central command node; indeed, firehouses and police stations throughout the city also needed to be nodes.

The answer is a modified hub network, known as a modular hierarchical network. Such a network has one central node that is connected to other nodes in a descending hierarchy of centrality and connectedness (Figure 5).

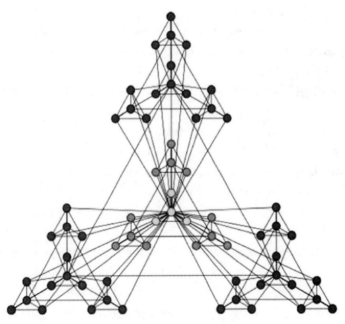

Figure 5. Modular hierarchical network: a central node is connected to other nodes in a descending hierarchy of centrality and connectedness. Everyone is connected but not for every purpose.

Not only is each central node connected to all the other nodes in its district, but they are all connected to one another. This degree of integration means that information flows to everyone in that subnetwork in real time, allowing someone in a collapsed building to communicate immediately not only to disaster central in that subcompartment of the system but also to the nearest firehouse, police car, or neighbor with a shovel. At the same time, however, that information is flowing to a local set of aggregators and curators who can assemble, map, and filter it before sending it up the chain.

The next question for the architects of a response network is *whom* to connect. It has been repeatedly demonstrated that responses to crises are much more effective when government coordinates closely with nongovernmental organizations such as Doctors Without Borders, Care, Oxfam, and others, both global and national. Businesses with global and local supply chains and employees also have valuable networks and materiel to offer. Technology companies such as Google and Twitter played essential roles in the Haiti earthquake and Japan's earthquake, tsunami, and radiological triple disaster, serving as emergency communications systems and creating tools such as Google's Person Finder and Palantir Gotham.[23]

In the immediate aftermath of the Haiti earthquake, the U.S. State Department reached out to telecommunications providers to create a short code, a truncated phone number for dialing or messaging, to which any Haitian could text information. A team of coders from an emergency response nonprofit then deployed to Haiti and built the infrastructure to receive messages sent to that four-digit number and transfer them to an adapted version of the crisis mapping platform

Ushahidi, which was originally created to identify election fraud and violence after the abortive 2007 Kenyan elections. A group of volunteers at Tufts University used Ushahidi to create a map of the distress calls from stranded and imperiled Haitian survivors. Coordinates were delivered to U.N. responders, the U.S. Coast Guard, and, through a personal connection at Tufts, the Marine Corps. As author and global trends consultant Andrew Zolli tells the story, many different groups—"tribes, networks, and teams"—came together spontaneously to form what came to be known as Mission 4636; he also emphasizes the value of short feedback loops from the ground to mission participants to let them know what was working and what was not, and to intensify commitment and maintain morale.[24]

The lessons from Haiti and elsewhere tell us that crisis planners should be creating, in advance, a hierarchical modular network linking key connectors from government, NGOs, and business within each central node. They should prepare and publicize key disaster response text numbers, much like 911 or 311, so that citizens know where to send information. At the same time, personnel within central nodes must be prepared to curate information from and distribute information to social media channels, radio broadcasters, and regular national, local, and regional news media. The structure of the network and the key players can be identified in advance, but planners must expect disasters to have a fluidity reminiscent of Clausewitz's "fog of war." They should be prepared to cull information from every possible source. The more public participation the better, as long as it is channeled and curated. Similarly, backup resilience must be built into the system itself, ensuring that neighboring nodes in the extended or more central hierarchy can pick up for each other.

This model of response networks may sound suspiciously tidy in the face of the often overwhelming chaos of a major disaster. But preparation saves lives and calms panic. Preparing to allow people to connect to one another can be particularly important; we are helping them do what they will want to do anyway. As Keri Stephens and Patty Malone explain in *The Handbook of Crisis Communications*, people in crisis are "likely to seek out others with similar stories and experiences"; social media and other mass channels mean that "victims and other publics can now turn to each other for virtual informational and emotional support."[25]

Network theory thus allows us to harness a natural community response in the service of efficient information flow to and from the responders who need it and to all citizens who want to help. Recall from Chapter 2 that network density—how tightly connected nodes are—can be good or bad depending on the goal. Development researcher and consultant Ben Ramalingam has also observed the way in which a disaster leaves an "institutional vacuum" that is immediately filled by informal networks of family and friends. He draws on research showing that "a dense, horizontal, kin-based network was in fact found to be more supportive than a sparser and more diverse network."[26] The University College London City Leadership Initiative calls these networks Informal Governance Systems and is conducting research with the Red Cross and World Bank in Nepal and Japan to better understand how they work in a crisis.[27] Immediate response efforts should focus on bolstering those networks.

## STABILIZATION NETWORKS

Recall the definition of resilience at the outset of this chapter: a system's resistance to change in the face of disturbance and its ability to recover. Stabilization networks are recovery networks. They are the networks necessary to restore an affected population, ecosystem, or community to its previous state before the attack or disaster, or even to build it back better. Recovery networks can also be defense networks in the sense of protecting against recurrence of a crisis or attack. They can be thought of more generically as "strengthening networks," putting in place the types and patterns of connections that will stabilize a fragile situation and strengthen a system's capacity to accomplish its goals.

As diplomats and development professionals will recognize, stabilization and support networks are a form of state building. "Reconstruction and stabilization" is U.S. military jargon for "winning the peace." Even without a war, plenty of governments around the world need help providing basic services to their citizens: security, health care, education, infrastructure, and economic opportunity. Improving "governance" and "capacity building" are well-established categories of foreign assistance. The lessons of network theory, however, suggest that we focus too much on the assistance we are providing—the transfer of knowledge and skills needed to carry out administrative tasks—and not enough on the relationships we are building.

Stabilization networks should operate at the level of both government and civil society, as strong self-government requires both. Both the hub and the mesh offer promising places to start. In this context each hub in a hub network can be thought of as a module, like the subgroups in the modular hierarchical response networks, or better yet as a pod, a small group within which it is possible to build strong relationships. These pod networks are likely to be better for strengthening specific government capabilities, although just as personal trainers warn of the impossibility of "spot reductions" when you're trying to lose fat, spot strengthening is difficult to achieve except as part of a wider regimen. Weaving a wider and more distributed web that can connect more people and communities is also crucial both socially and economically, particularly in a fragmented society that struggles to integrate diverse ethnic, religious, or racial groups.

The stabilization in these networks comes from the power of human connection. The impact of network participation on participants in many networks is rooted in a fundamental human desire to be connected to others and to be recognized by them as a peer.[28] Remember homo sociologicus. Legal scholar Ruti Teitel writes of "a will to live collectively that may well be inherent in what it is to be human."[29] In *The Social Animal*, journalist David Brooks reviews certain neuroscientific and biological underpinnings of precisely this point.[30]

That connection can be created and channeled far more systematically than we are doing. Think about resilience nets as the safety nets under a circus performer. We can make them stronger and wider and springier. We can change their pattern so that they are stronger than a straight mesh. The result will not only be increased resilience but at least the possibility of increased energy and entrepreneurship.

Transforming Clusters into Clubs

War-torn and plagued with dysfunctional governance, Ukraine needs a set of stabilization and assistance networks like the ones Europe and the United States put in place in Eastern and Central Europe after the fall of the Berlin Wall. One example from that time was the American Bar Association's Central and Eastern European Law Initiative (CEELI), which trained tens of thousands of lawyers, judges, and other legal officials in what the rule of law requires and looks like. Still, no matter how good the advice, one-time contact will not work. In the early years after the Wall came down, many U.S. assistance programs came under sharp criticism for relying on fly-in consultants who landed in a country they didn't know, spent two weeks dispensing expertise, and disappeared.

It is much better to build a longer-term professional association, which can be done by constructing professional networks. Social psychologists and researchers have shown that face-to-face interaction increases cooperation. In more than one hundred social dilemma experiments with thousands of subjects, cooperation nearly doubled when players were allowed to communicate face-to-face—even when the individuals involved didn't like each other.[31] Repeated contact, or "mere exposure," improves likability over time, at least in the aggregate.[32]

The best way to help government officials—judges, legislators, regulators, and bureaucrats—is to engage them in peer groups that both create a sense of belonging and exert peer pressure. As Tina Rosenberg writes in *Join the Club*, the creation of peer groups has spread revolution, taught high school kids algebra, and sharply reduced the incidence of AIDS in South Africa.[33] Knowledgeable peers can provide support and assistance as needed. The desire to keep up with those peers and have them think well of you can also create a set of higher expectations about professional behavior.

None of this will come as news to parents; we are bombarded with research showing that we have far less impact on our children than their friends do.[34] The study of networks tells us that these peer group connections will reverberate beyond the individuals involved; remember that our friends' friends' friends' choices and behavior affect our own. Applying this insight to stabilization networks means that sustained relationships within a peer group will influence not only the bureaucrats directly involved, but their colleagues as well.

The best structure for peer group networks is the pod form just discussed, which is a variation on a hub network. But whereas effective response networks needed a modular hierarchy, in which each member of a subnetwork—a module—was connected to a central source and each central source was then connected to a central aggregator for the entire network, pod stabilization networks require a different modification The trick is to ensure that the nodes off of each of the "branches" emanating from each hub are connected to one another, to turn the clusters into pods. The density and vibrancy of those cross-connections make the difference, as well as their link back to a larger network. And it is essential that the members of each pod assume they will engage in repeated interactions.[35] This is where social physics kicks in. Research at the MIT Human Dynamics Lab has shown that the frequency of direct interaction accurately predicts "the shared level of trust and the effectiveness of peer pressure."[36]

Imagine, for instance, that the new Ukrainian finance minister and her top officials are integrated into a pod network of ten or so EU finance ministers, a U.S. deputy or undersecretary of the treasury, and perhaps a Canadian, Japanese, or Australian member. The Ukrainian justice minister would be part of a similarly curated network of justice ministers. They would all be connected to one another and would meet during global and regional meetings twice or three times a year. Each pod or subnetwork would also be connected to the central node of the hub network. That central node is vital; it must be composed of the foreign and development ministers of the EU and the United States as well as the U.N. secretary general and representatives from other important powers or regional organizations concerned with stabilizing and strengthening the Ukrainian government.

Critical to the success of this pod network, however, is the additional appointment of a respected figure, perhaps a former finance minister or central banker, as a club leader. Peer pressure works only in groups whose members are sufficiently engaged with one another to care about each other's opinions. Another social physics axiom is that the number of direct interactions among group members is a "very good measure" of whether they would adopt and sustain cooperative behaviors.[37]

When governments need to be stabilized, trust is also necessary for officials of those governments to actually ask for support. The leader is not a figurehead; he or she must be willing to stimulate an ongoing level of activity in the group. The

leader can continually ping the network to trigger the exchange of information, create subgroups by connecting pairs
or trios of members to address specific issues, make valuable
introductions in the private and civic sectors, and foster regular side and submeetings. The leader must understand that
sparking and weaving relationships and orchestrating group
activity is a genuine job, and it should be compensated accord-
ingly.

Pod stabilization networks need not be limited to government officials. Equally important are people-to-people networks that government can facilitate. In 2010, the State
Department launched a Global Entrepreneurship Program designed to identify and train promising entrepreneurs in the
Middle East and elsewhere, and connect them to financing networks, mentors, market access contacts, and support networks
to create an "entrepreneurial ecosystem" modeled on Silicon
Valley.[38] It got off to a good start in Egypt and North Africa but
was never fully funded or embraced by traditional diplomats. If
we really want to help young Ukrainians imagine a different
future, we need to enable as many of them as possible to innovate and create jobs for one another, following the same principles of sustained engagement and relationship building that
we use with national leaders.

## Weaving a Civic Web

Connection itself is not necessarily a good thing. Think of organized crime networks or networks of spies and informers for
any kind of boss. High connectivity can maintain a negative
equilibrium as readily as it can a positive one. Duncan Watts
describes how high connectivity ensures stability: "Networks

that are too highly connected prohibit cascades" of disruptive behavior because "they are locked into a kind of stasis, each node constraining the influence of any other and being constrained itself."[39] On the other hand, network theorists have also shown that in the right circumstances, increasing the connectivity of actors increases the likelihood they will choose cooperative action.[40] Connecting the right actors for the right purposes holds out at least the possibility of shifting from a negative to a positive cooperative equilibrium, weaving a civic web to counter a criminal one.

Moreover, the more diverse and layered a civic web is, the stronger and more resilient it is likely to be. In his comparative study of Allentown, Pennsylvania, and Youngstown, Ohio—two rust belt manufacturing towns hit by the same economic crisis at the same time—organizational theorist Sean Safford documents how different types of social and civic networks produced different levels of trust and cooperation. The main reason Allentown bounced back and Youngstown struggled to recover was not the presence of civic networks; each city had a civic infrastructure linking business leaders, social clubs, arts and cultural institutions, and charities. It was the diversity of the people and organizations that were connected, in the same way that a diverse set of genes and organisms pooled in a biological ecosystem provides greater resilience in the face of natural or man-made threats. In Youngstown, the economic and civic networks largely overlapped, so that the virus of globalization and technological transition hit both equally hard. In Allentown the two networks intersected at critical points but diverged enough that when the local economic leadership was decimated, other civic leaders could connect "key constituencies who needed to cooperate in the face of the region's crisis."[41]

When the steel industry began to founder, the Garden Club couldn't save Youngstown because the Garden Club members were mostly the wives of the very business elite that was in trouble as the steel industry foundered. But in Allentown, the region's most important business leader, the head of Bethlehem Steel, focused his civic activity on the board of the Boy Scouts, a "cross-class-based organization" that connected him to a much wider array of civic leaders. This tale of two cities yields a larger lesson: "The key to rebuilding mature industrial regions lies in whether and how they have reknitted the fabric of civic participation."[42]

Remember the relative advantages of strong and weak ties. In Youngstown the ties were *too* strong, reinforcing one collective view and creating stasis. Allentown's civic network, by contrast, had more bridging than bonding capital, weaving together more disparate groups and illustrating "the strength of weak ties."[43]

When the governments of wealthy developed countries think about stabilizing poorer, less developed countries, they typically think in terms of sending in foreign advisers, consultants, and peers. But tapping into civic spirit—the basic human desire to improve one's circumstances—can start anywhere. Stabilization networks can thus be built by bringing people together within another society. Its government may be fragile, its civil society weak by Western standards, but people everywhere share affiliations—professional interests, hobbies, educational backgrounds, places of worship, charities, sports teams.

These affiliation networks are the "substrate" of social networks. A network strategy to build resilience across a society could start by searching for affiliation networks, with the idea that these repositories of social capital can be mobilized into civic capital. The next step is to create "short cut links" among these different networks to create a small-world network, which allows rapid movement between otherwise disconnected groups and organizations.[44] In a healthy, resilient society, these different social and civic networks will include business and political leaders or will intersect with business and political networks at key junctures. In a fragile society, criminal, family, and authoritarian networks often dominate at the elite level, so the initial focus should be on developing counternetworks.

Finally, network designers, weavers of civic mesh, can draw on the concept of structural balance: the principle that groups of friends are more stable than groups of enemies. More subtly, a triangle of three people in which two friends are connected to each other and to a common enemy is more stable than one in which one person is friends with two other people who do not like each other (Figure 6).[45] International relations theorist Zeev Maoz found that higher levels of conflict result when there are relational imbalances that violate structural balance.[46] These principles can be useful in creating networks in deeply divided societies.

A healthy dose of humility is required here. Network engineering can create the same unintended consequences and even disasters as social engineering generally. But we have new tools that allow us to map existing networks much more precisely and dynamically, which makes it possible to support

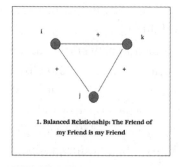

1. Balanced Relationship: The Friend of
my Friend is my Friend

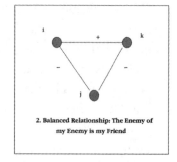

2. Balanced Relationship: The Enemy of
my Enemy is my Friend

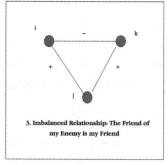

3. Imbalanced Relationship: The Friend of
my Enemy is my Friend

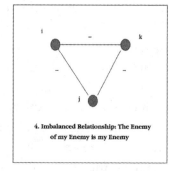

4. Imbalanced Relationship: The Enemy
of my Enemy is my Enemy

Figure 6. Balanced and imbalanced enmity relations. A plus sign
indicates the two nodes are friends, a negative sign that they are
enemies. In the top two panels (1 and 2), the relationships among
nodes i, j, and k are stable: in panel 1 all the nodes are friends, and
in 2 nodes i and k are friends and both dislike j. In the bottom two
panels, the connections are unstable: in panel 3, nodes k and i both
like j, but they dislike each other, and in 4 none of the nodes are
friends. In both these cases, the network won't hold.

and build on existing civic reservoirs rather than try to import
or create them. Moreover, as Moises Naim has shown, many
illicit networks have licit sections.[47] It is worth trying to find
and connect the right dots.

## Money from the Mesh

A healthy civic web can also be a vibrant economic web. Put on your rose-colored glasses, just for a second, and imagine a thriving mesh economy based on social and civic networks in towns and cities. In her 2010 book *The Mesh*, Lisa Gansky described a new business model based on "network-enabled sharing—on access rather than ownership. The central strategy is, in effect, to 'sell' the same product multiple times." Gansky wrote before Uber, Lyft, Airbnb, or TaskRabbit existed; today the "sharing economy" is also called the gig economy or crowd-based capitalism, all labels for a much bigger transformation in the way we create, provide, and harness value and think about ownership. But she emphasized a dimension of the sharing economy that is particularly relevant to fragile communities.

She called businesses based on sharing access to a particular good "mesh businesses" because a "mesh describes a type of network that allows any node to link in any direction with any other nodes in the system. Every part is connected to every other part, and they move in tandem."[48] Just so does information—about a car, a room, a service provider, a potential date, or anything else—flow through the mesh of social networks.[49] Moreover, the mesh businesses she focused on provide "shareable physical goods, including the materials used, which makes *local* delivery of services and products—and their recovery—valuable and relevant."[50] Sharing cars, bicycles, rooms, clothes, tools, and money helps reweave the physical community: a neighborhood, town, city, or region. In places with weak economies and fragile governance, enabling local entrepreneurs to profit by renting the goods they own will require the simultaneous weaving or reweaving of a civic and an economic mesh.[51]

Equally important, the mesh economy operates through social trust. The bigger the mesh, the greater the returns, but the mesh expands through social networks—word of mouth among friends.[52] Mesh entrepreneurs thus have every incentive to build not just a customer base but a community in which consumers talk to and share information with one another. That information also allows the provider of goods and services to customize offerings to individual customers, further building trust. Gansky describes how successful mesh businesses create a "virtuous cycle of trust" that mirrors Francis Fukuyama's account of how trust grows and spreads through economically *and* socially connected societies.[53]

Plenty can go wrong. Again, channels of connection are often channels of corruption or oppression. But anyone with a cell phone can operate a sharing platform. Moreover, enterprising individuals can buy goods with the aim of multiple consumption. The larger point here is not to offer an economic panacea but simply to point out that the very strength of the sharing economy, which has exploded since Gansky and others first wrote about it, is in the structure of an underlying network and the kinds of communications that flow across it. That is a structure of resilience.

## RESILIENCE BUILDING

Consider how many global problems have their roots in fragility: fragile ecosystems, fragile governments, fragile economies, fragile social fabric. Building resilience is vital, both in order to resist negative trends and to recover when bad things inevitably happen. From the chessboard perspective, however, strategies to build resilience are anomalous: they are preventive or temporary or remedial. They are not about winning in any measurable or sustained way.

The web view is different. Creating, maintaining, and strengthening resilience is weaving and bolstering webs of positive human relationships within and across borders. An excellent current example is candidate membership in the European Union: the officials of prospective EU members are absorbed into a vast web of official networks on every subject within the EU's jurisdiction. Other regional organizations could take a leaf from the European book here, but only if they are prepared to attach membership requirements, at least to regional subgroupings.

Most important, we can now fit specific networks to specific problems. We can build resilience through defense networks, response networks, and stabilization networks, each with a specific design and management structure. We can pour sufficient resources and attention into those networks to make them work. Geopoliticians may scoff. But some policy makers are catching on: the decision to adopt the Paris climate agreement calls for the appointment of two high-level "champions" to orchestrate networks of "non-Party stakeholders," such as cities, NGOs, and companies, to pursue complementary initiatives to combat climate change.[54] And if paying former ministers and distinguished elders to be network leaders sounds like summer camp, consider how cheap these investments are compared with imposing sanctions and fighting wars.

Building resilience is also a more modest and achievable aim than the grand project of nation building. The goal is to support people who want to build their own nation by providing peers who will reinforce their best version of themselves in the face of flagging will and periodic despair. Providing that support in the form most likely to be effective takes just as much energy and skill as negotiating a peace agreement or creating a diplomatic coalition.

# CHAPTER FIVE

# Task Networks

T HE goal of resilience networks is to strengthen, deepen, react, respond, bounce back, stabilize, and assist. Task networks, as the name suggests, are networks created to perform more precise and time-bound tasks. In their book *Team of Teams*, for example, General Stanley McChrystal and his coauthors describe how they transformed a hierarchical military command into a network tasked with defeating al Qaeda in Iraq. The task was clear, even if the best way to carry it out was not. The network that emerged was a collaboration network structured as a team of teams.[1]

Like resilience networks, task networks can have different structures and properties, such as the degree of integration and the nature of clustering. Terminology can also be tricky; many theorists and observers do not distinguish between cooperation and collaboration—often with good reason, as these categories are not mutually exclusive. Cooperation networks can become collaboration networks; collaboration networks certainly require cooperation but demand much more; and an innovation network is almost bound to involve both cooperation and collaboration. Understanding how to use networks effectively means understanding when to create, deepen, or loosen the relationships between nodes to affect the flow of information and ideas.[2] These relationships have many names and are continually evolving; the value of a typology is to create conceptual categories that provide a practical starting point for those who need to create custom-built networks.

I distinguish among task networks based on the initial preferences of the individuals and groups involved. It is possible to design a network primarily for cooperation, collaboration, or innovation, even if each category ultimately collapses into the others. That starting point will in turn depend on how well defined the task is at the outset of the project.

- A cooperation network is a linked group of individuals working together to carry out a prescribed task in a prescribed way.
- A collaboration network is a linked group of individuals figuring out together the best ways to carry out a prescribed task that itself may evolve.
- An innovation network is a linked group of individuals tasked with generating new ideas, processes, and/or products in the service of a prescribed general goal.[3]

Let us begin!

## COOPERATION NETWORKS

The classic cooperation problem in social science scholarship is the prisoner's dilemma; the classic strategy for turning conflicting incentives into cooperative behavior is tit-for-tat, which a player used to win Robert Axelrod's famous 1980 prisoner's dilemma tournament.[4] Each player's best strategy, from an individual perspective, is to defect, but if they all pursue that strategy, they will all be worse off than if they cooperate. Tit-for-tat works well enough in a game with a limited number of players—say the United States and the Soviet Union. But how to adapt it to the web world, with a potentially unlimited number of players?

The power of the prisoner's dilemma is that it captures the essence of collective action problems, situations in which private incentives conflict with the public good. This is the tragedy of the commons: where sheep owners, say, know that they all need a common grazing space, but to keep it usable, they cannot all graze all the time. Yet unless a way is found to make sure that everyone uses the space on a rotating basis, individuals have no incentive to refrain and every incentive to use the space before others graze it out.

The logical solution to the tragedy of the commons is the leviathan, a strong government able to enforce fair use of the resource and punish defectors. But Nobel Prize–winning research by Elinor Ostrom showed that in the real world the opposite was true. She found that in hundreds of common pool resource situations, such as irrigation systems, those managed by the farmers themselves performed better than those managed by a government.[5] In the real world, the farmers communicate with one another. The rational behavior assumptions of the prisoner's dilemma hold only if the players don't know each other and can't communicate. When participants are linked, they develop governance structures, resolve disputes, prevent overharvesting, and generate more product from a common pool resource than a government does.

As we saw in Chapter 1, an entire generation of distinguished political scientists has studied how to put these insights to work through the construction of international regimes, on the simple but powerful premise that states with common interests will cooperate to their mutual benefit if the transaction costs of cooperation can be made low enough. Network theory points to critical refinements that can be made across any negotiating table. It can also show us how to increase cooperation among populations by creating different kinds of groups that can be linked or not, depending on whether their members are likely to cooperate or not.

## Cooperation Among Adversaries

Consider the web perspective on problems such as conflict between China and the other countries bordering the South China Sea, between Iran and its neighbors, or between Venezuela and its neighbors in the Caribbean. In the chessboard world, nations are either allies, adversaries, or neutral. Their governments determine their national interests and implement strategies to achieve them; when those interests and strategies conflict with those of another nation, the two nations are adversaries.[6]

This frame wildly oversimplifies the way governments actually interact. When I was director of policy planning at the State Department, my office worked with our Chinese counterparts to organize the U.S.-China Strategic and Economic Dialogue. Secretary Clinton and Treasury Secretary Timothy Geithner led a delegation of ten heads of U.S. government agencies to meet with their counterparts in Beijing. Many of these agencies, such as the U.S. Department of Health and Human Services and the Nuclear Regulatory Commission, saw their Chinese equivalents as necessary allies in a common struggle against disease or environmental degradation. Even among the two countries' militaries, many high-level officials on both sides are deeply concerned about preventing an accidental encounter in the air or on the sea, or in the worst case keeping one from escalating.

Beyond the two governments, of course, plenty of citizens wish to turn enmity to amity—or at least to good business! Families, merchants, students, scientists, activists, artists, athletes, entrepreneurs, and many other groups can be activated as nodes in broader cooperative networks. Governments traditionally have turned to people-to-people diplomacy, often called public diplomacy, fostering educational, arts, and cultural exchanges of various kinds, broadcasting positive messages, and engaging foreign publics in dialogue and even heated debate. These exchanges have yielded valuable relationships, but in a fairly random way that is hard to track or use in a crisis.

A more systematic approach drawing on the full range of web actors within government and across societies would focus on building islands of cooperation in a sea of distrust. Studies of repeated games, the kind from which the tit-for-tat strategy arises, have shown that if the principal players come to know and engage each other, they become more patient and more likely to sustain cooperation over time. The structure of the networks that breed this kind of cooperation is shown in Figure 7.

Through this architecture, the fragile trust that is built up by the interplay of tit-for-tat can be deepened and strengthened through complete integration of the core network, meaning that everyone at the center is connected to everyone else. Each member of the core is connected to other, noncooperating players, at least some of whom will gradually shift to cooperative behavior.[7] In the core-periphery network, core players will tolerate the defectors on the periphery so long as they can count on the continued cooperative play of their core partners.

Diplomats will not exactly be surprised at this news. Legal scholar Gabriella Blum has written in *Islands of Agreement*

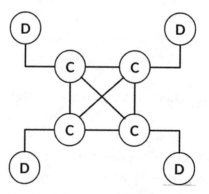

Figure 7. Core-periphery network. The core nodes are all maximally connected to one another, with defectors on the periphery. The core players will continue to cooperate with one another despite the uncooperative players on the fringe.

about managing the "enduring armed rivalry" between Israelis and Palestinians, arguing that it is possible to create space for cooperation beneficial to both sides even amid long-term armed conflict.[8] Another recent example is the P5+1/Iran nuclear deal, which would never have been concluded without the intense efforts of close-knit teams on both sides, who met repeatedly over the course of several years.

During his tenure as secretary of state, John Kerry has spent more time with Iranian Foreign Minister Javad Zarif than any other foreign dignitary. The duo, and their negotiating teams, which included Ali Salehi and Ernest Moniz, who had studied at MIT at the same time and also built a close relationship during the talks, formed a cooperative core dedicated to securing a deal despite resistance from hard-liners on the periphery.

That cooperation has persisted. When a last-minute snafu threatened to stymie a deal to release imprisoned *Washington Post* reporter Jason Rezaian, Kerry talked directly to Zarif, who resolved the issue. When a U.S. Navy patrol boat was captured in Iranian waters, Kerry called Zarif and the American sailors were released in less than a day. Before the nuclear negotiations, this level of cooperation would have been impossible. Note, however, the interplay of web and chessboard: the cooperative solution was underpinned by withholding funds due to the Iranians until the release was accomplished.

It should be possible to design a more structured and systematic "archipelago strategy," aimed at building strong pockets of cooperation among government officials, business leaders, church groups, universities, and many other groups in the private and civic sectors. The key is to pay attention to the composition of the initial group and to give each group a specific task that requires sustained contact and engagement. Counterintuitively, perhaps, it is also important to choose a task in an area of controversy, so that group members are likely to face criticism or opposition from others in their network. They will draw closer to one another as they reach agreements that they must then defend in other contexts.

Thus instead of creating a business round table of Chinese and Japanese executives, for instance, it would be more effective to task a working group of business leaders with developing a marketing campaign to increase the attraction of Japanese products in China and Chinese products in Japan. Similarly, a group of U.S. and Cuban environmentalists could be asked to create a joint plan for protecting the waters between the two nations. Or a group of university presidents from the United States, Europe, and various Muslim-majority nations could be charged with developing a code of conduct for coeducation consistent with both Islamic law and universal human rights.

Such projects will work only if the governments involved commit to monitoring the processes and implementing the results. Feel-good efforts under the broad umbrella of confidence-building measures are not enough. The architects of cooperation must deliberately seek out areas where any agreement would be hard won and controversial, and carefully select the core group members with an eye toward building deep relationships. The resulting cooperative networks in specific areas could then be mapped and connected to help build constituencies for broader cooperation.

## Cooperation Among Colleagues

One of the central insights of Robert Keohane's *After Hegemony*, the most influential book for international lawyers and international relations scholars of my generation, was that the presence of a common interest is a necessary but insufficient condition for international cooperation.[9] The literature on designing regimes—formal or informal principles, rules, norms, and decision-making procedures—seeks to overcome the obstacles of free-riding, cheating, reputational impact, and basic lack of time and information that prevent nations from getting to what political scientists and economists call the "Pareto-optimal frontier." That is jargon for social scientific heaven: the place where everyone is maximally well off and any party's move to improve its situation further will lower the total welfare of the group.

Many of the international agreements that have been negotiated based on these design principles provide public goods, like lower carbon emissions, lower barriers to trade, or a ban on chemical weapons. Network theory goes further: it tells us how network structure and degree distribution—how many links each node has—can lower the costs and increase incentives for individual actors to contribute to public goods.[10] In some cases, an actor is more likely to take an action if her neighbors do. This means that adding links to active players will increase the incentive for that player to act (in which case we say that the players are strategic complements). In others, the actor is less likely to act if her neighbors do (the players are strategic substitutes). Depending on how and to whom a node is connected, adding links can either increase or decrease cooperation.

In a world of strategic complements, adding connections to cooperators will make everyone more likely to cooperate. In a world of strategic substitutes, where one party's cooperation makes another's unnecessary, connecting one cooperator to another, or to a cluster of cooperators, may lead her to stop cooperating, as in Figure 8. Even in this world, however, adding links can increase cooperation, as in Figure 9.

A research team comprising physicists, ecologists, and biologists has demonstrated that connecting networks of coalitions and clubs has the potential to deepen cooperation and spur action on global public goods problems. In addressing climate change, for instance, we would think initiatives and organizations would be strategic substitutes—if one association is working on the problem, others would feel less compelled to contribute. But in fact, "an interacting ecosystem of agreements, coalitions and initiatives across multiple levels of governance"

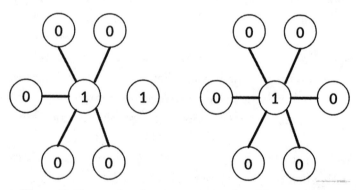

Figure 8. Connection decreases cooperation. Players who are strategic substitutes are less likely to contribute to a public good if their neighbors do. In this case, adding a link decreases total cooperation.

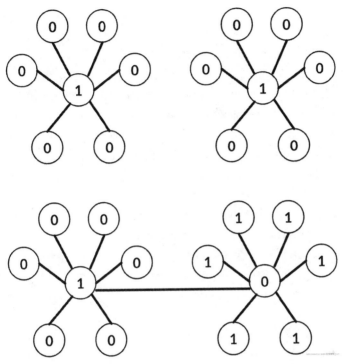

Figure 9. Connection increases cooperation. In this strategic substitutes case, adding a link increases overall cooperation.

may "substantially deepen international cooperation" and be more effective than a "single comprehensive regime with universal participation" under the U.N. Framework Convention on Climate Change.[11] Recent research has indeed demonstrated that national climate policies and transnational climate initiatives are strategic complements, not substitutes. Analysis of fourteen thousand instances of participation in international climate governance showed that strong national climate change policies in a country make that country's cities, companies, civil society groups, and other nonstate actors more likely to join international climate networks.[12]

More generally, overlapping building-block institutions allow for adaptation and flexibility: countries can "learn and change their preferences in one institution, which can have spillover effects in other institutional settings." Already this approach has shown success: the Financial Stability Board, then Forum, accelerated acceptance of global financial standards and deepened cooperation in the IMF after the 1998 Asian financial crisis; the Nuclear Suppliers Group, a network of countries that pushed for limiting the export of dual-use nuclear technology, brought about increased cooperation within the Non-Proliferation Treaty.[13]

Elinor Ostrom wrote extensively about the strength of such "polycentric systems," interconnected networks of formally independent decision-making enterprises at various levels pursuing a shared goal.[14] In tackling climate change, she observed, "encouraging the emergence of a polycentric system" that includes municipal utility energy-saving rebates, state and national clean air laws, "green" initiatives in cities, and various other laws, agreements, and programs could start the process of reducing emissions and prod "international regimes to do their part."[15]

The differences between the chess player and the networker, homo economicus and homo sociologicus, play out predictably in the literature on provision of public goods. In the economics literature on networks, punishment (or the threat of it) compels cooperation.[16] In repeated games, the effectiveness of punishing defectors depends on the availability of information: whether enough other players are aware of a player's reputation or history. More information thus leads to higher levels of cooperation.[17] Researchers in sociology and biology, by contrast, tend to recognize a wider range of motivation for cooperation: homophily (birds of a feather flock together), preferential association (wanting to do what the cool kids do), peer pressure, reputation, and indirect reciprocity (paying it forward).[18]

These insights open up new possibilities for policy makers who must connect nations, organizations, and leaders to solve the increasingly urgent global problems of our time. Network theory can help us think through the advantages of separate versus complete networks, different network architectures, and the management of different kinds of flows, from resources to reputation, through those networks. All can be deployed to increase cooperation, whether among states engaging one another as unitary actors or among the much wider universe of web actors.

## COLLABORATION NETWORKS

Collaboration problems arise when a group of individuals want to solve a common problem, or are required to do so, but cannot work together effectively enough to achieve their objective. General McChrystal, when he was in charge of the Joint Special Operations Command (JSOC), faced this problem in Iraq in 2004. Tasked with finding and destroying al Qaeda in Iraq, he faced a dilemma that he described in Figure 10.

The U.S. military is a hierarchy, even its special operations forces. Al Qaeda is a network, a structure that allows speed, flexibility, and constant adaptation. It includes many

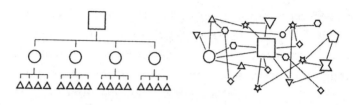

What we were designed for          What we were facing

Figure 10. Facing a networked adversary: U.S. Special Forces was designed to combat enemies organized in hierarchies. But al Qaeda was organized as a network.

individuals and groups who execute attacks against a wide variety of targets in the name of reestablishing a radically pure version of Islam. Some attacks are centrally directed; others are carried out autonomously by individual cells.

McChrystal had to create matching capabilities in his own organization, which meant somehow turning his hierarchy into a network. The task was more than to match organizational forms, however; as we saw in Chapter 2, different network structures can elicit specific behaviors from individuals within them. Research on open-source software development has found that "in a given time period, more centralized groups of developers fixed more bugs, whereas more decentralized groups developed more new features. Individuals working on the same problems behaved either productively or creatively depending on the structure of the network they worked in."[19] McChrystal thus had to design a network that would generate the behaviors necessary to respond to and defeat the enemy.

His first task was to build "trust and a shared sense of purpose," consciously forming and deepening relationships among small groups of people so that they could "act as a seamless unit," exercising "joint cognition" in changing circumstances.[20] His first answer was a command of teams (Figure 11).

Each team is an interlinked star. The presence of one clear central node allows for central management. At the same time, other nodes are connected to one another in ways that allow for decentralized intelligence to emerge.[21]

This structure quickly encountered a problem well known to organization theorists and behavioral psychologists: small-group cohesion works wonders as long as the group remains small.[22] As one SEAL put it: "The squad is the point at which everyone else sucks. That other squadron sucks, the other SEAL teams suck, and our Army counterparts definitely suck."[23] The feeling of belonging to a particular squad is a powerful source of motivation, strength, and resilience, but how then to create shared knowledge, cooperative action, and collaborative problem-solving among multiple teams?

Moreover, given the fast pace and ever-evolving tactics of the enemy, McChrystal needed teams to be able to act as individual units interacting continually in unexpected and unpredictable ways, allowing the emergence of "ingenious

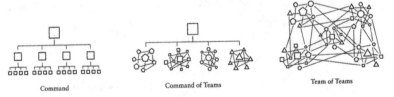

Command

Command of Teams

Team of Teams

Figure 11. Team of teams: McChrystal tuned the structure of the task force to improve its ability to share information and solve complex problems.

solutions . . . in the absence of any single designer." The solution, McChrystal and his coauthors argue, was a team of teams, a network capable of solving large, complex problems, relying on "both the visible hand of management and the invisible hand of emergence, the former weaving the elements together and the latter guiding their work."[24]

At first glance, the team of teams looks like a classic "small world" network, characterized by low average degree (most people are not connected to many other people), high clustering, and enough connections between clusters that the average distance between any two nodes in the network is small. But the team of teams is much more systematic than that, in important ways. McChrystal did not want everyone connected to everyone else; that would be hopelessly inefficient. But he needed "everyone to know *someone* on every team, so that when they thought about, or had to work with, the unit that bunked next door or their intelligence counterparts in DC, they envisioned a friendly face rather than a competitive rival."[25] Strategic network design meant ensuring a deliberate number of links between clusters, for efficiency but also for psychological purposes.

Equally important, the team of teams can transform itself into a complete network for communications while remaining a connected modular network for action. McChrystal relied on the twin pillars of "shared consciousness" and "empowered execution." To achieve shared consciousness, all members of the network received the same information, continually updated, a feat McChrystal accomplished by transforming the daily operations and intelligence briefing (the O&I) into a rich discussion that anyone on any team, whether from JSOC or any other partner agency, could dial into securely and both listen and speak.[26]

The O&I became the "neural network" of the entire team of teams, with almost seven thousand people engaging daily for more than two hours.[27] The forum completely contravened classic "need-to-know" military secrecy and fostered a culture of radical sharing. This was a complete network, in which we know both mathematically and empirically that the "probability of adopting optimal action can be increased to one by simply increasing the number of nodes."[28]

What McChrystal did not expect was that developing a shared consciousness strengthened his ability to implement his second principle, empowered execution. Empowered execution means pushing authority as far down the chain of command as possible, providing general guidelines and a shared sense of purpose, and then allowing team members at all levels to exercise their own judgment. Shared consciousness and empowered execution are interrelated; as McChrystal writes, when team members listened to superiors debate problems on the O&I, it allowed them to understand the perspectives of senior leadership, which in turn "gave them the skills and confidence to *solve their own* similar problems without the need for further guidance or clarification."[29]

Empowered execution is a management principle employed in highly adaptable, horizontal organizations. Information economics researcher Marshall Van Alstyne, who has written extensively on how people share information, finds: "Local agents are not only better positioned to *gather information* on specific local conditions, but vested with decision authority and ownership of the result, they are also more likely to look for problems and opportunities."[30] Similarly, businesses that have high connectivity with their customers and partners identify problems earlier than their more centralized competitors.[31]

McChrystal's "team of teams" goes by other guises in other literatures: many might call it a "distributed network with local agents." Duncan Watts calls it a "meta-team" composed of members from multiple scales of a large organization.[32] In many ways McChrystal faced the dilemma that large corporations did in the 1990s when they transformed themselves into network enterprises. Recall that in Chapter 2 Walter Powell described a "new logic of [business] organizing . . . built around project-based work and team organization."[33] Fluid project-based collaboration is the defining characteristic of the network enterprise, both within and between firms.

The genius of the "team of teams" approach, as McChrystal describes it, is the deliberate emphasis on both the number and type of connections between each module, combined with Janus-faced flexibility. The whole team can turn itself into a social learning network with a clear center, and then back into a distributed modular network with just enough connectivity to supplement internal competition with a common purpose. Both faces are essential for the combination of cooperation and adaptation that defines effective collaboration.

## INNOVATION NETWORKS

McChrystal's teams, whether operating as a team of teams or autonomously in carrying out individual missions, innovated every day. They were fighting a terrorist network that continually adapted to local circumstances and to what they themselves were doing; they thus continually had to find new ways to defeat the enemy.

Suppose, however, that innovation itself is the goal; that the reason to assemble a particular group of people is to come up with new products, services, ideas, or solutions to problems. The problem at hand could be how to monitor carbon emissions, how to monitor and report human rights violations, how to curb illegal fishing, or how to make desalinization easier and cheaper. These are all problems that governments, international organizations, development organizations, and other participants in global affairs must grapple with. Allocating research dollars is a traditional solution, but they would be much better spent within a network designed explicitly for innovation.

Such networks are the backbone of an approach—described by its creators as a "new paradigm"—called "open innovation" or sometimes "networked innovation." In his 2003 book *Open Innovation*, Henry Chesbrough distinguished that approach from traditional models of "closed innovation," in which companies invested in proprietary research and development and expected to harvest any new ideas, products, and processes that resulted. Ideas from outside were often quietly downgraded as "not invented here." Open innovation, by contrast, assumes "that firms can and should use external ideas as well as internal ideas, and external and internal paths to market, as they look to advance their technology" (Figures 12 and 13).[34]

Open innovation turns a firm into the hub of a set of nodes and networks that connect to value in many different ways. To take just one prominent example, companies like

The Closed Paradigm for Managing Industrial R&D

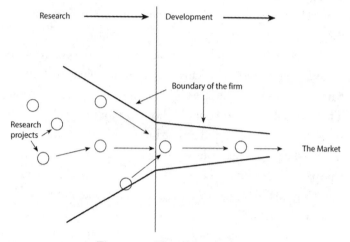

Figure 12. Closed innovation

The Open Innovation Paradigm for Managing Industrial R&D

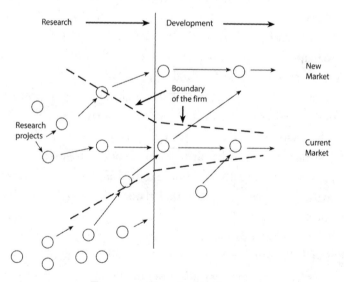

Figure 13. Open innovation

Procter and Gamble and Eli Lilly outsource many research problems to an innovation platform called Innocentive, which calls itself a "global network of millions of problem-solvers."[35] Multiple firms also play this game; Yochai Benkler describes "creation nets," loose networks of firms that work together "to come up with new products, processes, and ideas."[36] Even though these firms sometimes compete for the same market, they continually communicate with one another to innovate and improve their products' efficiency and competitiveness.

The U.S. government is following suit. The Pentagon and the intelligence community have created units to gather in technological innovation from a wide range of sources. The CIA's nonprofit venture capital organization, In-Q-Tel, receives business plans from commercial technology start-ups specializing in certain innovation categories useful to U.S. intelligence, such as advanced analytics, field deployable technology, mobility, and infrastructure and security.[37]

The Defense Department has launched DIUx, a Silicon Valley–based unit that connects with tech firms and invests in promising technologies with military applications. Start-ups pitch their ideas to DIUx—on one occasion to Secretary Carter himself in a "Shark Tank" event.[38] The Pentagon will soon open a second DIUx branch, in Boston.[39]

It is important to distinguish open innovation from open source. The open innovation paradigm described above is applicable to for-profit companies, or at least to organizations that intend to benefit from the resulting innovation. Open source is a more open-ended, less structured approach to innovation that I will discuss under scale networks. Some government agencies, like the intelligence community, the

Pentagon, and perhaps Treasury, may want to be able to ensure that some of the innovation they sponsor is proprietary. Others, like USAID and the State Department, will be more drawn to open-source innovation, since part of the value they seek to create is the generation of public goods.

What open innovation and open source have in common is what Jeff Jarvis, author of *What Would Google Do?*, describes as the "power of the link," the way that the ability to search for knowledge and then link to it liberates thinkers, writers, and researchers from having to master everything themselves; they can concentrate on their own areas of expertise and then link to other experts' work.[40] Aggregating knowledge and linking multiple problem solvers with different areas of expertise fosters a far more complex division of labor in the innovation process. This division of labor in turn underpins evolving theories of innovation, from the "hero" model embodied by the myth of Steve Jobs, to the team approach, and now to the open team or even crowd-sourcing.[41]

The optimal structure for open innovation places one firm at the center, as in a star or hub network, organizing and orchestrating the rest and harvesting value. Questions as to the network's "optimal density and size"—how many nodes and how connected those nodes should be—remain open.

Some clustering is certainly beneficial, implying some kind of hub structure. Van Alstyne finds that "networks of small groups . . . prove to be more innovative."[42] But how many small groups, and how much connectivity? Too many links among members will make the network unwieldy to manage and reduce the quality and novelty of the information it generates. Too few will dampen collaboration and cocreation.[43] It will be up to network designers to find the happy medium for their specific purposes.

Beyond structure, the details of "external network management" become central to the success of innovation networks. At their best, innovation networks are communities of practice as well as producers of value; indeed, open-source networks are explicitly both, producing internal social value. The leadership and management skills required to make these networks work are distinctive and crucial. We will discuss them later on in the book.

Foreign policy makers and global public problem solvers should turn to innovation networks when they have open-ended problems to solve. These problems should be specific enough, however, that bigger is not always better. Think "how to curb illegal fishing" rather than "how to save the oceans." The focal firms or organizations must be readily identifiable and must have sufficient resources and time to create, orchestrate, and harvest the results.

## THE GOLDILOCKS PRINCIPLE

Resilience networks come in many different forms: a mesh, a modified star, and a customized hub, among others. Task networks are all versions of a hub network: small groups, pods, or teams connected in various ways. That is not surprising, given that the specificity of a task requires a degree of direction and precision in its execution. When a task needs doing, it is not the time to let a thousand flowers bloom. Yet when a task needs doing in changing and unpredictable circumstances, too precise direction is a liability.

Hence the value of a task network. Tasks are best carried out by small, diverse, but cohesive groups. Diversity of team members provides multiple talents and perspectives, while small size builds sufficient trust and team spirit for the group to act as one and to adapt seamlessly to changing circumstances. Among adversaries, repeated interaction within a small group connected to a hostile larger group is essential to begin building the trust that is essential for common problem solving.

Among colleagues, the trick is to create the right kind of groups for the circumstances: peer groups of states or individuals who are more likely to go along if their friends or counterparts do; hub-and-spoke groups of potential free-riders. The team-of-teams approach to collaborative task execution creates a partially connected cluster network that can turn into a giant, completely connected star network for information purposes. And innovation networks harness the creativity and energy of small groups with input and ideas from as broad a community as possible.

The principal questions for task network designers are Goldilocks questions: when small groups are all charged with executing one large task, how densely or loosely should they be connected? Too many connections can paralyze; too few can cause vital information to be missed. As foreign policy practitioners become adept at designing networks for specific purposes, they are likely to develop a typology of task networks. But the categories of coming together to achieve a specific purpose, coming together to think and adapt as that purpose evolves and changes, and coming together to figure out new ways and means to do something that may never have been done before, cover a wide spectrum of jobs.

# CHAPTER SIX

# Scale Networks

M ANY global problems are really scale problems. In international development, for instance, we can use small-scale experiments to measure the effectiveness of different approaches to improving health, combating poverty, increasing literacy, and other initiatives. But even once we have identified programs that genuinely make a difference, how do we replicate them across millions of villages and communities? Alternatively, assume that a number of different approaches will work in fighting epidemic diseases, from bed nets to new treatments and vaccines. How do we align the thousands of large and small organizations, groups, and individuals working on a particular disease or cluster of health issues to coordinate their actions for the most impact? Finally, how do we assemble the ideas and knowledge that all these different players are generating in a way that builds rather than splinters?

Scale networks are part of the answer. They are particularly valuable for government policy makers because one of the great attractions of the chessboard world is that small, manageable initiatives, like starting negotiations or creating a working group of governments, have at least the potential to make a big impact. Some problems, meanwhile, arise from the interaction of people and groups but are frustratingly resistant to small-scale approaches. That is why the answer is so often a big convening, with the hope that bringing together hundreds of "key players" will somehow cause a solution to emerge. Knowing how to build scale networks that can implement these solutions opens a new box of policy tools.

It helps to think about scale networks in three basic ways: replication, gathering in, and parceling out. One type of scale problem is a replication problem: when a pilot project based on careful research, analysis, and testing works, yielding a successful approach to solving a particular public problem, how to repeat that success? The use of oral rehydration therapy to treat infant and child diarrhea is a good example. How to replicate the particular approach or organizational arrangements that made that idea work?

In other situations, many people know about, agree on, and are delivering the solution to a particular problem, but they are not working together effectively. Vaccine delivery and effective community pushback against religious radicalization are two examples. These are "gathering in" problems: connecting and coordinating many parts to create a larger and more effective whole.

The final category comprises "parceling out problems," in which an immense task requires that large numbers of people be reached and persuaded to help. Many hands make light work, but how to create the global equivalent of a barn raising or a quilting bee? Each of these categories requires a large-scale solution, but the network structure and management must be tailored a little differently.

## REPLICATION NETWORKS

Replication is a biological idea: the wonderful image of a DNA double helix unwinding to produce two identical copies of itself. This concept of spontaneous self-generation is one of the secrets of scale. Just imagine if we could design and implement a set of pilot projects, figure out which ones work, and then have those models effortlessly replicate themselves in other places. It is never that simple, of course, and replication run amok is cancer.

Network theory does provide a set of replication tools, for both organizations and ideas. Or, more accurately, it helps us understand the conditions under which the replication that we can see actually happening is most likely to occur. Recall from Chapter 2 the principle that individuals who are connected to other individuals make choices that are affected not only by their friends but also by their friends' friends and their friends' friends' friends. Is it possible to operationalize this phenomenon, to maximize the likelihood of scaling up either a club or a concept?

In the first section below we explore a template model for spreading self-organized groups. In the second we look at how marketers are already using network theory to help them spread information and ideas. No one has figured out precisely how to make a meme go viral, but it is certainly possible to create a more conducive environment for mass replication.

## The Seeds of Self-Organization

"At Alcoholics Anonymous, no one's in charge. And yet, at the same time, everyone's in charge." In *The Starfish and the Spider*, entrepreneurs Ori Brafman and Rod Beckstrom point to AA as a quintessential example of a decentralized "starfish" organization. "Spider" organizations are centralized, with a leader in charge and a headquarters that functions as a central nervous system. Decapitating this organization will destroy it. Starfish organizations, by contrast, have no one in charge, no "permanent location or central headquarters," and no clear division of roles. They consist of autonomous decentralized units that can be individually destroyed without harming the whole, with knowledge and power distributed throughout the organization.[1]

We will return to the question of whether an organization can really operate with "no one in charge" when we discuss network leadership in Chapter 8. For present purposes, what is most illuminating about starfish organizations is the way information spreads and groups replicate one another. With AA, founder Bill Wilson chose to create a twelve-step recovery program that anyone could adopt by forming his or her own AA chapter, without central direction. He created the template but "trusted each chapter to do what it thought was right." Anyone could start a chapter "without asking permission or getting approval."[2] The result was a global network, powered by what AA members call "the big book," the story of how Wilson got sober.[3]

A more contemporary example is TEDx, the rapid spread of TED conferences on themes of every description. TED's mission is "ideas worth spreading." The two "mainstage" TED conferences every year are carefully curated; organizers scour the world to find scientists, technologists, futurists, artists, activists, and authors to present beautifully groomed talks. TEDx "supports independent organizers who want to create a TED-like event in their own community." The program began in 2009; it has generated ten thousand events with almost fifty thousand talks held all over the world. TEDx has a detailed template of what its events must look like, but anyone can get a license to hold a TEDx event as long as the proposed event meets the template requirements.

Still another example comes from the foreign policy world, at least as I am defining that world in this book. Team Rubicon is a disaster response network composed of veterans. Founded by two former marines who assembled a team to go to Haiti after the 2010 earthquake, this NGO now has thirty-eight thousand volunteers who have deployed to more than one hundred disaster sites in the United States and abroad. Members organize into teams to deliver emergency assistance in disaster zones. They deploy within twenty-four hours and can operate independently or integrate into NGO or government command structures.

The secret sauce of Team Rubicon is that veterans have the mission-based community and sense of purpose often absent from civilian life. Team Rubicon is growing as a replication network, spawning AA-style chapters in foreign countries—so far, the United Kingdom, Norway, and the Philippines. Local veterans run the organizations, receiving only seed money, guidance, best practices, and norms from the central platform, which serves as a "coach" and the "glue" for the network rather than a "head office."[4]

Replication networks combine the power of decentralization with the uniformity (or at least consistency) of a central template and the community of fellow travelers. They offer a resource and a product that people need and want, within a structure that rewards local initiative. At the same time, however, many rely on what Tina Rosenberg calls "the social cure": the creation of "peer group[s] so strong and persuasive that the individual adopts a new identity."[5] AA gives recovering alcoholics a new sober identity and a support group to go with it; TEDx is simply cool, building on TED's cachet as a conference on Technology, Entertainment, and Design.

Rosenberg tells the story of a Serbian opposition group named Otpor—"resistance" in Serbian—that succeeded in bringing down dictator Slobodan Milosevic's government in 2000. "Otpor turned passivity into action by making it easy—even cool—to become a revolutionary." Young people were attracted by edgy graphics, street theater, rock music, and acts of political opposition. In the words of one of Otpor's leaders, Ivan Marovic, "Our product is a lifestyle. . . . It's about being cool. We're trying to make politics sexy."[6]

Otpor succeeded, and not just in Serbia. Rosenberg focuses on the mechanisms of political mobilization, the harnessing of positive peer pressure. But Otpor's message spread—to Georgia, Tunisia, and Egypt—not only because of its content but because of a replication network launched and funded by investor Peter Ackerman. Ackerman created the International Center on Nonviolent Conflict, which holds seminars and training on nonviolent political strategies for opposition groups from all over the world. He made Otpor's story into a film, which has been translated into more than ten languages, and also created a video game that lets activists practice their strategies in virtual space.[7] In short, he has turned successful revolutions into a template and created channels and platforms that make that template available to groups all over the world. The product is good; the audience is there; the template is available and no one is in charge to stop any group from making it their own. Imagine how many other successful strategies could replicate themselves the same way!

## Going Viral

Foreign policy officials and nonprofit groups fighting Islamic radicalization frequently lament that ISIS, al Qaeda, and similar groups seem to be able to spread their ideas quickly and effectively via social media, whereas the stories of ISIS recruits who now reject radical Islam, or the sermons of more moderate imams, do not have the same reach. Similarly, anti-immigrant groups succeed in spreading narratives of crimes committed by immigrants much faster and more effectively than pro-immigrant groups can propagate stories and statistics of immigrant value to their communities. Social media are simply the rumor mill made manifest: networks have always hummed and buzzed with the latest news, ideas and fashions. Today, however, that humming and buzzing is now actually visible electronically and can move at the speed of millions and billions of clicks. Now that we can see and monitor those networks, is it possible to shape and tweak them for positive purposes?

One of our design principles is that a network lives only when something flows across it. A corollary principle is that networks succeed and fail depending on how effectively and efficiently information moves between their nodes. Organizational sociologist Walter Powell envisions workers in a modern firm as information processors; to MIT's Alex Pentland, teams are like "idea-processing machines combining individual thinking and social learning."[8] The productivity of an organization, the impact of a social movement, and the staying power of a fad all depend on whether the structure of the network facilitates the optimal flow of information.

Malcolm Gladwell's 2000 book *The Tipping Point* popularized scientific work on norm cascades through the concept of a single tipping point, "that magic moment when an idea, trend, or social behavior crosses a threshold, tips, and spreads like wildfire."[9] Gladwell's division of the world of influence into connectors, mavens, and salesmen led marketers to search for "influentials": specific individuals with these attributes, who could help the marketers' ideas and products go viral. What Gladwell omits, however, is that an idea can cascade only if the structure of the network is right. Too little connectivity among nodes and an idea has nowhere to spread; too much and a single influential gets drowned out in a sea of competing ideas.[10]

Today, marketing guru and social network designer Paul Adams focuses not on "overly influential individuals" but on "small, independent yet connected groups of friends." He argues that for "spreading ideas, the structure of the network is more important than the characteristics of the individual." Only relatively small groups share enough and are sufficiently influenced by one another for an idea to take hold among them; only when those groups are connected through individual members to many other small groups will the infrastructure exist for rapid spreading. Moreover, the composition of each group matters: the first adopters of a new idea must be a group of people with a low threshold for change (innovative hubs), but those groups are typically outliers, with fewer connections to others than groups that are more resistant to change (follower hubs).[11]

Adams is offering concrete marketing advice. Duncan Watts makes the same point from a broader perspective, observing that cohesive, isolated groups tend to reinforce a set of attitudes and resist change (think North Korea or the Branch Davidians). At the opposite end of the scale, highly connected individuals who participate in many groups are less likely to be dominated by a single worldview; they have many sources of information and influence, and may triangulate among all those sources; and they are also less likely to get continual reinforcement from like-minded peers. That is why cults cut their members off from society.

We come to another Goldilocks rule: viral communication requires just the right balance "between local reinforcement and global connectivity."[12] The MIT Human Dynamics Lab team found exactly the same pattern in their study of 1.6 million day traders on the eToro platform, which allows one to see and copy orders placed by other traders. The most successful traders were connected enough to a diverse enough group of other traders that they could see and learn from the behavior of a wide range of others, but not so many that they ended up in an echo chamber in which only a few behaviors, not necessarily the best ones, drowned out the others.[13] This practice of "social exploration"—seeking out a broad range of ideas and forming connections with the right number and range of people when making a decision—is a central element of social physics.

The key, then, is to find individuals who are, in Pentland's phrase, "susceptible" to social learning, in the same way that some of us are more susceptible to catching the flu. The data miners at MIT have found that people are more susceptible if they are influenced by someone else showing a new behavior (a role model) who is "sufficiently similar" to them that the new behavior will be useful, if the level of trust between them and the role model is high, and if the new behavior or idea is consistent with previously learned behaviors. The researchers showed the influence of role models in a study of smartphone app downloading behavior in a community of young adults. They found that the two predictors of which apps someone would download were being similar (in gender, age, job, religion, and so on) to others who had downloaded that app, and, to a greater extent, the frequency of interaction—an indicator of trust—with peers who had downloaded it.[14]

Watts offers a formal model of this susceptibility, based on what he calls an individual's "critical threshold for change."[15] It sounds obvious that an individual is more likely to adopt a neighbor's idea or behavior if she is open to change—that is, has a low critical threshold. But less obvious and equally important is the density of her network, the total number of neighbors she is connected to. She may be either too connected or not connected enough to change her behavior.

To make this concrete, consider a young professional in Kiev at the outbreak of the Maidan uprising in the winter of

2014. Let's say he is gainfully employed, largely apolitical, and a bit socially conservative—not the type to rush to the streets and erect a barricade. He has a high critical threshold to joining the uprising, meaning that a large percentage of people in his social network would have to take to the streets before he did too. Let's say he has ten friends who have joined. If his social network is sparse, say only fifteen people, then those ten friends will be enough to get him to join the protests. But if his network is dense, say fifty people, then he will continue to stay home.

Here we arrive at the gulf between academic theory and practical action. Even if we can reliably find out whether a given person in a population has a positive orientation (opposes radical Islam or carbon emissions, say), how do we connect her to the right number of the right people? We can understand, from looking at existing networks, why something is happening in the lab, but we have no idea how to apply that knowledge to achieve a chosen outcome out in the world. Watts's answer is that we need to identify a "percolating vulnerable cluster," which sounds to some of us like an exploding coffee pot, at least to those of us old enough to remember when coffee was something made in a percolator, or even in a pot.[16]

Remember, however, that we now have vast troves of data about who is connected to whom and the frequency and even emotional valence of those connections.[17] Data mining—of GPS location fixes, phone call records, credit card statements, and survey data, all voluntarily provided—allows us to identify a group of individuals and figure out whom they interact with and trust. Once these trusted individuals are identified, it should be possible to create groups of susceptible individuals around them and to connect those groups in the right ways to other groups to maximize the chance of positive behaviors spreading.

As media analyst and scholar Nadia Oweidat notes, the war of ideas in the Muslim world is not about "good Islam" versus "bad Islam," or even extremists versus moderates. It's about whether governance should be informed by modern, secular values or by religious, patriarchal ones. Oweidat told me that "when Wael Ghonim started the Facebook page 'We Are All Khaled Said,'" a reference to a young man whose death under police custody had catalyzed antigovernment activism in Egypt, "It was a call to have real citizenship, human rights, accountability, and the rule of law." It was a rejection of both authoritarianism and sharia, under which certain persons are less equal than others in the eyes of the state. These ideas flared up during the Arab Spring; the debate between the two paradigms continues today even under newly authoritarian governments. But the voices supporting secular values of equality and personal freedom have failed to take hold and percolate the way those supporting religious violence and intolerance have. Liberal ideas, though alive on social media throughout the Muslim world, are often overpowered by extremist ones.[18] But what if it's not, as network theory suggests, the content of the ideas themselves that is responsible for their spread, but rather the structure of the network and the clusters into which they are born?

Simply putting these ideas out on social media will not guarantee their adoption; they will probably be drowned out or ignored. Instead, we should start by creating small groups composed of some influential individuals committed to modern values—a civil state, equality, the rule of law—and a number of others who trust them, combined with at least a few contrarians to create a lively culture of debate and exploration. A minority of group members should also have connections to individuals who belong to groups that espouse (but do not necessarily practice) religious governance and even violence. Support the creation of a number of these small groups within individual countries and in different countries. Then connect them, but not too tightly.

Google Jigsaw, the tech giant's geopolitically focused technology incubator, has been experimenting with the first steps of such an approach. The Redirect Method, as the program is called, uses Google's advertising algorithms to direct those searching for extremist content toward curated YouTube videos that feature credible, organic content debunking ISIS narratives.[19] Attempts to block ISIS propaganda—shutting down Twitter accounts or removing YouTube videos—have largely failed to keep would-be extremists from viewing it. But Jigsaw's approach is showing promise, with 300,000 people drawn to the anti-ISIS YouTube channels in just two months. The next step would be to connect those who watch the videos into the types of communities described above.

In a chessboard mindset, if you want a person to behave a certain way you focus on creating incentives or disincentives to change that person's behavior. But network theory and social physics have shown that if you want an innovation or behavior to spread, you shouldn't focus on the individual; rather, you should change the connections *between* people. In their eToro trading platform study, the MIT team showed that this adjustment means sometimes increasing connectivity (for isolated traders who didn't learn from others) and sometimes reducing connectivity (for hyperconnected traders caught up in echo chambers).[20]

In her pioneering work on the corruption networks that run kleptocratic states, Sarah Chayes of the Carnegie Endowment for International Peace has found that most acutely corrupt regimes coalesce around a densely connected "kinship kernel."[21] These kernels, like the trader's echo chamber, circulate the same pernicious ideas and block out other ways of thinking and acting. U.S. military and civilian officials in Afghanistan and other corrupt states have tried, in vain, to persuade individuals in these networks to be less corrupt. A web-based anticorruption strategy would devote less effort to persuading individuals to change and more to trying to change the pattern of connections within the kernel and to stem the flow of resources into it.

Identifying the dispositions and connections of individuals in a society may seem an impossible task. But in a world in which the vast and unpredictable tides of human connection are instantly turned into billions of dots of data, we can see ideas, templates, and behaviors flowing and changing in real time. It is hard to resist trying to nudge and channel those flows in a positive direction. In the web world, it is not a reach to imagine foreign policy makers consulting social physicists the way their Cold War forerunners consulted natural physicists. The flow of atoms through carefully constructed channels threatened to blow up the world; the flow of ideas through equally carefully constructed channels can help knit it back together.

## COORDINATION NETWORKS

As we saw with innovation networks, the power of the digital link is that it allows for a vast division of labor. It is now possible to specialize in one area of expertise or experience and simply link to other specialists rather than try to master their fields. It is as if each individual were a single cell that can now link other single cells to create multicellular organisms. The business world has adopted this molecular form through the "growth of interfirm networks" composed of various small and large companies that collaborate to perform different components of the research and development and the production processes.[22] These networks distribute the costs of expensive projects, allow for experimentation and innovation, and are highly resilient in the face of disruption.[23]

The international development world needs a similar way to coordinate collective action. For global problems like pandemics, climate change, youth unemployment, or refugee housing, many organizations around the world are working on the problem. They simply aren't working together. Coordination networks, gathering in and connecting many different efforts, are the answer.

The best example of such a network is the Global Alliance for Vaccination and Immunization, or GAVI. Many small organizations and some larger ones have been working on vaccination and immunization against multiple diseases for decades. But GAVI has been a game changer. It has brought together foundations and multilateral organizations to work with developed and developing country governments, civil society organizations, the developed and developing country pharmaceutical industry, and research and technical institutes around the world. Each member of the network leverages its comparative advantage: The Gates Foundation provides funding, pharmaceutical companies develop vaccines, the World Health Organization regulates vaccine quality, and civil society organizations implement immunization programs. Since its founding in 2000, GAVI has immunized more than 500 million children and aims to vaccinate another 300 million by 2020.[24]

Scale makes the network work. Without the cumulative demand from many countries, the market for vaccines against infectious diseases in poor countries is simply not great enough to spur the needed research and development.[25] Modularity and division of labor enable large organizations to perform local tasks, from a global development bank to a research institute, to a local nonprofit health organization committed to delivering actual vaccines to actual babies in remote communities. Similarly, David Kaye, a law professor and U.N. special rapporteur, has argued that rather than make the International Criminal Court the single body responsible for the prosecution of mass human rights abuse cases, the United States and its multilateral partners should devote resources to helping national courts try such cases and thus coordinate an "international approach to national justice."[26]

In June 2016, two networks of cities working to combat climate change merged to form the Global Covenant of Mayors for Climate and Energy—which, with more than 7,100 cities from 119 countries, may be the world's largest coordination network.[27] Cochaired by Michael Bloomberg and European Commission Vice President Maroš Šefčovič, the Covenant is a central platform that coordinates and connects the efforts of cities and local governments to reduce carbon emissions, build climate resilience, and develop sustainable energy infrastructure. It provides technical assistance, helps member cities collect comparable data to drive accountability and competition in meeting emissions reductions targets, and, through an advisory group of financial institutions, advises cities on how to attract private investment in sustainable infrastructure. Cities account for an estimated 75 percent of global carbon emissions and 70 percent of energy consumption. The Covenant thus creates and mobilizes a network of actors on the front lines of climate change, bypassing the cumbersome processes of negotiating, ratifying, and implementing a legally binding international agreement.

All of these coordination networks must be structured as star networks with a clear center that is tasked with the considerable work of doing the coordination. Both GAVI and the Global Covenant of Mayors have a central secretariat with enough resources to get the job done. Simply finding and linking many different organizations dedicated to the same ultimate goal is not enough (although if you are the Gates Foundation, people will pay attention!). The central platform cannot give orders; the many organizations of many different types being pulled together will be independent to a fault.

The work of leadership in this context, as we will discuss in Chapter 8, is both specialized and underrecognized. It requires cultural competence across a wide range of public and private actors as well as a distinct set of skills: finding, connecting, cross-fertilizing, aligning interests, troubleshooting, problem solving, and continual orienting and reorienting toward the larger mission.

Network leaders can also maximize the appeal and power of their network by creating a "pull" platform. As John Hagel and his coauthors explain in *The Power of Pull*, many of the most successful information-age businesses operate on the principle of "pull" rather than "push." The push economy assumes that businesses and organizations know what their customers need, decide on the products and platforms that will meet those needs, and push them out. The pull model, by contrast, assumes that the *customers*—or clients or subscribers or followers—know quite well what they need and want and can build, and will be most productive if they have access to resources, knowledge, and platforms of creation and connection.[28]

A pull platform is not just a random assemblage of material. The value to customers, or in this case coalition members, lies in curation. In a world of too much of everything, abundance is a problem. Consider the value of playlists, curated podcast lists, best-seller lists of all kinds, and the quirky sensibilities that inform many of our favorite websites and stores. Providing the right material, the most useful and user-friendly material, and the most diverse, culturally sensitive material will make a central coordination platform the most attractive to the organizations you seek to coordinate. Curation, says entrepreneur Steven Rosenbaum, is fundamentally about "adding quality *back* into the equation and putting a human filter between you and the overwhelming world of content abundance."[29]

With its access to big data and the processing power to mine and curate it, Google is a leader in developing these types of platforms for organizations and individuals. Google Jigsaw has created data-gathering and mapping platforms that cast a wide net and then curate the results to make them accessible and useful. The platform Montage compiles and curates the thousands of hours of conflict zone footage uploaded daily to YouTube and provides tools for human rights organizations and reporters to analyze it and share their insights. Investigative Dashboard scrapes national business records to build accessible and navigable databases for investigative journalists and watchdog groups working to identify the shell companies through which illicit money flows.[30]

Former Duke University President Nannerl Keohane describes leading a university as guiding "a flotilla made up of several schools of different sizes, all generally agreed on the destination, each with its own resources and some degree of independence in charting the course."[31] For the admiral on the flagship at the head of the flotilla, the trick is finding common interests among self-directed deans and faculty members, setting a broad general destination, providing attractive incentives, and coordinating just enough to keep everyone sailing toward that destination in their various distinctive ways. Just so with coordination networks. The opportunities to create collective value with the millions of nonprofit organizations, corporations, government agencies, philanthropies, and concerned citizens seeking to make a difference on global problems are legion. The key skill is a deft hand at creating and maximizing the opportunities for do-it-yourself public problem solving.[32]

## CUMULATION NETWORKS

If gathering-in networks are coordination networks, parceling-out networks are cumulation networks: scale networks that pull together knowledge, expertise, or some common activity.

They break a single piece of work into myriad small pieces and cumulate the results. They can be set up for cooperation, collaboration, or innovation, depending on how fixed the work is. But they operate at a scale that poses special challenges.

At the simplest level, think Amazon's Mechanical Turk, an online marketplace for digital labor, gone global. The social enterprise Samasource, working with large technology companies, breaks up big data projects into smaller pieces that it then farms out to a workforce in developing countries. It describes this as "global sourcing for data projects that require a human touch."[33] This kind of modularity also encourages cooperative participation in public good endeavors. Massive, crowd-sourced projects rely on breaking large volunteer projects into small, low time-intensity modules, making people more likely to contribute.[34]

The next level up is a collaboration network in which contributors show much more creativity and work together, even if sometimes at cross-purposes. The best example is Wikipedia, an encyclopedia created by cumulating the knowledge of anyone who wants to contribute. Wikipedia is an example of an open source project, a collective endeavor that succeeds when "a broad group of contributors recognize[s] the same need and agree[s] on how to meet it."[35]

Tim O'Reilly, whose company O'Reilly Media runs the Open Source Convention, describes collective participation in distributed small tasks to create a common whole as "the architecture of participation."[36] Rendered as a network, that participation results in cumulation on a central platform. The structure looks like a star network, with some clusters among participants who know one another. Once again, however, weak ties for input, strong ties for output. Too many links among the community of contributors will make the final product less accurate or valuable. Peers not only source information, they weigh in on one another's contributions; if their ties with one another are too strong, they lose the "wisdom of crowds" quality that results from weak ties.

The romance of the open source paradigm is considerable. As one journalist describes it, "think of it as the triumph of participation by the many over ownership by the few." According to political scientist Steven Weber, "property is something to be distributed rather than protected."[37] It goes beyond peer-to-peer sharing to peer-to-peer production, and ultimately from collaboration to cocreation.

The iconic example of a cumulation network is the open-source software Linux, which is accessible to any developer who wants to contribute to it and which has become a genuine rival to Microsoft's and Apple's proprietary operating systems.[38] The critical difference between open source and open innovation, which has expanded to embrace entire innovation ecosystems, is that open source is not driven by a profit motive.[39] It is less a directed task network than a networked ecosystem that arises out of a collective desire to take on tasks that continually evolve as the whole evolves. Online hosting repositories and distributed revision control platforms that allow users to post and revise code such as GitHub now enable programmers across the world to make and merge changes to open-source code without even knowing of one another's existence. This is, in the words of social media theorist Clay Shirky, "cooperation without coordination."[40]

The cumulation of knowledge and the cumulation of code, which is a form of knowledge, are also features of distributed coordination networks. A Global Water Network modeled on GAVI, for instance, might mobilize individuals and organizations around the world to work on water problems, including marshaling volunteers to create a global map of water quality and availability.[41] The coordination piece is the parceling out; the cumulation piece is the gathering back in and the creation of a product that is continuously updated.

The critical ingredient for success here is a small degree of hierarchy injected into the center of the network. With a broad community of disparate individuals contributing to a common product, vetting and quality control matter. Networks are empowering in many ways, but when it comes to mobilizing and directing resources, controlling quality, organizing commitments, and making quick decisions, hierarchy is necessary.[42] Even Wikipedia—a nearly pure coordination network with volunteer content production, editing, and policing—is centrally managed by the Wikimedia Foundation, whose paid staff designs the platform's software, vets contributions, and mediates disputes, and whose board sets standards and compels administrators around the world to accept updates.[43]

Another way to combine hierarchy and networks is to create a cumulation network within an existing hierarchy, as Amazon has done with its reviews. The Amazon system allows anyone to write a review and everyone to comment on the helpfulness of that review, but it has clear checks in place—hierarchically enforced—to prevent abuse of the system. As any blogger knows, trolls can quickly destroy open debate and even the will to write in the first place, so a strong hand is often needed. All of Twitter essentially works the same way, allowing individuals to block other individuals but also to report bad behavior to an authority that can take definitive action.

The potential for creating these kinds of large-scale coordination networks to provide information on how well states are living up to their international obligations is enormous. Consider, for instance, equipping citizens around the world with apps for monitoring water and air quality, or radiation, or violence, in ways that can be certified and gathered. In the Syrian civil war, members of the Syrian opposition initially sent horrific pictures of government atrocities out through social media networks. Soon, however, some of these pictures were exposed as fakes; Syrian government activists began sending pictures as well in a deliberate effort to complicate the already complex narrative. A network run by the United Nations with a template for gathering and verifying information would have been far more trustworthy, and a better instrument for pressuring international actors.

## A PLACE TO START

Resilience, task, and scale networks are necessary tools for formulating and implementing strategies of connection and disconnection in the web world. They all draw on our basic architecture of centralized, decentralized, and mesh (centerless) networks. All are modified in various ways for different purposes, just as strategies of conflict can almost always be reduced to a version of chicken, prisoner's dilemma, or stag hunt. All require connecting the right people or institutions in the right ways: neither too many connections nor too few.

The basic templates described here are just that: a toolbox for getting started. The annals of web diplomacy are not yet written. But, as noted in the introduction, some policy makers are beginning to tinker. As discussed in the Introduction, Secretary of Defense Ash Carter announced the establishment of an Asia-Pacific "principled security network" just as I was finishing this book. He was adopting a web strategy to promote distributed regional security and address the rise of China.[44] Whereas a chessboard approach might seek to isolate or balance against China, Carter invited it and every other Asia-Pacific nation to join the network. The goal is to use connection to limit China's maritime expansion.

The United States and other governments are thus already implementing web strategies, but we do not yet know how to test or improve on the basic idea of a "network." It is impossible to have slang without a standardized vocabulary, impossible to be ungrammatical without a common grammar. The categories of resilience, task, and scale, and the subcategories within them, are a start at that basic grammar. They will evolve and mutate, but will provide an anchor, I hope, for a systematic new way of thinking about and practicing foreign policy.

Structure alone is not enough, however. Even with the right connections to the right people or institutions, making networks work requires a human factor. No form of human organization can escape power and politics; no purpose-built organization can escape the need for some form of leadership. Power in networks is different from power in hierarchies. Leading in networks is different from leading in hierarchies. Understanding and operationalizing those differences is as critical to successful strategies of connection as understanding network architecture.

# PART III

Power, Leadership, and Grand Strategy

CHAPTER SEVEN

# Network Power

P OWER fascinates everyone, from lovers to generals. The power of networks has already generated several books with that exact title, as well as a raft of ruminations on the changing nature of power in a networked age. After spending a year in Shanghai in 2007 and 2008, I came to think about power differently. In the article that emerged from that rethinking, "America's Edge: Power in the Networked World," I argued: "The emerging networked world of the twenty-first century . . . exists above the state, below the state, and through the state. In this world, the state with the most connections will be the central player, able to set the global agenda and unlock innovation and sustainable growth."[1] In *The Seventh Sense*, Joshua Ramo asserts that nothing less than mastery of the future is at stake, power over "billions of connected lives" joined to "tens of billions of linked sensors and machines."[2]

The traditional definition of power rests on the ability to achieve your goals either on your own or by getting someone or something—a group of people, an organization, or a state— to do what you want them to do that they would not otherwise do. In his celebrated book *Power: A Radical View*, political theorist Steven Lukes defines three faces of that kind of power: command, agenda setting, and preference shaping.[3] In the language of parenthood, command is a direct order: "You are going to camp this summer." Agenda setting is structured choice: "Would you like to go to computer camp or sports camp?" Preference shaping is appealing to family values: "In this family we go to camp; we believe in the importance of learning new skills and making new friends."

Joseph Nye prefers a dichotomy, distinguishing between hard power, the power of coercion, and soft power, the power of attraction. Hard power makes others do what they do not want to do by diplomatic, economic, or military compulsion. Soft power is a variation on preference shaping: it rests on co-opting others by creating something sufficiently attractive that other people want to be part of it or imitate it.[4] Nye and Suzanne Nossel both developed the idea of smart power, which Secretary of State Hillary Clinton later made her own. Smart power is the selective use of all the tools at a nation's disposal: military power, but also trade, diplomacy, foreign aid, national values, and leveraging influence through a "stable grid of allies, institutions, and norms."[5]

Ramo sees smart power as the guiding principle of the Obama administration's foreign policy, but he asserts that it is "no more a foreign policy vision than 'good weather' is a strategy for farming." More fundamentally, he argues, the "team of white American men" currently directing U.S. foreign policy are "network-blinded." They simply miss the great possibilities of networks, in which "power is defined by both profound *concentration* and by massive *distribution*."[6] Remember that scale-free networks exhibit a "rich-get-richer" pattern: since power comes from connection, the networks with the most connections attract the most newcomers. You join a social network like LinkedIn because lots of people are on it; banks use the SWIFT network because other banks do; and nations join the WTO because it has the most members. As we shall see, the power of massive distribution is equally salient.

All of these authors, however, including Ramo, employ a very traditional definition of power itself. They distinguish between the power *of* networks and power *in* networks, between power as capabilities and power as connections, and between the power of states and the power of people. But they miss a deeper shift: a shift not only in who holds power and how best to exercise it, but in the very essence of what we think power is.

Power *over* differs fundamentally from power *with*. For the still highly homogeneous foreign policy elite—the statesmen and CEOs who still today pull the levers of global power—"power with" will seem touchy-feely and New Age. As important as it is to have a formal understanding of the structure and properties of networks in foreign policy, an intuitive grasp of "power with" is just as essential. Let us begin, however, with more conventional ways of thinking about networks and power.

Defining and measuring the power of a network is another way of asking what networks are good for as foreign policy tools. What attributes do networks have that make them particularly effective in specific circumstances, relative to hierarchies or markets? When, for instance, would we strive to create a network of states or web actors rather than a more formal organization or simply an informal group or club?

The first answer rests on the need for "efficient, reliable information." According to Walter Powell, "The most useful information is rarely that which flows down the formal chain of command in an organization, or that which can be inferred from shifting price signals."[7] The speed with which information can travel across a relatively flat network is perhaps best illustrated by the story of Mona Eltahawy, a well-known Egyptian-American blogger with sixty thousand Twitter followers, who was arrested and beaten in November 2011 in the Egyptian Interior Ministry in Cairo. Somehow she managed to tweet five chilling words: "beaten arrested in Interior Ministry."

Eltahawy tweeted those words at 5:44 P.M. U.S. Central Time. At 6:05 P.M. I got a direct message on Twitter from National Public Radio's Andy Carvin, the top English-language curator of tweets from Arab protesters in multiple countries, telling me of Mona's tweet. I immediately sent an email to my former colleagues at the State Department. Within five minutes, I had heard back and was able to send out a general tweet that the U.S. embassy in Cairo was on top of the case. Nicholas Kristof of the *New York Times* sent out a similar message to his more than one million followers. By then the hashtag #FreeMona was trending on Twitter, and a few hours later Mona was free, though with two broken bones and a traumatic story of sexual assault to tell. Maged Butter, an Egyptian blogger who was arrested with Eltahawy, was also released. In a world of hierarchies we would have still been trying to figure out whom to call.

A second property that makes networks effective in global affairs is their adaptability. Network members build relationships rather than routines. In crises and rapidly evolving situations, routines can be a handicap. The trust that comes from established relationships allows rapid shifts in course while keeping everyone involved on board. Walter Powell identified this feature of networks as well. Because they are "typified by reciprocal patterns of communication and exchange" (another way of saying that they depend on relationships more than structures, rules, and processes), they build the trust and tacit knowledge that support sustained but open-ended cooperation.[8] In a world of uncertainty and rapid change, trust is the key ingredient of adaptability.

Transnational criminal and terror organizations draw power from adaptability. When U.S. law enforcement declared war on Colombian drug cartels in the 1980s and 1990s, these criminal networks changed their structure to maintain both secrecy and coordination. The decision-making hierarchies flattened out, ties weakened, and the peripheral nodes—the crop harvesters, processing labs, distributors, and so on—became more independent. The cartels' structure went from a wheel to a chain, in which "drug shipments proceeded through a series of transactions among independent nodes that coordinated their activities, largely on an ad hoc basis." The core had less control and enforcement ability, but with time and repeated interaction, "participants from different groups" built "trust and reciprocity."[9]

Another dimension of adaptability is the network's ability "to incorporate elements of hierarchy and centralization" into its structure.[10] At first glance, Amnesty International is an organizational paradox: it is both a sprawling grassroots collective of nearly two million activists and a highly centralized bureaucratic core in London that controls membership and sets the normative agenda for the entire organization. Though such centralization flies in the face of the organization's democratic ideals and volunteer spirit, Amnesty's vast network has flexibility and agency in implementing the center's decisions. Trusted domestic NGOs help disseminate the agenda to activists, who, for example, flood targeted government personnel with letters on behalf of a prisoner. The size of Amnesty's network gives it influence; the centralized core enables quick, coherent, and coordinated action.[11]

The third pillar of network power is scalability—the ability "to grow rapidly at relatively low cost" without creating huge problems for the organization.[12] This ability to grow quickly and cheaply is the key to activist campaigns and social movements. Such networks feature loose ties, an agenda with wide appeal, and a powerful narrative.[13] The Make Poverty History and Jubilee 2000 debt cancellation coalitions reframed debt as a justice issue to attract a broader range of actors and organizations into the network.[14] During the Egyptian uprising of 2011, the protesters shared little more than a desire to oust the Mubarak regime, and "cheap, constant connection," whether via Facebook or SMS or ham radio.[15]

Social movements and political campaigns, the extreme examples of the network power of scalability, often have short shelf lives. Again, hierarchy matters. The Occupy movement grew explosively, but the breadth of its agenda, the lack of a centralized core, and its refusal to engage in ordinary politics caused it to fade. Sustainable transnational advocacy organizations that scale up often set narrower agendas. Amnesty International's loose grassroots network is, almost like Occupy's protests, relatively cheap and easy to join. But as the periphery of the organization has expanded, the central core has had to become more powerful to steer the direction and information flow of the larger organization. Here again is a symbiosis of distribution and concentration.

## POWER IN NETWORKS

When we talk about the power *of* networks, we are speaking from the Archimedean platform of government, corporate, or civic policy making—the perspective of architects and designers of networks choosing when and how to create them. Understanding power *in* networks, by contrast, means knowing where and how the United States or its state and web allies should position themselves within existing or new networks to be able to advance their own interests. The two kinds of power interact, of course. When a participant in a network understands that the network's structure can enhance its power, it will try to influence the overall structure as well as improve its position within it.[16] This partly explains why the late ambassador Richard Holbrooke took great pains to personally arrange the seating chart for official dinners.

Very simply, power in hierarchies flows from the ability to command or manipulate others, which requires a position at the top. Power in networks flows from connectedness: the number, type, and location of connections a node has. In a star or hub network, the most central nodes have the most connections and the highest likelihood of gaining more. That is why network theorists describe power in networks in terms of centrality. We reviewed the different types of centrality in Chapter 2: "degree centrality," "closeness centrality," "betweenness centrality," and the truly obscure but nonetheless important "Eigenvector centrality." It's hard to imagine the corridors of national capitals ringing with these terms, but I will review the basics here in English, with examples.

Recall that degree centrality is a simple measure of a node's number of connections, which determines how much access it has to other nodes. The most connected person is the one with the biggest Rolodex (for my generation) or the highest number of Facebook friends. Degree centrality is a measure of social power, highly relevant for information flows, as the most connected have the widest range of information sources and are thus the first to hear any news.[17] Some international relations scholars argue that smaller states can maximize their position relative to larger states by accumulating social power. Switzerland and other small European countries do this in the diplomatic world by hosting peace talks and treaty negotiations and by maintaining embassies, consulates, and missions to multilateral organizations.[18] But as any power broker knows, quantity of contacts does not trump quality.

Betweenness centrality measures the extent to which a particular node lies on the shortest paths between other nodes in the network. A node with high betweenness centrality is usually influential, as it sits at the crossroads of flows of information, money, or goods and is thus able to exert control over the interactions of other nodes in the network. This is what enables a tiny city-state like Singapore to be a global trade powerhouse. Some 40 percent of the world's trade flows through the Strait of Malacca, the chokepoint between East Asia and the Middle East and Europe. Singapore has capitalized on its strategic location astride this chokepoint to build itself into the second-busiest port in the world.

We can also think of betweenness centrality as an opportunity for brokering. A real estate broker sits at the intersection of buyers and sellers of houses in a particular community. She doesn't necessarily have the greatest number of friends or contacts in town, but she knows many people who are likely to sell and many who are likely to buy. That means she is the most efficient person to go to if you want to buy or sell a house. Power brokering works the same way; in the old days, if you wanted a job in Washington, you went to a handful of senior lawyers and former high government officials who knew everyone inside and outside of government. They knew who was looking to hire and who wanted to be hired, as well as the key people to call to get recommendations or perhaps to spike a particular application. The Obama administration tried to open this system to ordinary citizens without inside connections by requiring all candidates to go through the USAJOBS website, but political power and power brokering still go hand in hand.

Brokering power also means bargaining power. A broker's contacts constitute a valuable asset that she can use to set terms and conditions for those who want to join her network. The same applies for a brokering state. The European Union has wielded this power expertly, offering access to the European common market in exchange for commitments to adopt European standards and values. Nonmember states sign bilateral association agreements with the EU not just for the immediate benefits of any one agreement, but for the access they gain to the "wider networks represented by the EU."[19] (We have heard a great deal about the EU's bargaining power and will no doubt hear more in the coming months, as Great Britain tries to figure out how best to negotiate its exit from the Union.) The World Trade Organization, which grants its members benefits like freer international trade and access to dispute resolution mechanisms if they accept its rules, holds a similar power.[20]

Manuel Castells identifies an especially powerful class of network power brokers: those who "operate the connections between different networks."[21] These "switchers," as he calls them, include politically wired media moguls, Wall Street executives who fund congressional campaigns, and university trustees who also sit on corporate boards. Switchers invariably have high Eigenvector centrality, which measures the importance of a node by not only its number of connections but also by the number of its connections' connections. Truly powerful people in networks are well connected to people who are themselves well connected.

The power that comes from being able to broker valuable exchanges—whether of houses, jobs, political influence, or stock—also translates into network vulnerability, in the sense that removing a node with lots of connections needed by other network participants can damage or even destroy the whole network. Now we are back to the point about scale-free networks; they naturally create a few massive winners connected to vast numbers of minimally connected nodes, which means plenty of robustness against accidents but vulnerability to attack.

Finally, consider the power of the periphery—the absence of any centrality at all. Unlike the bargaining power of highly connected brokers, the "power of exit is often wielded by less embedded nodes at the margins of networks."[22] The social media platforms that are *not* Facebook, Twitter, or LinkedIn are all desperately trying to build their networks; even the biggest ones continue to compete actively for nodes. Ramo assumes that the biggest just keep getting bigger due to network effects, but entire subnetworks—say, all Facebook users in a particular country or business—actually have leverage: they can credibly threaten to depart or not to join. This possibility compels the architects and central nodes atop a hierarchy to make sure the network provides value for its members.[23]

This point is somewhat counterintuitive, but it demonstrates the distinctive nature of network logic. At first glance, the location of the major digital platforms in the United States is a source of power. Countries with many different economic, political, and social ties with the United States will find it difficult to wean their citizens off U.S. platforms. China, however, while central for many purposes in the world, is on the periphery of U.S. digital networks. Chinese citizens are tied much more to one another than to other countries. Thus China can control its netizens and seal them off with much less protest, precisely because it has fewer connections to U.S. networks. Other more digitally peripheral countries may well learn how to deploy their virtual populations as power assets in the same way that they deployed a leaning toward communism or capitalism as a power asset during the Cold War.

## "POWER OVER" VERSUS "POWER WITH"

All of the above definitions of power are variations on the idea of power over others, of dominion. They all fit within Steven Lukes's basic framework. This kind of power is traditionally measured in terms of capabilities; indeed, in the chessboard world, one of the familiar measures of state power is a mathematical equation adding up a state's population, iron and steel production, energy consumption, and military expenditure and military personnel, then calculating its percentage of the world's total on each of these dimensions.[24]

Power *over* is also a function of credibility and will. The problem with nuclear weapons as tools for exercising power is precisely that they are so destructive that using them is not a credible threat except in existential situations. States that rank high on the scale of capabilities may be seen as less powerful if they have a weak leader or a government hamstrung by history or fractious domestic politics. Still, it is essentially an ironclad rule in chessboard politics that big states matter more than small states, because they have more ability to coerce, to control and to set agendas, and more ability to deploy the resources necessary to shape their preferences.

Network power adds an additional capability: the number of connections a state has, the ability to create more, and the control of who can and cannot connect.[25] For Joshua Ramo, the key to wielding network power is gatekeeping: the ability to include and exclude. That is a very old form of power, now being exercised in a new virtual world. When I first wrote about networks I emphasized how they enabled governments that could no longer get things done in traditional international institutions to come together for action in faster and more flexible ways. That amounts to using new means—networks—for old ends: end-running a stalemate or forum shopping.

Power *with* starts from a different place. It is the power of many to do together what no one can do alone.[26] Consider the power of water. Each drop is harmless; enough drops together, moved by sufficient energy, create a flood that can level a landscape.

Power with is not a capability but rather an emergent property. Like power over, power with enables an individual (or an institution) to do what she could not otherwise do. But where power over starts with an agent—an individual, group, or institution—power with can be exercised only in connection with others. Think of the difference between the power of a mayor and that of a mob. The mayor can order things to be done in her city; she can call out the police in case of trouble, hire and fire officials, and propose a budget. No one member of a mob has that power. But the mob can topple the mayor.

Power With as an Alternative to Fordism and Fascism

The concept of power with was introduced in the 1920s and 1930s by pioneering organizational theorist Mary Parker Follett, the "mother of modern management." In a world of mechanistic production lines and rigid industrial hierarchy, she championed worker empowerment and participation, writing that "power-over" was actually "pseudo power" and that only "power-with" was real: "genuine power is not coercive control, but coactive control . . . the enrichment and advancement of every human soul." Her interest was not in how to locate and amass power but in how to develop it. "Genuine power," she wrote, "can only be grown, it will slip from every arbitrary hand that grasps it."[27]

The great twentieth-century political philosopher Hannah Arendt picked up on this theme in a quite different context, theorizing about the legitimacy and durability of government. Arendt conceived of power as entirely relational, emerging from "sheer human togetherness."[28] She wrote: "Power corresponds to the human ability not just to act but to act in concert."[29] It is an emergent property: it cannot be held or amassed; rather, it occurs spontaneously and must continually emerge anew. Arendt again: "Power springs up between men when they act together and vanishes the moment they disperse."[30]

Unlike power over, Arendt's version of power does not rest "upon subjugation and obedience, but upon consent (with [an] initiative) and support (for the initiative taker)."[31] She thus believed that no government would last without the consent of the governed, a true power base. When that power is absent, rulers resort to power over, often enforced by violence and other means of coercion. From this perspective, Assad's actions in Syria, for instance, reflect his *lack* of enduring power to rule the country.

But in Follett and Arendt's time, power with was like a flash flood: fearsome but relatively rare. With virtual means of connection, communication, and assembly, "flash" anything is easier to create. "Flash mobs" are groups that gather for a short period of time for an unusual or apparently senseless activity; "smart mobs" are groups created for more purposeful activity.[32] Power with thus bears much closer examination. Like power over, power with can be defined, measured, and augmented or diminished. But whereas power over can be wielded, like a weapon, power with can only be practiced, like a discipline. Power over can be amassed, stored, and used when necessary; power with can be channeled only once it has emerged.

Recall our discussion about homo economicus and homo sociologicus in Chapter 2. Power over and power with come from different sides of human nature. As always in this book, we are talking about both/and rather than either/or. Understanding a new kind of power does not negate the existence or importance of an older kind. Homo economicus calculates her interest and reasons how best to advance it. Homo sociologicus feels the strength of his connection to others and adapts his behavior to theirs.

That is why discussions of power with emerge in very different literatures from the study of foreign policy. Deanna Zandt, for instance, in the civic technology community, describes how sharing increases an individual's power and agency: "How we share information, find community, and both connect and disconnect will give us unprecedented influence over our place in the world."[33] Entrepreneur Lisa Gansky similarly describes the psychology of sharing as a disruptive economic force.[34] These authors are speaking to the human desire for connection, belonging, and sharing power from the inside out, a power that cannot be exercised by decision makers and policy architects but, if properly understood, can be encouraged or nurtured.

To understand the full differences between power over and power with, consider two very different accounts of power in our networked age, both of which draw from the foreign policy and business worlds.

### Gatekeeping: The Power of Exclusion

One approach to understanding network power is gatekeeping, "the various processes by which nodes are included or excluded from the network."[35] In *The Seventh Sense*, Joshua Ramo argues that networks have reshaped the world's landscapes by reducing time. The New World used to be three months away from Europe by ship; now, because of the transatlantic airline network, it is just six hours by air. A live video feed from anywhere on the planet is milliseconds away. These networks superimpose new topologies on our world, virtual maps that can be rapidly rearranged "as a result of connection." They "change instantly, depending on their design, on who is connected, and as the speed and thickness of the connection shift."[36] Power lies in controlling them, having mastery over the design, speed, and members of a given networked landscape. In other words, gatekeeping.

In Ramo's view, "power is in the construction and control of gated spaces," what he calls "gatelands." These closed, in-or-out network worlds pervade our lives: financial markets, Facebook, the Internet, U.S. citizenship. The creators and masters of these gatelands, the gatekeepers, hold the most "important, formidable, influential," and "profitable" positions in today's society—

not least because survival depends on managing who is in and who is out.[37]

### Participating: The Power of Engagement

Chess is competition. The strategies of the chessboard world are all about winning. The great debates in international relations theory over the past half century, as we saw in Chapter 1, are all about whether competition has to be zero-sum or can be positive-sum, allowing for multiple winners. But the desire to *win* is never in doubt.

Competition, however, is only one side of human nature. Connection is the other. We know that viewing pictures of family members, or indeed representations of love between any human beings, makes us less competitive. Unlocking our caring side reminds us of the enormous pleasure we take in connection to others. We no longer need to win, but we do need to be seen and recognized, to belong, to matter, to share, and to participate.

Jeremy Heimans runs Purpose, a "public benefit corporation" that launches social movements, creates tailored media tools, and consults with organizations to advance progressive causes such as gun control and gay rights by engaging large numbers of people.[38] Henry Timms is the president of the 92nd Street YMHA, a venerable Manhattan institution that for decades has provided intellectual stimulation, culture, and connection for a tightly woven New York community. Recently he has been behind #GivingTuesday, a global philanthropic movement that has co-opted the Tuesday after Thanksgiving for communities, businesses, organizations, and individuals to celebrate generosity and give.[39]

Following in the footsteps of Follett and Arendt, but from the vantage point of twenty-first-century civic engagement, Heimans and Timms call power *with* "new power," which they define as power based on mass participation and peer coordination.[40] We see it at work in Wikipedia, peer-to-peer lending, the Arab Spring protests, and ISIS.

The difference between "old power" and "new power" is precisely the difference between power that can be held and contained and power that cannot. Old power "works like a currency. It is held by few. Once gained, it is jealously guarded, and the powerful have a substantial store of it to spend. It is closed, inaccessible, and leader-driven. It downloads, and it captures."[41]

New power, by contrast, "operates differently, like a current. It is made by many. It is open, participatory, and peer-driven. It uploads, and it distributes. Like water or electricity, it's most forceful when it surges. The goal with new power is not to hoard it but to channel it."[42]

Most interesting, new power can be created out of nothing more than the stuff of human connection, the way Bitcoin can be mined out of data. Heimans and Timms describe an ascending scale of participation that runs from consuming through sharing, shaping, funding, and producing to co-owning (Figure 14).

Participation taps into homo sociologicus's deep desire to belong to some larger entity. It can arise spontaneously from two or more people coming together and deciding to undertake a project, like kids deciding to build a clubhouse or a fort or hold a tea party. Or it can be designed and structured, by businesses inviting their customers to participate in designing a product, or terrorist groups calling teenagers to join a new family united in its devotion to an angry God.[43]

New power gains its force from people's growing capacity—and desire—to go far beyond passive consumption of ideas and goods.

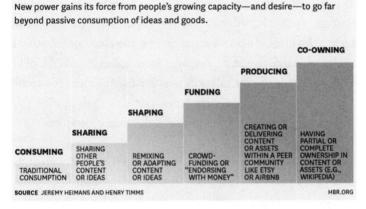

| CONSUMING | SHARING | SHAPING | FUNDING | PRODUCING | CO-OWNING |
|---|---|---|---|---|---|
| TRADITIONAL CONSUMPTION | SHARING OTHER PEOPLE'S CONTENT OR IDEAS | REMIXING OR ADAPTING CONTENT OR IDEAS | CROWD-FUNDING OR "ENDORSING WITH MONEY" | CREATING OR DELIVERING CONTENT OR ASSETS WITHIN A PEER COMMUNITY LIKE ETSY OR AIRBNB | HAVING PARTIAL OR COMPLETE OWNERSHIP IN CONTENT OR ASSETS (E.G., WIKIPEDIA) |

**SOURCE** JEREMY HEIMANS AND HENRY TIMMS                    HBR.ORG

Figure 14. The participation scale

When it is deliberately practiced, the power of participation is a strategy of engagement, of creating collective projects. Connecting two nodes in a network creates only a formal relationship between them. It is the flows of energy, conversation, debate, shared experience, and collaboration that tie them together. These flows become even more important when they can move in multiple directions as part of a larger network. The parts that participate in a common enterprise, or a linked set of common enterprises, draw power and comfort from the awareness of being parts of a larger whole.

Another approach, described by technology writer Tim O'Reilly, is to design open systems that channel the efforts of self-interested individuals into contributions to a greater whole. Such an "architecture of participation" undergirds the most successful collective projects, such as the World Wide Web. Often associated primarily with proprietary software developers, the development of the Web was actually an open source triumph.

HTML, "the language of web pages," was accessible and simple enough to enable ordinary users to participate. Each amateur coder who created a page for whatever reason was contributing a node to the greater construction—*automatically.* Unlike Wikipedia, which depends on a degree of selflessness, the architecture of the Web is such that "users pursuing their own 'selfish' interests build collective value as an automatic byproduct."[44]

Note that the transition from gatekeeping to participating demands a shift in perspective. Gatekeeping assumes a gatekeeper: a person, institution, or machine that can decide whom to include or exclude. Gatekeeping is a power that can be exercised in the first person.

Participating is done in the first person, but the power it generates can be exercised only in the first person plural, "we," not "I." Consistent with ancient religious parables and the riddles of Chinese philosophers, it can be obtained only by giving it to others. A person, institution, or machine can create opportunities for participation and can invite or urge others to participate. But only they can decide to do so—think of the citizens of the former Soviet Union who saw their state as an elaborate charade: "We pretend to work and they pretend to pay us." And if they do participate, then *they* hold the power, but only collectively.

## ORCHESTRATING POWER

For all of our discussion of power in the web world, power in the chessboard world remains alive and well. Courts enforce laws; international alliances maintain recognized borders; navies patrol shipping routes. Dictators can drop barrel bombs on their people or order their armies to invade another country. Nations that fear for their existence can cut their populations off from the world's networks, even at great cost to their economies and societies.

Any understanding of the power of networks and power in networks, as well as the deeper distinction between power *over* and power *with*, must be meshed with these older concepts of power. Teddy Roosevelt's maxim "Speak softly and carry a big stick" is still perfectly relevant to U.S. policy in Syria, for instance, where the U.S. failure to use force in defense of a red line made it far harder to practice diplomacy.

And just as in the chessboard world, the actual practice of power in the web world still comes down to decisions made by leaders, even if those leaders make up a far bigger and more diverse group than traditional foreign policy elites, and even if they understand the extent to which their power rests on collective decisions—not of "followers" but those taken by their coparticipants in a common enterprise.

In 2009 I wrote that in a networked world, "the measure of power is connectedness": the "ability to make the maximum number of valuable connections." There were some early adherents to this view. The 2007 joint maritime strategy of the U.S. Navy, Marine Corps, and Coast Guard called for building cooperative relationships with more nations. The strategy recognized that U.S. interests are "best served by fostering a peaceful global system comprised of interdependent networks of trade, finance, information, law, people, and governance."[45]

Today, the idea that connectedness is a key measure of power is gaining currency across the government. The National Intelligence Council's 2016 Global Trends Report predicted that in the years to come "the ability to foster relationships and leverage information" and to "cultivate trust and credibility will become as important as military and economic might in shaping future events."[46] The report's authors add, "The most powerful entities will leverage states as well as corporations, social or religious movements, and some individuals to create webs of cooperation across issues."

It is critical, however, to understand how the power of connectedness works. As I put it in 2009, "it is not the power to impose outcomes. Networks are not directed and controlled as much as they are managed and orchestrated. Multiple players are integrated into a whole that is greater than the sum of its parts—an orchestra that plays differently according to the vision of its conductor and the talent of individual musicians."[47] It is the power to evoke rather than to impose.

An actual orchestra conductor, of course, has plenty of power over as well as power with. At least in some orchestras, she can hire and fire musicians; even without that authority, she can advance some careers and retard others, and she can decide what music they will all make. Still, a conductor and a general must lead in very different ways.

As we will see in the next chapter, some generals are thinking very differently about leadership, as are university presidents and serial entrepreneurs. Ori Brafman and Rod Beckstrom insist on the possibility of starfish organizations, in which the participants move in a kind of synchrony, without central direction of any kind. Power with can work that way, but only for a while. Leaders remain essential. But we need a much broader understanding of who they are and what they actually do in a world of both chessboards and webs.

CHAPTER EIGHT

# A Different Way to Lead

M<sup>Y</sup> favorite definition of leadership was put forward by my mentor, role model, and friend Nannerl Keohane in her book *Thinking About Leadership.* Keohane was a highly successful president of Wellesley College and Duke University; as we saw in Chapter 6, she compares leading a university to captaining a flotilla. Her broader definition of leadership applies far beyond ivy-covered walls: "Leaders determine or clarify goals for a group of individuals and bring together the energies of members of that group to accomplish those goals."[1]

This description can apply equally to a university, a corporation, or a social movement. *Thinking About Leadership* opens with the example of a homeless settlement in Providence, Rhode Island, where the chosen leader stepped down after members questioned his legitimacy. The camp rapidly de-

POWER, LEADERSHIP, AND GRAND STRATEGY

scended into bickering and predation, showing that even the most rudimentary organizations require leadership and that any member of a group can provide that leadership as long as other members consent.[2]

Keohane's definition of leadership is particularly apt for leading in networks because it does not assume any formal structure of command. Her reference to a "group of individuals" allows for the possibility of a completely horizontal structure in which a leader has no ability to "determine" the group's goals, in the sense of deciding them herself, but can only "clarify" them.

Clarifying a group's goals assumes that group members have objectives independent of the leader's wishes or commands. That is characteristic of a network: the nodes are independent actors with their own views. The next step is for the leader to "bring together" the energies of group members in order for those goals to be accomplished. "Bring together" could be a euphemism for "command," but it suggests evoking more than directing, a horizontal process of collective motivation rather than a vertical "snap to!"

Clarifying goals and bringing together energies may seem like altogether softer stuff than many traditional definitions of leadership, in which we imagine a leader with the vision, charisma, or power to rally followers behind her. One of the reasons I favor Keohane's definition is that it works equally well for power *with* as for power *over*, for the chessboard and the web. But unlike some visions of power with that assume an absence of leaders, as in the supposedly "leaderless revolutions" of the Arab spring, Keohane's view is that effective collective action requires direction, however gentle or hidden the hand.[3]

So too with leadership in networks. The verbs applied to leadership in networks are instructive: the commonest one is musical rather than military. Leaders are often described as "orchestrating" a network, which in its original definition means to figure out which instruments should play a particular piece and how to weave their different sounds together.[4] Open-innovation scholars inspired by Henry Chesbrough, for instance, insist that innovative network organizations have a central hub with "orchestration capability" to integrate the resources and abilities of various internal and external network participants.[5]

Other verbs include "manage," "mobilize," "connect," "troubleshoot," "program," "direct," "compose," "devise," and "assemble."[6] The nouns, too, do not always recognizably refer to leaders: "curator," "collaboration manager," "partnership broker," "networker," "systems integrator," "systems entrepreneur," "facilitator," "troubleshooter," "problem solver."[7] Make no mistake, however: these words all describe ways of *making things happen*. They all fit within the definition of leadership adopted here. Without them, networks will not work.

Network leadership and network leaders are distinctive enough to merit their own subcategory, in the sense that an individual could advertise himself as a network leader with a specific set of skills and attributes. Moreover, network leadership takes different forms in different networks: the position and actions required of leaders in resilience, task, and scale networks will often differ. It is possible, however, to identify common skills and attributes that form the core of network leadership.

I describe those skills and attributes in this chapter as the "five Cs": clarification, curation, connection, cultivation, and catalysis.[8] The last is an odd word but a vitally important process. Understanding each of these five Cs, practicing them, and learning how they fit together is essential for anyone, in the public, private, or civic sector, who seeks to lead in the web world.

CLARIFY

Leadership begins with the clarification of goals, which Keohane describes as "providing solutions to common problems or offering ideas about how to accomplish collective purposes." At its most basic, clarification starts when someone in a group "steps forward and makes suggestions" about how to fix or achieve something.[9] But that's not where it ends. Clarification is constant and iterative. It may include behind-the-scenes conversation, deft steering of debate, and effective persuasion. Effective leaders put forth ideas in a style specific to their type of institution. A general issues commands after receiving information from his subordinates, whereas a magazine editor may suggest rough story ideas that solidify after being kicked back and forth with reporters.

From the perspective of a network architect, clarifying goals often means deciding who should be in the network in the first place. Building a scale coordination network, for instance, requires determining what goals all nodes must share—not just improving global health, for instance, but fighting a specific disease. Building a successful stabilization network would similarly depend on identifying a clear set of goals and choosing the right government officials with whom to connect—individuals with a reputation for integrity, for instance. Clarifying goals in these cases folds into curation.

Alternatively, clarification of goals may overlap with cultivating trust through consensus building. Assume that all members of a network share common goals at a fairly abstract level: they all want to defeat terrorists or drug traffickers; they all want to bring clean water to the world's people; or they all want to be part of an innovation ecosystem. Clarifying goals, then, means continually refining what those goals mean in practice through facilitated discussion and working through disagreements—essentially tilling the earth and pulling weeds.

That process of refining what a common goal means in practice also requires continually reminding and refocusing network members when they stray from those goals—a process that any parent finds all too familiar. The general goal is to get good grades; the specific goal is not to spend hours watching YouTube videos and Facebooking friends. In that context, "leading" feels remarkably like nagging. In fact, however, motivating your children to do something you have both agreed is vitally important for their future is a more horizontal form of parental leadership: it works far better over the longer term than hierarchical command.

## CURATE

As we saw in Chapter 6, in many networks more is actually less. The careful selection of whom to connect to whom is a key part of network construction and leadership. Recall the coordination network GAVI—the Global Alliance for Vaccines and Immunization. GAVI brings together the Gates Foundation with the World Health Organization, UNICEF, and the World Bank to work with developed and developing country governments, those countries' pharmaceutical industries, civil society organizations, and research and technical institutes around the world.

GAVI won't work without a strong central node of leaders exercising all the attributes described here. But the first stage is to identify as precisely as possible the criteria for network members and to put in motion a process of both active and passive selection. Think of a great disc jockey: she knows how to find new songs that will fit a particular playlist through active looking, openness to suggestion, and even self-selection; she may glean songs from Spotify Discover Weekly based on her prior preferences, listeners who write or tweet in, and composers who put forward their own work. The curation process for a successful network must be simultaneously broad and focused.

Curating members is equally important in an innovation network. The architects of the open innovation paradigm for businesses describe ideal combinations of deep and wide ties, as well as formal and informal ties.

Deep and wide ties resemble Mark Granovetter's analysis of strong and weak ties; deep ties create trust and easy collaboration, but they are less successful at bringing new flows of ideas and information into the innovation process. Wide ties cast a broad net to capture the new, but they are harder to activate for purposes of cocreation. Formal ties can be directed; informal ties are unexpected but bring the value of serendipity.

Curating people or institutions or whatever else constitutes a node is critical, but so too is curating the resources available on a central platform. Recall the volunteers sifting through distress texts during the Haiti earthquake, or the platforms being developed by Google's technology incubator, Jigsaw, that compile and curate swaths of YouTube videos, financial data, and other information to aid investigators and journalists.

Curation is so important that a good network leadership team running a stabilization, response, coordination, or cumulation network should have a full-time curator as a member. The same combination of concentrated resources and mass distribution that Ramo sees as the essence of network power is also the secret of great curation: to be useful to a mass distribution network, the resources available must be capacious but also carefully selected.

## CONNECT

Given that a network is a set of connected nodes, to say that a network leader must be able to "connect" network members seems redundant. "Connecting," however, is more challenging and time-consuming than it seems. When we describe a good "networker," we mean someone who is good at connecting herself to others who can be useful to her. A connector is someone who is skilled at connecting people to each other.

Good connectors are synergy spotters. Much of what I do as CEO of New America consists of realizing that two people whom I know, either both within New America or one in and one outside, are doing similar or complementary work and would benefit from knowing each other. It is up to me to make that connection in such a way that the value of the introduction is quickly apparent to both parties. If I am the only one who sees its value, then I have wasted everyone's time, including my own.

This part of connecting is essentially cross-fertilizing: spreading knowledge like compost to help lots of things grow. It is driven in part by self-interest—I benefit when two New America nodes connect in ways that benefit their work. But a good connector is also a compulsive sharer, driven by the same human impulse that animates so much of social media, crowd-funding, and various new economic models based on sharing and collaboration. We find something we like and immediately think of someone else who would like it too, benefit from it, and spread it in turn.

This urge to connect and share, so dear to homo socio-logicus, can create and reinforce a culture of generosity that undergirds the architecture of participation. Where power over narrows and controls a specific set of choices, power with broadens access to the circle of power and connects as many people as possible to one another and to a common purpose. That culture must be cultivated, but it begins with connection.

A third critical dimension of connecting is ensuring repeated flows across a network—an activity best described as pinging. Back to our design principles: a network of individuals or organizations that are connected only formally or through a routinized set of communications is dead. It lives only to the extent that energy flows across it, in the form of ideas, emotions, or news. Social physics requires sociability. A great connector is someone who continually checks in with members of his network, sending them notes to see how they are doing, reading and rebroadcasting their news, responding to happy, sad, or proud events in their lives. We all know these kinds of connectors; they brighten our lives. They are also leaders, even if often unsung.

## CULTIVATE

Although tanks and helicopters have long replaced the horse cavalry, say "general" and many of us still summon a quick mental picture of a man waving a sword on a white horse, leading his troops into battle. That vision lies at the heart of a classic image of leaders and followers. Imagine my surprise, then, when I came upon Stanley McChrystal's discussion of leadership in his book *Team of Teams*.

The chapter subheading reads: "From chess master to gardener: The leaders we need now." McChrystal then lays out the characteristics of "leading as gardening." The principal idea is that instead of directing, a leader-gardener "creates an environment in which the plants can flourish. The work done up front, and vigilant maintenance, allow the plants to grow individually, all at the same time."[10] Planting seeds is important, but it is that vigilant maintenance, the tending, that makes a leader effective.

George Shultz, who has held cabinet positions as secretary of labor, secretary of the treasury, and secretary of state, describes his work as the nation's chief diplomat in the same terms. The work of diligently cultivating and tending relationships, he has written, is among the "most underrated aspects of diplomacy." He once spoke at a freshman seminar I was teaching at Princeton and mesmerized the students with his account of tending relationships with other nations, nurturing their growth, and pulling weeds before they grow big enough to choke channels of communication or undermine the trust so critical in a crisis. "The way to keep weeds from overwhelming you," he said in an interview years later at the Council on Foreign Relations, "is to deal with them constantly and at their early stages."[11]

Still another image of leading as gardening comes from Dame Stephanie Shirley, a successful British serial entrepreneur, who talks about the ways she "nurtured and cared" for her enterprises. She always allowed her employees to have flexible, home-based schedules, and she reaped the benefits of this arrangement when she needed to take three months off to care for her autistic teenage son.

"What happened was that they managed very well without me, which might have upset me. So, that is when you build an organization: it has to be more than just me," Shirley told National Public Radio's Rachel Martin. "And so as I was developing management, I think of myself . . . as a sort of gardener. I grow organizations, I grow people, I've grown not only my company but four independent charities, which are now totally freestanding."[12] Barclays Vice Chair Barbara Byrne, a charter member of the tiny circle of top women in finance, describes her greatest satisfaction at work as coming "from investing and growing talent just like I grow my garden. I nurture both into bloom."[13]

The understanding of leadership as cultivation may come particularly easily to women, as the gender traditionally in charge of "raising children," itself an agricultural metaphor. But many wise men have come to the same place. It is a kind of leadership particularly well suited to alliances and networks, loose arrangements held together as much by trust and commitment to a mutual mission as by law and bonuses. A good piece of Henry Chesbrough's work on network orchestration in innovation networks focuses on trust building.[14] A leader weaving an interorganizational open-innovation network must diligently tend to and deepen those external relationships: "Repeated interactions breed trust in networks."[15]

The cultivation skills necessary for effective network leadership include delegation and empowerment, troubleshooting and conflict resolution, and setting and enforcing boundaries. Delegation and empowerment are the nurturing side of cultivation: sharing responsibility and authority in a way that encourages others to grow, while also creating the conditions that help them succeed. Troubleshooting and conflict resolution are weeding: looking for problems before they arise and ensuring that when trouble does break out, it can be managed and resolved.

Finally, as any parent or manager knows, creating an environment of trust and self-reliance requires the establishment and enforcement of limits. If anything goes, nothing goes. Codes of conduct, an ethical culture, and clear definitions of what is acceptable and unacceptable behavior establish a safe space within by demarcating the wilderness without.

Intense cultivation may not be possible throughout a large network. In such cases it is important to cultivate trust and empowerment among a small group of leaders responsible for the rest of the network. Philanthropist Jeffrey Walker has studied how to create "cause-based collaborations," which I would describe as a subset of collaboration networks focused on producing and spreading social goods. He identifies the central importance of an "honest/unbiased broker," a "person, group, or entity" to act as a "superb networker," troubleshooter, and problem solver who can "bring people together and can find the common linkages among members of a disparate group."[16]

That broker alone, however, is not enough. He or she needs a "small group of focused individuals" who can provide the "collaborative glue" for the entire network. In practice, this means "convening meetings, sharing knowledge, gathering resources, tracking outcomes, and holding stakeholders accountable for their commitments until the shared goal is achieved."[17] If the broker plots and seeds, the members of this group weed and maintain the watering schedule.

An example of such a group was the Prime Minister's Delivery Unit in Great Britain, created by Tony Blair in 2001 to guarantee that government departments would implement the prime minister's promised public service reforms. Led by Sir Michael Barber, the delivery unit helped set targets, held departments accountable for meeting them, and developed and shared techniques to help solve problems. But most important, it built "trusting relationships" among the network of responsible government actors.[18] Delivery units based on the U.K. model have been adopted by governments around the world and by the World Bank.

In the business world, Chesbrough and his collaborators reach similar conclusions regarding innovation networks. They suggest that in cases of "radical innovations"—a better mousetrap, or (their example) a tastier genetically modified tomato—"a small clique of central players" must manage "the external network with all the actors that are necessary to launch" the innovation. Because introducing an entirely new innovation or product upsets the established distribution of value in the network, the central clique must work actively to "manage the potential tensions between partners." Here again, cultivation is the key: the "total value created depends on the quality of the relations between the partners" in the network.[19]

Leadership as gardening is perhaps the most dramatic departure from the chessboard world. It is impossible to think of a geopolitical chess master "gardening" or "cultivating." Networks require nurture in a way that hierarchies do not (though they too flourish better with cultivation). The resulting harvest is one of cooperation, collaboration, innovation, and resilience.

CATALYZE

When networks are constructed of many different agents all acting on their own, the connection itself is the catalyst for common action. Think of Arab Spring protesters or the Occupy movement. But in other networks, particularly resilience and task networks, it is necessary to add the agent that generates the reaction.

For Stanley McChrystal and his joint task force in Iraq, the catalyst was his presence on every Operations and Intelligence call, calls that were never canceled or postponed. That signaled their importance. As he and the senior leadership elicited ever more valuable intelligence and insights from participants, other agencies, some initially reluctant to share, began contributing and attending every O&I call as well.[20] For an innovation network, the catalyst is the call for a specific invention or solution to a particular problem that spurs a response. In a replication network, it is the injection of the idea or formula to be replicated.

Catalysts not only spark but sustain and rekindle action in a network. Mapping the human genome was the largest collaborative biological project in history, bringing together a network of scientific agencies and institutes such as the U.S. Department of Energy and the National Institutes of Health. One participant was the British biomedical research charity Wellcome Trust.[21] The Trust singlehandedly triggered British involvement in the project, founding a sequencing center called the Sanger Institute and bringing together key partners. In 1998, to accelerate the project, Wellcome doubled its investment to more than £200 million.[22] And the Sanger Institute ended up decoding one-third of the human genome, more than any other single institution.[23]

In still other cases, particularly in the small groups that make up a central leadership hub for networks, catalyzing action requires uncommon abilities of persuasion. Human beings are not chemicals; the agent alone may create disturbance but not decision. The consensus builder must often be a persuader.

The chief attribute necessary to persuade, however, is neither command of facts nor rhetorical gifts. The first step toward persuading others is an evident and sincere willingness to be persuaded yourself. Remember, the science of information cascades tells us that an idea, no matter how good, will not spread if those in the network have high critical thresholds for change. A persuasive leader can lower those thresholds by modeling acceptance. If you signal that nothing the other side can say will change your mind, it becomes evident that any discussion taking place is serial monologue, not real dialogue.

Contrast this posture with the third face of power in Lukes's trilogy: the ability to shape preferences through culture and ideology. That is power *over*. Practitioners of power *with* must proceed from existing preferences and seek to change them. To do so, they must first be willing to adapt their own preferences, not for show but for real. The network leader who would be a catalyst must be prepared to change himself as much as he would change others.

## FROM NEW CASTE TO NO CASTE

Follow the leader. It's a game we play as children and an assumption we still make as adults: effective action in any organization requires some to lead and others to follow. As McChrystal has told students, even when just two people are walking down the street, someone has to be in charge. That may be true of two military people walking down the street; my husband and I manage without hierarchy. But for more complex action, we are accustomed to look for a leader.

In early 2011, that assumption motivated many news stories about who was really leading the protesters in Tahrir Square, captured in a *New York Times* headline on February 9: "A Quest for an Opposition Leader."[24] The story listed Facebook activist Wael Ghonim, Nobel Prize winner Mohamed El Baradei, Muslim Brotherhood leader Mohamed Badie, Ghad party leader Ayman Nour, and another Nobel laureate, the chemist Ahmed Zewail.

The protesters themselves, however, refused to appoint a leader. Even Ghonim, who mobilized tens of thousands of protesters with his Facebook page and Twitter feeds, rejected the leadership mantle. They rightly feared that identifying themselves as leaders would lead to immediate arrest, an assumption that proved all too true as the Egyptian revolution progressed to the stages of reaction and restoration.

Another reason for their refusal, however, is that Ghonim and his contemporaries had a conception of leadership that was almost pure power *with*. As digital natives, they saw the world not in terms of atomized actors requiring leaders to represent them and organize cooperation, but as a vast network of individuals who needed only to be coordinated and activated to take to the streets and demand change. What the people in Tahrir Square, and countless squares in many smaller Egyptian cities and towns, needed above all was the assurance that they were not alone; that others wanted decent government and an end to corruption as much as they did.

That is the assurance Ghonim provided when he created the Facebook page "We are all Khaled Said," giving tens of thousands of people a place to come together, make their views known, and draw strength from their gathering numbers. In a *Newsweek* interview, Ghonim insisted that his purpose was "to increase the bond between the people and the group through my unknown personality. This way we create an army of volunteers."[25]

The power Ghonim and his fellow leaders unleashed was enough to overthrow a government and even to remind successive governments that they governed at the sufferance of the people. In some respects, General Abdel Fattah al-Sisi's government has heeded these lessons: he has been more mindful of economic hardship endured by the poor. But power with quickly gave way to power over; the "leaderless revolution" gave way to a government very much in charge. In the end, the Egyptian masses were not a network built to sustain lasting change. All of the hopeful people who connected to Ghonim's Facebook page could destroy but not create, protest but not prioritize, intoxicate but not implement.

Social media and other technological platforms make it possible to democratize both power and action to a far greater extent than ever before in human history. The mob could always assemble, but we now have the possibility of continued connection long before the mob gathers and after it goes home. Networked democracy is still in its infancy, failing more than succeeding.[26] But the possibility of governing, or self-governing, through networks is alive, well, and inspiring a new generation of politicians around the world. Like all connections, these networks are not necessarily good. They may coalesce around profoundly disturbing visions and values, connecting the dispossessed with bigotry, brutality, and ignorance. But they are forming.

To sociologist Manuel Castells, network power is held primarily by the programmers, those who design the network and set the protocols, rules, and structures that determine how information flows and who can join. Seizing on this idea, Joshua Ramo views leadership as belonging to the "masters," a "new caste" of tech-savvy mavens who build and run networks: Mark Zuckerberg, the NSA, the coders and directors of the New York Stock Exchange.

Such a new caste could only exercise power *over*. Power *with* is deeply democratic. Networks will not work with no leaders, but new leaders are emerging from every walk of life. Far more than the current crop of foreign policy makers and leaders, they are best defined by no caste. They are young (and not-so-young) civic and social entrepreneurs, activists, and new politicians. Pia Mancini cofounded and leads Argentina's Partido de la Red (Net Party), which fields candidates who pledge to cast votes and introduce legislation according to the will of citizens using the open source platform DemocracyOS. Mancini and her team built the platform as a tool to make governments more participatory and accountable, and activists and politicians in Tunisia, Mexico, Kenya, and other nations have begun using it.[27] Another new network leader is Adalberto Verissimo, a Brazilian ecologist whose NGO Imazon's processing and publishing of publicly available NASA data showing the rapid deforestation of the Amazon galvanized government, industry, and the public to take meaningful action. In 2014, eleven years after Verissimo began, the rate of Amazon deforestation had dropped 76 percent from 1990 levels.[28]

It is critical that these new leaders understand the skills and attributes of network leadership. Network leaders will not chart a course for others to follow, or even represent the views of their followers in our traditional understanding of representative government. Rather, they will be individuals who clarify the goals of their followers, whom they will see not as followers at all but as fellow participants; they will curate those participants and the information and resources they make available to them, connect their network members to one another and to ideas and action, cultivate both individuals and institutions in their networks and an overall environment and culture, and catalyze action as carefully, thoughtfully, and effectively as they can.

These leaders will also have to lead in stereo just as they will have to see in stereo. They cannot escape the need for at least some hierarchy and the power of command, just as hierarchical leaders will have to master network skills. The most effective leaders will be able to determine and clarify goals for whatever group they are leading, and mobilize the group's energies to achieve them, whether that group is a hierarchy, a network, or, most likely, some of both.

CHAPTER NINE

# A Grand Strategy

"GRAND strategy" refers to how a state harnesses all its instruments of power—military, political, economic, cultural, technological, and moral—in harmony to further its prosperity and security.[1] The grand strategy of all grand strategies, assuming mythical proportions, is George Kennan's strategy of containment: the simple idea of blocking the expansion of the Soviet Union and holding the line until it collapsed from internal strife and contradiction.[2] Bill Clinton's grand strategy was democratic enlargement—expanding the circle of democracies; George W. Bush favored "promoting freedom" and "ending tyranny": using American power to eliminate breeding grounds for terrorism.[3] Barack Obama, as we saw in the Introduction, initially chose engagement, a strategy of connection, but without a clear theory of what specific connections to make or how to manage them to advance U.S. national interests.

A grand strategy for the Digital Age must be at least partly a strategy of connection. It must accept the ubiquity and power of networks and internalize both their opportunities and their threats. But just as the Digital Age subsumes the Industrial Age, so must a grand strategy for our world operate both on the chessboard and in the web. It must acknowledge the state-based international order even as it makes room for a people-based order.

I propose a grand strategy of Open Order Building based on the three pillars: open society, open government, and an open international system. The defining choice of our age is not democracies versus autocracies, but open versus closed.[4] In *The Industries of the Future*, Alec Ross, one of the architects of the Open Government Partnership (OGP), lines up countries on an "open-closed axis" and notes that countries like China, Saudi Arabia, and Kuwait are trying to pioneer hybrids of open economies and closed societies. He predicts that "the societies that embrace openness will be those that compete and succeed most effectively."[5]

Open versus closed means more than openness to trade, people, and ideas. As we have seen throughout this book, the network form creates its own logic and mindset.[6] Where networks are superior to hierarchies, it is because their logic drives them to be open. Open in the sense of participatory: networks accommodate the participation of the many rather than the few and derive power from that participation. Open in the sense of transparency: they defeat efforts to control and limit information, just as the July 2016 coup in Turkey was defeated by the ability of President Recep Erdoğan and his supporters to use FaceTime, Facebook Live, and Twitter to circumvent the army's control of the television networks. And open in the sense of autonomy: unlike a rule-governed hierarchy, networks encourage self-organization within a framework of principles.[7]

"Open versus closed" thus incorporates a whole set of principles about how society and government should be organized, principles that are consistent with America's history and values, even if we often fall short of achieving our ideals. A grand strategy of Open Order Building means standing for and supporting those principles around the world, as well as applying them as much as possible to the international system itself. The need is urgent, as the battle of open versus closed is being joined right now, within and between nations, and the forces of closed are gathering strength. In historically open nations like the United States and those of Western Europe, political leaders are channeling populist anger against globalization. They call for building walls, expelling immigrants, restricting trade, and withdrawing from the alliances and organizations that have underpinned global stability for generations.[8] In more closed nations like China, Russia, and Iran, autocratic governments seek to block and contain networks and the technologies that enable them. Indeed, Jared Cohen and Eric Schmidt argue that national filtering and restriction of the World Wide Web will intensify and balkanize the global Internet into separate nation-state networks.[9]

To explicate the concepts and principles of Open Order Building, I will contrast them with another grand strategy of connection, Joshua Ramo's proposed strategy of Hard Gatekeeping. I choose Ramo because he is a foreign policy thinker and practitioner who fully appreciates the drama and scale of the transition to the age of networks, but differs sharply from me in the lessons he draws and the prescriptions he offers. But I also choose him because he is a digital Kissingerian, whereas I am a digital Wilsonian.[10] The debate between us is but the newest round of a decades- and indeed centuries-old debate between supporters of a power-based foreign policy versus adherents to a values-based foreign policy. As we saw in Chapter 1, those camps have many labels: Kissingerians versus Wilsonians, realists versus liberal internationalists, or, as I prefer to frame it, statists against humanists.[11]

For Ramo, it's all about power. The axis of division between nations in an age of "collapse and construction" will be over the question *"Are you the gatekeeper or the gatekept?"* The gatekeepers control the networks that control our lives. The "gatekept" are inside those networks and controlled by their designers. "Hard gatekeeping" is a grand strategy based on the deliberate construction of "secure, carefully designed communities to manage everything from trade to cyberinformation to scientific research." These "gatelands" can be either physical or virtual.[12] Some will be exclusively for Americans; others will include allies; all will be designed to ensure that the United States is always the gatekeeper, never the gatekept.

Each power's gatelands will be "flavored" by its national values; U.S. gatelands will reflect "American values of democratic choice, freedom of thought, and privacy," as well as "rule of law, transparency about how decisions are made, and democratic accountability." Other nations "will design their gated enclosures" differently, depending on their history, culture, and domestic politics.[13] Traditional great-power competition will thus move into the digital realm, with each nation jostling to expand its "sphere of online influence."[14] The goal of hard gatekeeping as a national security strategy is to make "American-led gatelands" the most attractive in quality and reliability, so that small and medium-sized countries will want to join them.[15] This will be our competitive advantage over other great powers.

The Chinese government should be very happy with this vision. Indeed, Ramo writes: "America should be relaxed as Europe and Russia and China build gated systems."[16] Putting Europe and other U.S. allies in the same camp as Russia and China contrasts sharply with a vision of the world that assumes deep ties among governments based on the embrace of common values grounded in universal human rights. Equally worrisome, Ramo is content to replicate the physical barriers of the twentieth century in the virtual world of the twenty-first, replacing iron curtains with digital ones.

The U.S. government has already taken a stand on this issue. In a historic speech on Internet freedom in 2010, Secretary of State Hillary Clinton pointed out that "even as networks spread to nations around the globe, virtual walls are cropping up in place of visible walls." Building on Franklin Roosevelt's Four Freedoms, she championed "the freedom to connect—the idea that governments should not prevent people from connecting to the Internet, to websites, or to each other."[17] Just because gatelands *can* happen does not mean that they should, or that the United States should not oppose their emergence.

Let us take each pillar of Open Order Building in turn: open society, open government, and an open international system. For students of international relations, note that this grand strategy begins with domestic rather than international politics and indeed starts with society rather than government.[18] It offers an integrated conception of society, state, and international system. It thus marries the worlds of the chessboard and the web, recognizing states as powerful and important actors on the global stage while also acknowledging and validating individuals, groups, businesses, and institutions not simply as state subjects but as actors in their own right through global networks.

## OPEN SOCIETY

The first principle of every grand strategy is to protect the American people and safeguard the security of our allies. At its most elemental level, that is what national security means. Ramo concurs: the first element of hard gatekeeping is to "keep America and anyone inside the country's gated order safe." He imagines not only better physical security but also "rebuilding a new Internet designed for an age of digital threats."[19]

It is impossible, however, to guarantee personal safety in a radically and constantly connected age, no matter how high the wall or thick the gate. The very promise of safety is an irresistible temptation to hackers, the invading hordes of the twenty-first century. So too with lone-wolf attackers. Dictatorships fare little better than democracies at stopping such attacks, at far higher cost to civil liberties.

One of the constants of a networked age is thus a measure of irreducible uncertainty. It is the nature of connection and complexity: even tiny perturbations can ripple through the web in unpredictable, sometimes devastating ways. Better to embrace openness and strive for deep security, a promise not of safety but of resilience and self-reliance. In their forthcoming follow-up to *Team of Teams*, Chris Fussell and Charles Goodyear describe how organizations adopt structures of connection to bypass traditional bureaucratic limitations and cope with the inherent uncertainty of complex environments. They show how companies ranging from Airbnb to Intuit (maker of Quicken) have connected functional silos, increased flexibility, and adopted other lessons of Stanley McChrystal's task force in Iraq.[20]

Living in an open society requires taking calculated risks. We should expect government to develop webs of surveillance and protection, but consistent with citizens' civil rights. Much of the civil rights work of this century will be articulating and championing digital rights. And we must accept that the government cannot guarantee absolute safety. A measure of insecurity is the price of liberty and democracy. It's a price worth paying.[21]

## Citizen Participation

In this world, as former Assistant Secretary of Homeland Security Juliette Kayyem argues, citizens can and should do much more to provide for their own security. "No government," she writes, "ought to guarantee perfect security, because no government can provide it."[22] Government's role is to "invest in creating a more resilient nation," which includes briefing and empowering the public, but more as partner than as protector. Government benefits as well. Resilience expert Stephen Flynn has pointed out all the ways that Americans armed with more information from the government, rather

than less, would have been able to help stop or at least mitigate disasters.

What would have happened, Flynn asks, had U.S. authori-
ties given a press conference in August 2001, apprising the public of intelligence about the threat from al Qaeda and the known
risk of hijackers blowing up a plane or using one as a missile?
Many would have called such a briefing alarmist, but some of
the passengers on the planes that hit their targets in Washington
and New York would have suspected that the hijackers were
lying when they said they were returning to the airport. Perhaps
some would have taken action as did the passengers of Flight
93, who, because they took off later, had heard that other planes
had been flown into the Pentagon and World Trade Center.[23]

Government places more and more faith in algorithms and
data integration to keep us safe; but old-fashioned community,
in which individuals know one another and can instantly spot
an anomaly, still goes a very long way. Sharing information in a
much more open security network and building strong community nodes is also likely to reflect, and thus protect, the actual America we are becoming, more than the gatelands designed by the young white and Asian men who overwhelmingly
compose Ramo's "new caste" of educated technocrats.[24] We
can keep ourselves safer not by demonizing our neighbors, but
by getting to know them again, and by harnessing diversity as
a pillar of our security.

## Distributed Power

The self-reliance necessary for open security depends on the
ability to self-organize and take action. Society-wide, this approach requires limiting power, both public and private.

Excessively concentrated power, whether in private, public, or even civic hands, is an invitation to abuse.

Ramo argues that the winner-take-all nature of network effects means that the current platform monopolies are here to stay. Nine of the twelve most popular mobile apps are connected to systems owned by American companies like Google, Apple, and Microsoft.[25] Facebook, Whattsapp, and YouTube all have more than one billion users. On the other hand, Ramo assumes that Russia, China, and Europe will be able to extract their citizens from American-owned platforms and build their own gatelands, which shows that government can, if it chooses, disrupt even the most powerful private monopolies.[26]

Once again, the power of networks is concentration and distribution at the same time. Ramo assumes that the concentrations of power that flow from the scale-free architecture of many networks are inevitable and unchangeable, but networks are created by human action. Their effects are not new. They were the backbone of the railroad and telephone monopolies of the nineteenth and twentieth centuries; these networks used their size to dominate their markets, but they eventually faded away. The Northern Securities Company, which briefly monopolized transcontinental railroad traffic in the United States, was one of the first trusts broken up under the Sherman Antitrust Act of 1890. The American Telephone and Telegraph Company, known when I was growing up as Ma Bell, discovered that no matter how "natural" its monopoly, the government can still intervene and break it up—fortunately, or we might all still be using rotary-dial phones! It was Google's turn in the early 2000s, at the hands of the EU commissioner for competition.

Over my lifetime, antitrust law has effectively been neutered by theories that privilege efficiency and low prices (to the extent that monopolies provide these goods) over competition and smaller businesses. But intellectual fads and legal theories change, and the strain of American political economy that runs from Jefferson to Brandeis is reemerging, challenging concentrations of economic power on the grounds that competition is good for its own sake, no matter how well intentioned and indeed beneficial monopolies may be.[27]

Regardless of the outcome of this renewed debate, in the digital age data is a precious asset. In a democracy the data *about* the people belong *to* the people. We currently sign away our rights to that data in return for the wonderful free goods and services that big tech companies provide. Over time, however, the people will catch up to the data masters and also insist on a slice of the value that data creates when it is aggregated.[28]

Smaller, more distributed hubs have many advantages. Over time, as Microsoft and Apple have come to realize, the key to competitive success will shift from dominating the platform to ensuring the interoperability of many platforms. Currently, start-ups compete intensively with one another, but for many the goal is to be bought by one of the big players. Those start-ups should instead be growing into midsized and large companies on their own, creating competition and jobs along the way.[29]

The growth of the sharing economy entails a move toward greater distribution. NYU professor Arun Sundararajan writes that "the economic models of crowd-based capitalism may actually be able to distribute production across millions of smaller providers without having to sacrifice significantly on the gains from scale that 20th-century organizations enjoyed." The ability of people to increase the impact of their assets via platforms such as Airbnb means "the traditional gatekeeping mechanisms that have prevented many . . . people from moving from worker to owner or worker to investor are loosened."[30]

Still, the power imbalance between Airbnb itself and any individual renter, or Uber and any individual driver, is enormous, just like the difference between individual miners or railway workers and the owners of mines and railroads in the late nineteenth century. Unions were the twentieth-century answer; some form of collective bargaining and some legal leveling of the industrial playing field must be part of the answer in the twenty-first.

The United States and other governments will gradually find the golden mean of network power—not too concentrated and not too distributed. The megahubs have power *over*, but power *with* may be exercised by vast numbers of distributed but connected users. Wise governments will promote a balance between the two. Rather than accepting that other great powers will build their own gatelands, creating a global "splinternet," the United States should champion and defend an open global Internet.[31] Paradoxically, however, encouraging others to continue to play on turf where the United States is currently so dominant may well mean accepting measures that will strengthen competitors to U.S. platforms. Better to have robust competition on one Internet than to have multiple national internets, which would become the twenty-first-century equivalent of autarky.[32]

The United States was famously founded as a government of limited powers; suspicion of concentrated private power as well as public power has surged in periodic waves throughout our history. Size ultimately becomes oppressive even to the big. Buildings and empires really do topple under their own weight. Moreover, the masters of new technologies cannot master the power of politics, even if they are right to challenge the current deep dysfunction of the American political system. Washington and Silicon Valley, right and left, populists and elitists will have to find a way to forge a new social and political contract: one that marries new technologies and the efficiencies and citizen participation they enable with principles of limited power in both the political and commercial realm.

The international order of 1945 was based on the principle of "embedded liberalism," meaning that the insecurity of open money and trade was cushioned by domestic safety nets.[33] An open international order of the twenty-first century must be similarly anchored in secure and self-reliant societies, in which citizens can participate actively in their own protection and prosperity. The first building block is open society; the second is open government.

## OPEN GOVERNMENT

In September 2011, President Obama launched the Open Government Partnership with seven other nations: Brazil, Indonesia, Mexico, Norway, the United Kingdom, the Philippines, and South Africa. By 2016 OGP had grown to include seventy nations. Participants sign the Open Government Declaration, a set of principles that they pledge publicly to implement to make their governments more open and accountable. They must then commit to specific action plans;

participants have made more than 2,250 commitments to date.[34]

The Declaration's three major principles are transparency, civic participation, and accountability. Transparency means increasing the availability of information about governmental activities and making those activities open to as many people as possible, a commitment that is likely to lead to open data standards. A commitment to transparency does not mean abolishing secrecy in all government deliberations, a step that quickly brings government (or any organization) to a halt, but making information about what government knows and does visible and usable in a way that invites citizen engagement.

The second principle of civic participation thus follows from transparency. Signatories to the Open Government Declaration agree to "creating and using channels to solicit public feedback" in policy making and "deepening public participation in developing, monitoring and evaluating government activities."[35] Making this commitment real will require a regulatory as much as a technological revolution. Instead of antiquated "notice and comment" procedures, in which legislatures and regulators deliberate for months and years about the text of proposed rules, taking input from vested interests and then ultimately passing what political forces will allow, governments must move to methods that alert all affected citizens to proposed actions in real time. In many nations, legislatures and government agencies have begun publishing draft legislation and legal codes onto open source platforms like GitHub, enabling their publics to contribute input and monitor the revision process.[36]

The third major principle of open government is accountability, defined in large part as professional integrity. Under the Declaration, participating countries commit to having "robust anti-corruption policies, mechanisms and practices," transparent public finances and government procurement, and efforts to strengthen rule of law.[37] In practice, governments must have a legal framework that requires the disclosure of the income and assets of all high government officials and must put in place a whole set of deterrents against bribery.

## Government *with* the People

Taken together, the principles of open government frame a much more horizontal relationship between a government and its people than the traditional vertical relationship of either representative democracy or certainly of autocracy. Open government experiments currently under way in cities and countries around the world are inventing government *with* the people rather than government *for* the people.[38] The result is a side-by-side relationship of government officials and citizens that offers a template for how chessboard and web actors can co-exist in the international system.

Writing about "connexity" twenty years ago, Geoff Mulgan argued that in adapting to permanent interdependence, governments and societies would have to rethink their policies, their organizational forms, and their morality. Constant connectedness, he wrote, would place a premium on "reciprocity," "the idea of give and take," sometimes thought of as "the golden mean," and a spirit of openness, trust, and transparency would underpin a "new way of governing." Governments would break down their command-and-control silos and "provide a framework of predictability, but leave space for people to organise themselves within flatter, more reciprocal structures."[39]

Mulgan was prescient: in many ways the principles of the Open Government Partnership are designed to operational- ize the new social contract he envisioned. But people are not only organizing themselves; they are working directly with government officials to "coproduce" government services.[40] Coproduction embodies a very different philosophy of self- government from the republican forms of representative de- mocracy the American founding fathers envisaged. Instead of governing ourselves *through* those who represent us, citizens can partner directly with government to create and imple- ment solutions to public problems.[41] As NYU professor Beth Noveck writes, "This shift from top-down, closed and professional government to decentralized, open and smarter governance may be the major social innovation of the 21st century."[42]

Networks of citizens are already participating in open data challenges in cities across the United States and around the world; they are assisting crisis communications in natural and man-made disasters; and they are helping draft govern- ment budgets, legislation, and even constitutions.[43] That do- mestic role for citizens in open government will penetrate the international system as well. As foreign, finance, justice, de- velopment, environment, interior, and other ministers—as well as mayors—take a greater role on the global stage, they will bring with them the corporate and civic networks they are accustomed to engaging as coproducers of government services at home.

## Open, Connected Governments

The evolution of open government illustrates the ways in which common values give rise to common structures, aided by the enormous potential of digital platforms. Keohane and Nye pointed out fifty years ago that industrialized, pluralist states are the most tightly networked.[44] Nations willing to sign up to the Open Government Partnership and implement their commitments are embracing values and developing structures that will allow them to knit their societies and economies closely together. Instead of championing a world of great-power "gatelands," a strategy of Open Order Building starts from a community of allies and partners woven together by many different government, corporate, and civic relationships. Imagine a set of school friends on Facebook, who stay connected to one another and add connections to their life partners, their business associates, the parents of their children's friends, their fellow churchgoers and volunteers in civic causes, fellow sports fans and hobby enthusiasts, spreading out but also binding many of the most connected members of intersecting networks ever more closely together.

The United States should similarly maintain and deepen relationships with its current allies, assuming that they are willing to embrace both open society and open government principles. The alliances the United States built in the second half of the twentieth century were not just bulwarks against the Soviet Union but were anchored in a common commitment to the values enshrined in the Universal Declaration of Human Rights. Neither the United States nor any of its allies has fully lived up to those values; we all continually struggle with our national shortcomings. But we do so openly, through a free press and freedom of expression for our citizens and a public willingness to respond to our citizens' demands, even when those demands include changing the government.

The United States should not serenely contemplate Europe's or Japan's creation of its own gated communities for finance, industry, services, communications, education, medicine, or other vital economic and social transactions. We should of course recognize our allies' desire for autonomy and self-protection, but we should encourage integrated physical and electronic networks and work to ensure that interoperability ripens into community.

More fundamentally, U.S. policy makers should think in terms of translating chessboard alliances into hubs of connectedness and capability. Many of our most farsighted leaders are already doing just that. NATO is in the process of transforming itself into a "hub of a network of international security partnerships and a centre for consultation on global security issues."[45] In Asia, which is much less connected in security and economic terms than Europe, Ashton Carter's principled security network is designed to expand and deepen connections between nations currently on the periphery of a security web with those that are the hubs of that web.[46]

AN OPEN INTERNATIONAL SYSTEM

The final pillar of Open Order Building is the maintenance and expansion of an open international system. It must be open to both chessboard and web actors and to shifting power relationships among them. Systems theory teaches us that the level of organization in a closed system can only stay the same or decrease. In open systems, by contrast, dynamic feedback processes make it possible for the system to adapt and for its level of organization to increase in response to new inputs and disruptions.[47] An open international system should be able to ride out the disruptions caused by changing power relationships and at the same time incorporate all the different kinds of global networks discussed in Part II as critical tools for solving global problems.

The current international system is fixed and hierarchical. Some nations are more equal than others. The permanent members of the United Nations Security Council, the founding members of the World Bank and the IMF: these nations, which ruled the world in 1945, designed an international order to preserve peace and prosperity and to secure their own interests. Though they had a far more universalist understanding of international order than many of their predecessors, they created a set of inevitably self-interested arrangements for a world of seventy-three states, including empires with scores of colonies.

It is time not for destruction but for reform. The institutions that a generation of statesmen built after the cataclysm of World War II are important repositories of legitimacy and authority. They should become the hubs of a flatter, faster, more flexible system, one that operates at the level of citizens as well as states.

That means finally tackling the job of opening up post–World War II international institutions to create more room within the established councils of decision. We must also flatten the hierarchy between the United Nations and regional organizations, so that regional organizations can act more autonomously, with either advance or subsequent Security Council approval of their actions.[48]

Revising the U.N. Charter is obviously a Pandora's box. Substantive changes in the past have required a cataclysm, which we now cannot afford. But rising powers will not wait forever. They will simply create their own orders—either virtually, as with Ramo's gatelands, or physically, with their own regional institutions and security networks. If the international order proves too brittle to change, it will simply crumble. Like the once-great European dukedoms, it will keep the buildings and pageantry, but the power will have moved on.

The power shift that must take place is not only between twentieth- and twenty-first-century states, accommodating the rise of Asia and Africa and giving visibility and voice to states that existed only as colonies—or not at all—in 1945. It is also, as Jessica T. Matthews wrote presciently in 1997, between states and what she labeled nonstate actors—the same people and organizations we have learned to think of as web actors.[49] Networks of bad web actors threaten global security and well-being on a daily basis; we must respond by creating and supporting integrated networks of good web actors—corporate, civic, and public.

Some of these networks link only national government officials. The Proliferation Security Initiative, for instance, enables its 103 endorsing nations to interdict weapons of mass destruction and related materials going to and from states, groups, and individuals that present a high risk of proliferation. It should have some connection to the United Nations. It should retain its voluntary character and its decision rules, but "docking" with some part of the United Nations will help counter criticism from India and other nations that the initiative is illegitimate. The IMF, World Bank, Organisation for Economic Co-operation and Development, and other international financial institutions and standard-setting bodies are members of the Financial Stability Board, a consortium of networks of central bankers, finance ministers, securities regulators, and other financial officials from twenty-four nations and the European Commission.[50]

Many other regulatory, judicial, and legislative networks should be formally anchored or docked with global or regional institutions. Among the most promising new developments are networks of mayors, men and women who have both the authority and the ability to make policies that will affect 54 percent of the world's population.[51] We live in a rapidly urbanizing age; cities and their governments will become increasingly important global actors.[52]

Moving beyond government officials, networks of global charitable organizations are already closely connected to entities like the U.N. High Commissioner for Refugees, which partners with more than nine hundred NGOs and U.N. organizations.[53] The vaccine network GAVI relies on funding from industrialized governments and helps developing country governments apply for grants and develop self-sustaining financing for immunization programs.[54]

These examples are only the beginning. For every NGO that has been granted hard-won observer status at a U.N. meeting, the state gatekeepers of the current international system have barred the door to thousands more.[55] The chess players are still firmly in control. For networks to nest within or have formal connection to traditional hierarchical international

POWER, LEADERSHIP, AND GRAND STRATEGY

organizations, those traditional organizations must flatten out. They have to open their hierarchies and formalized routines to allow for more flexible arrangements among their members, as well as mixed citizen, corporate, and civic networks. After all, if Facebook—at 1.5 billion members larger than any nation in the world—can function as a network of networks, plenty of networks have the money, energy, and ideas to contribute as decisively to global order as a group of often weak member states.

To see the difference between the twentieth-century international system and the twenty-first-century open system that I am proposing, consider the negotiations for the Trans Pacific Partnership trade agreement and the Paris negotiations for a new international agreement on climate change. The TPP negotiations were closed, were conducted in private, and involved only national trade representatives. This secrecy generated mistrust among U.S. citizens and lawmakers and cast a shadowy, elitist pall over the TPP that has contributed to the intense opposition to ratification it faced during the 2016 presidential campaign.

The Paris negotiations, on the other hand, were not only for governments. The negotiators recognized that business, academia, civil society, and ordinary people all have a role to play in tackling climate change. So the negotiations, as sprawling and messy as they were, involved everyone from corporations to advocacy groups to billionaire philanthropists. The agreement reached does not set targets that are binding in international law, but it may be our best hope for saving the planet. Implementing that agreement will require state action but also web action, mobilizing many different civic, economic, scientific, and political networks.[56]

Over time, the shells of twentieth-century interstate organizations can become global and regional platforms for multiple types of associations among both chessboard and web actors. The United Nations, the IMF, the World Bank, the WTO, the European Union, the Organization of American States, the African Union, the Association of Southeast Asian Nations, and a host of other global and regional organizations can all build on and perhaps transcend their original form and function. Right now they are still state-dominated, constrained by the formalities of their founding. They should become docks for all kinds of networks, those composed of government ministers and those composed of mixed government, civic, and corporate actors.

Recall the design principle that sees network boundaries as markers of identity rather than separation. International and regional organizations can retain their intergovernmental rules and character for some purposes while becoming network hubs for others, anchoring an overlapping set of groups, clubs, and associations of all actors dedicated to addressing a particular set of issues. The result will be a complex and open problem-solving international system.

## ANCHORING THE CHESSBOARD AND THE WEB IN AN EVOLVING INTERNATIONAL LEGAL ORDER

A U.S. grand strategy of Open Order Building seeks to advance U.S. national interests in the world by building an open global order, comprising open societies, open governments, and an open international system. We seek a world in which American citizens and human beings around the world are safe, prosperous, and endowed with opportunities to live full and productive lives. That is a world in which Americans can protect and advance themselves as Americans, but also pursue the universal values that define us as a nation.

That open global order, which marries the chessboard and the web, must be anchored in an international legal order that recognizes and protects both states and people. The international legal order of the chessboard is an order that recognizes only sovereign states as both agents and subjects of international law, with a separate and untouchable sphere for domestic law.[57] The international legal order of the twenty-first century must be a *double* order, acknowledging the existence of domestic and international spheres of action and of law but seeing the boundary between them as a permeable one. Again, a boundary of identity more than of separation.

In this order, states must be waves and particles at the same time. They must continue to be the principal actors in the global system for addressing many circumstances: interstate war, weapons proliferation, state-sponsored terrorism and other criminal networks, ethnic and religious conflict, boundary disputes, and the many other issues of foreign and commercial diplomacy. But they must also be the places where web actors reside, reaching across boundaries as they engage in commercial, civic, political, and criminal justice pursuits that reverberate in global affairs just as much as state actions do.

It is impossible to say what form that double order will ultimately take. But it is emerging before our eyes—slowly, painfully, but inexorably. The foundations of sovereignty itself are shifting.[58]

The deep origins of this shift lie in the human rights movement of the twentieth century, beginning with the Hague Conventions of 1899 and 1907, which laid down rules of war for both soldiers and civilians. But human rights themselves became politically polarized during the Cold War, with the West championing civil and political rights, the East championing economic, social, and cultural rights, and both sides tending to ignore violations in their client states. When many frozen conflicts thawed and then exploded in the 1990s, the world turned once again to the urgent question of what the world owes to citizens who are suffering atrociously at the hands of their own governments.[59]

The first step was the development of international criminal law, moving from the "victors' justice" of the Nuremberg Trials to a fast-growing body of law and courts holding individual officials internationally accountable for actions against other individuals.[60] Then came a sea change in the law of humanitarian intervention.

In 2000, responding to an appeal from U.N. Secretary General Kofi Annan to find a path between the purported illegality of the NATO intervention in Kosovo and the illegitimacy of the U.N. failure to intervene to prevent the genocide in Rwanda, the Canadian government gathered a group of distinguished foreign policy practitioners and international lawyers. The group, the International Commission on Intervention and State Sovereignty, redefined sovereignty itself for the networked age by addressing the "'right of humanitarian intervention': the question of when, if ever, it is appropriate for states to take coercive—and in particular military—action, against another state for the purpose of protecting people at risk in that other state."[61] They called this the Responsibility to Protect, later shortened to R2P.

The Commission argued that the core meaning of U.N. membership had to change. Nations are free to choose whether or not to sign the Charter. If they do, they are accepted as sovereign members of the community of nations. But they must also accept the "responsibilities of membership" flowing from that acceptance. The Commission sought not to repeal or dilute state sovereignty but to "re-characterize" it "from *sovereignty as control* to *sovereignty as responsibility* in both internal functions and external duties." Moreover, this obligation has teeth: "Sovereignty as responsibility has become the minimum content of good international citizenship."[62] When a state abrogates its internal responsibility to protect the basic rights of its people, other states have a responsibility to protect those citizens, if necessary by military intervention.

In 2003 another step toward an open international order with people *and* states at the center was taken by the Commission for Human Security, launched after the U.N. Millennium Summit by the government of Japan and chaired by Sadako Ogata and Amartya Sen. The Commission's report put citizens and states on the same plane even as it recognized the complicated relationship between the two: "The state remains the fundamental purveyor of security. Yet it often fails to fulfill its security obligations—and at times has even become a source of threat to its own people." Human security aims to "protect the vital core of all human lives in ways that enhance human freedoms and human fulfillment."[63]

The United Nations General Assembly adopted a watered-down version of the Responsibility to Protect doctrine at its sixtieth anniversary summit in 2005. The U.N. text reads: "Each individual state has the responsibility to protect its populations from genocide, war crimes, ethnic cleansing and crimes against humanity."[64] Should states fail to do this, the responsibility shifts to the "international community," which should employ all "peaceful means," and if necessary take "collective action" through the Security Council to protect a population. Since then, the doctrine's application has been controversial, most acutely regarding its use to justify the U.N.-sanctioned intervention in Libya to protect the people of Benghazi from a threatened massacre (or the perception of a threat) by the Libyan government under Moammar Ghadaffi.

The wheels of international law grind wondrous slow, measuring change across decades and centuries. The Peace of Westphalia was not one treaty but a complex of agreements among the multiple states involved in the Thirty Years' War. The principle of sovereign equality purportedly enshrined in that peace took hundreds of years to implement. In contrast, the U.N. Security Council has invoked the responsibility to protect fifty times in the past decade.[65] By the end of the Obama administration it was deeply out of fashion, but that is surely temporary. What is important is that fifty years after the adoption of the revolutionary Universal Declaration of Human Rights, the relationship of a sovereign to its subjects is receiving yet another level of international scrutiny. International law is recognizing states and citizens at the same time. The double order is emerging, as the masters of the chessboard, willy nilly, make room for the web.

The logic is inexorable; Henry Kissinger himself explains why. The Thirty Years' War engulfed Europe from 1618 to 1648, a holocaust that killed perhaps one-third of the people in the German lands. In Kissinger's account, the Peace of Westphalia was meant above all to create a system that would better protect the people of Europe from "forced expulsion and conversions and general war consuming civilian populations." Further, while "the right of each signatory to choose its own domestic structure and religious orientation" was affirmed, "novel clauses ensured that minority sects could practice their faith in peace and be free from the prospect of forced conversion."[66]

In other words, the Westphalian world order mandated the sovereign equality of states not as an end in itself but as the best way of protecting the subjects of those states—the people. It was itself a double order, but one in which the gamesmanship of the chessboard could be too easily detached from the humanity of the web. *Cuius principio, eius religio* (whose realm, his religion) protected citizens in the seventeenth century, but not in the twentieth, and certainly not in the twenty-first.

The people must come first. Where they do not, sooner or later they will overthrow their governments. The technology that fuels the transformation of the social and economic order within nations—from hierarchies to networks—gives the people more power to overturn and destabilize than ever before. Their governments too have more power than ever before, but the course of human history bends away from both tyrants and philosopher kings and toward self-government. An open global order, anchored in a double international legal order, is the best hope of humankind for addressing planetary problems that now touch us all.

# Conclusion:
## The Rise of Webcraft

N 2004, the British think tank Demos published an edited volume on networks that opens: "Networks are the language of our times. Think about al-Qaeda. The Internet, eBay, Kazaa. The mobile phone, SMS. Think about iron triangles and old school ties, No Logo and DeanforAmerica. Think VISA and Amex, the teetering electricity grid, the creaking rail network." Helen McCarthy, Paul Miller, and Paul Skidmore, the editors of the volume, explained that although "networks shape our world," we do not actually understand their logic well enough to structure our institutions, our "organizational and public power," to harness their potential.[1]

When I first leafed through this volume, I was in the midst of a seven-year tour as dean of Princeton's Woodrow Wilson School of Public and International Affairs. We educated young people aspiring to go into government or nongovernmental organizations in order to analyze and make policy. We made them learn a lot of economics and statistics, some politics, and some psychology focused on judgment and decision making. We taught them to write crisp, concise, focused memos. And we offered them electives in international relations, international development, domestic policy, and more economics.

We did not require our students to study technology; not even the structure, physical properties, and governance of the Internet, the world we increasingly all inhabit. And although we taught the politics of hierarchies, we taught nothing about the nature and structure of networks.

Policy schools, like law schools, are in the business of teaching students to solve public problems. In the future, they must include courses in digital and human geography, bringing together the work of all the many disciplines I have drawn on in this book. A network map will become the new memo: it will be how you lay out the dimensions of a particular policy problem for your boss.

Even more important will be the network mindset: the ability to convert three-dimensional human relationships into two-dimensional maps of connections, and to see the relationships between people or institutions—the links—as clearly as the agents themselves, the nodes. We should be teaching students the architecture of the Internet, the types and properties of networks, and how to manage and lead within networks. Over the longer term, the more we know about how and when networks emerge and what their impact is both on the people or institutions within them and the world outside them, the more we will know about how to create and orchestrate them for specific purposes.

Students steeped in networks will see policy and politics differently. They will appreciate how objects and people are changed by connection. They will quickly size up problems of too few connections or too many, of centralized, decentralized, and distributed structures. They will see resources where a chess player sees only weakness; they will understand leadership as empowerment, structures as information flows.

These students will graduate and move into government, civic organizations, and the growing number of private companies concerned with public problems. They will join the new generation of foreign policy practitioners who work far outside national embassies or the halls of the State Department. They will continue to see a world of geopolitics and gamesmanship, of difficult military, diplomatic, and economic decisions aimed at averting conflict or at least converting it into a measure of cooperation.

But they will also see an ever denser web of networks, perhaps including entirely new topologies of space and time. Connection will be their modal state—with one another, with organizations, with governments. The map of those connections will become their personal geography, just as much as it will become national and international geography. Solving public problems will become a matter of whom and what to connect and disconnect, when, where, and how. Public problem solvers will include diplomats, civil servants, activists, CEOs, and civic leaders, web actors wielding power and exercising leadership alongside governments. They will all need strategies of connection.

# *Notes*

INTRODUCTION

1. For a history, see Peter Hopkirk, *The Great Game: The Struggle for Empire in Central Asia* (New York: Kodansha, 1992).

2. See, e.g., Gideon Rachman, "Chess Moves to Transform World Politics," *Financial Times*, December 8, 2014, http://www.ft.com/cms/s/0/38378ebe-7bd2-11e4-a695-00144feabdco.html#axzz4DGvmY8Oi.

3. Henry Kissinger, *On China* (New York: Penguin, 2011), 23–25.

4. Joseph S. Nye, Jr., "The Future of American Power," *Foreign Affairs*, November 1, 2010, https://www.foreignaffairs.com/articles/2010-11-01/future-american-power. Stanley Hoffmann also used the metaphor, writing that competition among states played out on a variety of chessboards; see, e.g., Stanley Hoffmann, "International Organization and the International System," *International Organization* 24, no. 3 (1970): 389–413.

5. See Manuel Castells, *The Rise of the Network Society* (Oxford: Blackwell, 1996); as well as the second and third books of the trilogy, *The Power of Identity* (1997) and *End of Millennium* (1998). A significantly updated second edition of *The Rise of the Network Society* was published in 2010 (Oxford: Blackwell).

6. Castells, *Rise of the Network Society* (2010), xviii.

7. Geoff Mulgan, *Connexity: How to Live in a Connected World* (Boston: Harvard Business School Press, 1997).

8. Joshua Cooper Ramo, *The Seventh Sense: Power, Fortune, and Survival in the Age of Networks* (New York: Little, Brown, 2016), 11, 36, 37.

9. Thomas Schelling, *The Strategy of Conflict* (Cambridge: Harvard University Press, 1960).

10. Robert Axelrod, *The Evolution of Cooperation* (New York: Basic, 1984).

11. Anne-Marie Slaughter, *A New World Order* (Princeton: Princeton University Press, 2004). In Chapter 4 I will discuss these types of networks in greater depth and detail.

12. See Ash Carter's remarks at the IISS Shangri-La Dialogue in Singapore, June 4, 2016, http://www.defense.gov/News/Speeches/Speech-View/Article/791213/remarks-on-asia-pacifics-principled-security-network-at-2016-iiss-shangri-la-di.

13. See James G. Stavridis, *Partnership for the Americas: Western Hemisphere Strategy and U.S. Southern Command* (Washington, DC: National Defense University Press, 2010).

14. See Chris Fussell's section in "What Is the Future of War?" *Defense One*, February 23, 2015, http://www.defenseone.com/ideas/2015/02/what-future-war/105807/.

15. For a discussion of the intellectual genesis and variations of the term, see Terry L. Deibel, *Foreign Affairs Strategy: Logic for American Statecraft* (New York: Cambridge University Press, 2007).

16. Long Deng, "China: The Post-Responsible Power," *Washington Quarterly*, January 26, 2015, https://twq.elliott.gwu.edu/china-post-responsible-power.

17. "Shared Vision, Common Action: A Stronger Europe: A Global Strategy for the European Union's Foreign and Security Policy," June 2016, http://eeas.europa.eu/top_stories/pdf/eugs_review_web.pdf; quotations at 43, 44.

18. See "Canada in the World: A Global Networks Strategy," 2011, http://www.liberal.ca/files/2011/08/CANADA-IN-THE-WORLD.pdf.

19. Barack Obama, "First Inaugural Address," delivered January 20, 2009, https://www.whitehouse.gov/blog/2009/01/21/president-barack-obamas-inaugural-address.

20. Credit for the subheading goes to Elmira Bayrasli and Lauren Bohn, whose organization Foreign Policy Interrupted seeks to amplify the voices of women and other underrepresented groups in foreign

policy; see the home page of Foreign Policy Interrupted, http://www.
fpinterrupted.com.

21. Business strategist and author Don Tapscott calls collaborative,
web-based platforms and organizations that are committed to solving
international problems global solution networks (GSNs). His GSN
Program identifies, catalogues, and researches these organizations; see the
GSN Program home page, http://gsnetworks.org/.

22. See the About page of the MIT Practical Impact Alliance,
http://impact-alliance.mit.edu/about.

23. See the Environment page of Bloomberg Philanthropies, http://
www.bloomberg.org/program/environment/#intro.

24. Laurie Spengler, "Why Strivers Are Essential to Inclusive
Growth," Mastercard Center for Inclusive Growth, July 12, 2016, http://
mastercardcenter.org/action/strivers-essential-inclusive-growth/.

25. See John G. Ruggie, *Just Business: Multinational Corporations and
Human Rights* (New York: Norton, 2013).

26. Nesrine Malik, "Too Big and Too Scary, but the Global Fat
Cats Can Be Chopped Down to Size," *Guardian*, December 10, 2014,
https://www.theguardian.com/commentisfree/2014/dec/10/big-scary-
global-fat-cats-multinationals-tax-dodgers.

27. See Steve Coll, *Private Empire: ExxonMobil and American Power*
(New York: Penguin, 2012).

28. For example, the Public International Law and Policy Group, a
pro bono firm that provides legal assistance to states and governments
in peace negotiations, postconflict constitution drafting, and prosecut-
ing war criminals. See the group's website, http://publicinternationallaw-
andpolicygroup.org/.

29. Various thinkers, practitioners, and commentators have described the post–Cold War proliferation of "non-state actors." In her
1997 *Foreign Affairs* article "Power Shift," Jessica T. Matthews heralded
the rise of global civil society and the dispersion of national power among
a widening variety of nonstate actors, such as businesses, international
organizations, and NGOs; and Margaret Keck and Kathryn Sikkink analyzed the rise of transnational advocacy networks in their groundbreaking
book *Activists Beyond Borders* (Ithaca, NY: Cornell University Press, 1998).

30. From a Council on Foreign Relations event moderated by
Gideon Rose called "Digital Power: Social Media and Political Change,"

March 31, 2011, transcript available at http://www.cfr.org/social-media/digital-power-social-media-political-change/p24576#.

31. See Diane Rogers-Ramachandran and Vilayanur S. Ramachandran, "Seeing in Stereo: Illusions of Depth," *Scientific American*, July 1, 2009, http://www.scientificamerican.com/article/seeing-in-stereo/.

32. See episode 7 of Ken Burns's documentary *The Roosevelts: An Intimate History*, PBS, 2014.

CHAPTER 1. OF GREAT POWERS AND GLOBALIZATION

1. Joseph S. Nye, Jr., and Robert O. Keohane, *Power and Interdependence* (Boston: Little, Brown, 1977).

2. Robert Cooper, *The Breaking of Nations: Order and Chaos in the Twenty-First Century* (New York: Grove, 2003), 29–30.

3. One major exception is Margaret Keck and Kathryn Sikkink, who in *Activists Beyond Borders* (Ithaca, NY: Cornell University Press, 1998) study advocacy networks from both a descriptive and prescriptive approach.

4. See Nye and Keohane, *Power and Interdependence*, 37.

5. Ibid., 37.

6. For a recounting of this history see Robert Keohane, "Twenty Years of Institutional Liberalism," *International Relations* 26, no. 2 (2012): 125–138.

7. See Joseph Greico, "Anarchy and the Limits of Cooperation: A Realist Critique of the Newest Liberal Institutionalism," *International Organization* 42, no. 3 (1988): 485–507; and Joseph Greico, Robert Powell, and Duncan Snidal, "The Relative-Gains Problem for International Cooperation," *American Political Science Review* 87, no. 3 (1993): 727–743.

8. See Robert D. Putnam, "Diplomacy and Domestic Politics: The Logic of Two-Level Games," *International Organization* 42, no. 3 (1988): 427–460; and also Peter Gourevitch, "The Second Image Reversed: The International Sources of Domestic Politics," *International Organization* 32, no. 4 (1978): 881–912.

9. See Andrew Moravcsik, "Taking Preferences Seriously: A Liberal Theory of International Politics," *International Organization* 51, no. 4 (1997): 513–553.

10. Andrew Moravcsik, "The New Liberalism," in *The Oxford Handbook of International Relations*, ed. Christian Reus-Smit and Duncan

Snidal (Oxford: Oxford University Press, 2008), 234–254; emphasis in the original.

11. G. John Ikenberry, another leading thinker in liberal international relations theory, has written about interdependence in the context of the U.S.-built liberal international order of institutions and alliances; see, e.g., *Liberal Leviathan: The Origins, Crisis, and Transformation of the American World Order* (Princeton: Princeton University Press, 2011).

12. Miles Kahler, "Networked Politics: Agency, Power, and Governance," in *Networked Politics: Agency, Power, and Governance,* ed. Miles Kahler (Ithaca, NY: Cornell University Press, 2009), 1–20, 2. In addition to Professor Kahler, scholars working on network theory and international relations include Emilie Hafner-Burton and Alexander Montgomery, who have written an excellent overview of network analysis and international relations with Kahler, as well as publishing their own network analyses. Zeev Maoz has also applied social network analysis methods to international relations.

13. See the following chapters in *Networked Politics:* Helen Yanacopulos, "Cutting the Diamond: Networking Economic Justice," 67–78; Michael Kenney, "Turning to the 'Dark Side': Coordination, Exchange, and Learning in Criminal Networks," 79–102; Kahler, "Collective Action and Clandestine Networks: The Case of al Qaeda," 103–124; and David A. Lake and Wendy H. Wong, "The Politics of Networks: Interests, Power, and Human Rights Norms," 127–150.

14. Hafner-Burton and Montgomery have tested hypotheses about how network position and structure influence conflict among states, finding that indeed intergovernmental network position affects relative distributions of power and the likelihood of military conflict. Hafner-Burton and Montgomery, "Power Positions: International Organizations, Social Networks, and Conflict," *Journal of Conflict Resolution* 50, no. 1 (2006): 3–27.

15. Kahler, "Networked Politics," 13.

16. Lake and Wong, "The Politics of Networks," 127–128.

17. Paul Ingram, Jeffrey Robinson, and Marc L. Busch, "The Intergovernmental Network of World Trade: IGO Connectedness, Governance, and Embeddedness," *American Journal of Sociology* 111, no. 3 (2005): 824–858. The authors found that "trade between two countries

increases by an average of 58% with every doubling of the strength of IGO connection between the countries" (824); note, however, that although the authors demonstrated correlation between trade and like IGO membership, proving a causal relationship is difficult.

18. Michael Kenney proves this point through his analysis of the evolution and resilience of Colombian drug cartels; see Kenney "Turning to the 'Dark Side.'"

19. See Robert B. Ahdieh, "Coordination and Conflict: The Persistent Relevance of Networks in International Financial Regulation," *Law and Contemporary Problems* 78 (2016): 75–101; Abraham L. Newman and David Zaring, "Regulatory Networks: Power, Legitimacy, and Compliance," in *Interdisciplinary Perspectives on International Law and International Relations: The State of the Art*, ed. Jeffrey L. Dunoff and Mark A. Pollack (New York: Cambridge University Press, 2013), 244–265; David Zaring, "Finding Legal Principle in Global Financial Regulation," *Virginia Journal of International Law* 52, no. 3 (2012): 683–722; Benedict Kingsbury et al., "The Emergence of Global Administrative Law," *Law and Contemporary Problems* 68, no. 3 (2005): 15–62; Kal Raustiala, "The Architecture of International Cooperation: Transgovernmental Networks and the Future of International Law," *Virginia Journal of International Law* 43 (2002): 1–92. The breadth of work on the phenomenon of international regulatory networks has perhaps inevitably occasioned some criticism; see, e.g., Pierre-Hugues Verdier, "Transnational Regulatory Networks and Their Limits," *Yale Journal of International Law* 34, no. 1 (2009): 113–172.

20. Francesca Bignami and David Zaring, eds., *Comparative Law and Regulation: Understanding the Global Regulatory Process* (Cheltenham, UK: Edward Elgar, 2016).

21. The literature on complexity theory is vast. For a popular overview, see Steven Johnson, *Emergence: The Connected Lives of Ants, Brains, Cities, and Software* (New York: Scribner, 2001); Neil Johnson, *Simply Complexity: A Clear Guide to Complexity Theory* (London: Oneworld, 2009); James Gleick, *Chaos: The Making of a New Science* (New York: Viking, 1987); Steven Strogatz, *Sync: How Order Emerges from Chaos in the Universe, Nature, and Daily Life* (New York: Hyperion, 2003); John H. Miller and Scott E. Page, *Complex Adaptive Systems: An Introduction to Computational Models of Social Life* (Princeton: Princeton University

Press, 2003); Scott E. Page, *Diversity and Complexity* (Princeton: Princeton University Press, 2011).

22. Didier Sornette, "Dragon-Kings, Black Swans, and the Prediction of Crises," *International Journal of Terraspace Science and Engineering* 2, no. 1 (2009): 1–18, 1.

23. Robert Axelrod, *The Complexity of Cooperation: Agent-Based Models of Competition and Collaboration* (Princeton: Princeton University Press, 1997), 4.

24. Zeev Maoz, *Networks of Nations: The Evolution, Structure, and Impact of International Networks, 1816–2001* (Cambridge: Cambridge University Press, 2011), 365.

25. Axelrod, *Complexity of Cooperation.*

26. Lars-Erik Cederman, *Emergent Actors in World Politics: How States and Nations Develop and Dissolve* (Princeton: Princeton University Press, 1997).

27. Emilie Hafner-Burton, Miles Kahler, and Alexander Montgomery, "Network Analysis for International Relations," *International Organization* 63, no. 3 (2009): 559–592, 559.

### CHAPTER 2. NETWORKS EVERYWHERE

1. Before the Digital Age, writes network scientist Duncan J. Watts in *Six Degrees: The Science of a Connected Age* (New York: Norton, 2003), the "only way to get social network data was to go out and collect it by hand." Nowadays, "technology capable of recording social interactions electronically, from phone calls to instant messaging to on-line chat rooms, has increased the size of network data sets by several orders of magnitude" (59).

2. I am indebted to Christina Prell, *Social Network Analysis: History, Theory and Methodology* (Thousand Oaks, CA: Sage 2012). Prell maps the origins of social network analysis in three trajectories from psychology, sociology, and social anthropology, providing an excellent review of the scholarship and major contributors to the field.

3. Social network analysis emerged as a field of academic inquiry unto itself thanks in large part to mathematical physicist-turned-sociologist Harrison White, who in the 1970s established a research program in the Harvard sociology department to study the social network not just as a metaphor but as an analytical concept. White has

taught or influenced many of the most notable scholars in network analysis. See Prell, *Social Network Analysis*, 42–45.

4. For an example of some tools and approaches in use by social media companies, see Derek L. Hansen, Ben Shneiderman, and Marc A. Smith, *Analyzing Social Media Networks with NodeXL: Insights from a Connected World* (Burlington, MA: Elsevier, 2011). For an overview of how companies can use social network analysis to improve their organizations, see Rob Cross and Robert J. Thomas, *Driving Results Through Social Networks* (San Francisco: Jossey-Bass, 2009); and Linton C. Freeman, *The Development of Social Network Analysis* (Charleston, SC: BookSurge, 2004).

5. For a complete introduction to the basic concepts of network science see M. E. J. Newman, *Networks: An Introduction* (New York: Oxford University Press, 2010).

6. Nicholas Christakis and James Fowler, *Connected: The Surprising Power of Our Social Networks and How They Shape Our Lives—How Your Friends' Friends' Friends Affect Everything You Feel, Think, and Do* (New York: Little, Brown, 2009), 28; also see Sanjeev Goyal, *Connections: An Introduction to the Economics of Networks* (Princeton: Princeton University Press, 2007), 6–7, for an overview of empirical work in economics on how membership in different groups explains variation in individual behavior.

7. Mark S. Granovetter, "The Strength of Weak Ties," *American Journal of Sociology* 78, no. 6 (1973): 1360–1380.

8. Prell, *Social Network Analysis*, 34, 166–171.

9. See ibid., 46, in reference to Robert D. Putnam, *Bowling Alone: The Collapse and Revival of American Community* (New York: Simon and Schuster, 2000); and James S. Coleman, *Foundations of Social Theory* (Cambridge: Harvard University Press, 1990).

10. Ronald S. Burt, *Structural Holes: The Social Structure of Competition* (Cambridge: Harvard University Press, 1992).

11. For another approach to forms of social capital, see James S. Coleman, "Social Capital in the Creation of Human Capital," *American Journal of Sociology* 94 (1988): S95–S120.

12. See the help page for network measurement software NetworkAnalyzer, http://med.bioinf.mpi-inf.mpg.de/netanalyzer/help/2.7/#node.

13. Walter Powell, "Neither Market nor Hierarchy: Network Forms of Organization," *Research in Organizational Behavior*, no. 12 (1990): 295–336.

14. See Manuel Castells's three-volume Information Age Trilogy: *The Rise of the Network Society* (Oxford: Blackwell, 1996), *The Power of Identity* (1997), and *End of Millennium* (1998). A significantly updated second edition of *The Rise of Network Society* was published in 2010 (Oxford: Blackwell).

15. Don Tapscott and Anthony D. Williams, *Wikinomics: How Mass Collaboration Changes Everything* (New York: Penguin, 2006).

16. Ibid., 225.

17. Castells, *The Rise of the Network Society* (2010), 180; emphasis in the original.

18. See the PWC website "Hierarchy vs. Network—A New Business Model for Success?" 2014, http://www.digitalinnovation.pwc.com.au/hierarchy-vs-network-business-models/.

19. Karen Stephenson, "Towards a Theory of Government," in *Network Logic*, ed. Helen McCarthy et al., *Demos* 20 (2004): 35–48, 40.

20. Ibid., 45; see also Gillian Tett, *The Silo Effect: The Peril of Expertise and the Promise of Breaking Down Barriers* (New York: Simon and Schuster, 2015).

21. Watts, *Six Degrees;* the first experimental evidence for the existence of small worlds was provided by Stanley Milgram in 1967 (see ibid., 38–39).

22. Albert-Laszlo Barabasi, *Linked: How Everything Is Connected to Everything Else and What It Means for Business, Science, and Everyday Life* (New York: Penguin 2002), 66–72, 135.

23. Fritjof Capra, "Living Networks," in *Network Logic*, ed. Helen McCarthy et al., *Demos* 20 (2004): 25–34.

24. Ibid., 26.

25. McKinsey Global Institute, "Digital Globalization: The New Era of Global Flows," February 2016, http://www.mckinsey.com/business-functions/mckinsey-digital/our-insights/digital-globalization-the-new-era-of-global-flows.

26. Capra, "Living Networks," 28.

27. Ibid., 32, 27.

28. Cited in Barabasi, *Linked*, 231–232.

29. Simon Levin, *Fragile Dominion: Complexity and the Commons* (New York: Basic, 2000).

30. Simon Levin and Jane Lubchenco, "Resilience, Robustness, and Marine Ecosystem-Based Management," *Bioscience* 58, no. 1 (2008): 27–31.

31. Levin, *Fragile Dominion*, 202.

32. I draw heavily here on the work of economist Sanjeev Goyal, whose book *Connections: An Introduction to the Economics of Networks* (Princeton: Princeton University Press, 2007) offers an excellent overview of the economics literature on networks. He references much of the literature on networks from other disciplines and identifies the key difference as one of methodology: economists operate on the methodological premise that "social and economic phenomena must ultimately be explained in terms of the choices made by rational agents" (7).

33. Ibid., 1.

34. Several economists, however, have rejected this approach, arguing that economic incentives can crowd out prosocial behavior; see, e.g., Samuel Bowles, *The Moral Economy: Why Good Incentives Are No Substitute for Good Citizens* (New Haven: Yale University Press, 2016).

35. Example from Goyal, *Connections*, 8.

36. Ibid., 4, 7; see also David Easley and Jon Kleinberg, *Networks, Crowds, and Markets: Reasoning About a Highly Connected World* (New York: Cambridge University Press, 2010), 681–692.

37. Alex Pentland, *Social Physics: How Social Networks Can Make Us Smarter* (New York: Penguin, 2014), 62–70.

38. Ibid., 77–78, 80–84, 88.

39. Paul Adams, *Grouped: How Small Groups of Friends Are the Key to Influence on the Social Web* (Berkeley, CA: New Riders, 2012), 12.

40. Pentland, *Social Physics*, 16.

41. Recall that denser networks feature strong ties, sparse networks weak ties.

42. Economists call this the social multiplier and have sought to quantify it: see, e.g., Edward L. Glaeser, Bruce I. Sacerdote, and Jose A. Scheinkman, "The Social Multiplier," National Bureau of Economic Research Working Paper Series, http://www.nber.org/papers/w9153.

1. See Abram Chayes and Antonia Handler Chayes, *The New Sovereignty: Compliance with International Regulatory Regimes* (Cambridge: Harvard University Press, 1998).

2. Susan T. Fiske, *Social Beings: Core Motives in Social Psychology* (Hoboken, NJ: Wiley, 2010), 35; Nicholas Christakis and James Fowler contrast homo economicus with *homo dictyous*, meaning "network man." Homo dictyous has motivations that "depart from pure self-interest"; he or she "take[s] the well-being of others into account" in making choices about what to do. Homo dictyous is embedded in society—in networks of people—and thus is shaped by those others in many ways: desires, preferences, tastes, behaviors. Christakis and Fowler, *Connected: The Surprising Power of Our Social Networks and How They Shape Our Lives— How Your Friends' Friends' Friends Affect Everything You Feel, Think, and Do* (New York: Little, Brown, 2009), 222–228. I prefer my construct, based on Fiske and others, of homo sociologicus because it assumes that human beings are in networks or groups to begin with, owing to a desire to connect and belong is itself a deep preference, a default setting, shaped by evolutionary adaptation. But the two constructs certainly overlap.

3. Fiske, *Social Beings*, 35.

4. According to Fiske, social psychologists consider the desire to belong to groups as the predominant social motive.

5. Fareed Zakaria, "Bigger Than the Family, Smaller Than the State: Are Voluntary Groups What Make Countries Work?" *New York Times*, August 13, 1995.

6. David Brooks, in his book *The Social Animal: The Hidden Sources of Love, Character, and Achievement* (New York: Random House, 2011), turns to psychology to argue that our unconscious mind is driven to become one with others: "We seek, more than anything else, to establish deeper and more complete connections" (xvi).

7. See Yochai Benkler, *The Penguin and the Leviathan: How Cooperation Triumphs over Self-Interest* (New York: Crown, 2011); and Samuel Bowles, who in *The Moral Economy: Why Good Incentives Are No Substitute for Good Citizens* (New Haven: Yale University Press, 2016) recounts various experiments that show explicit incentives that assume human selfishness often fail to compel and can even deter a desired

behavior; he concludes, "policies premised on the belief that citizens or employees are entirely self-interested often induce people to act exactly that way" (84).

8. Benkler, *The Penguin and the Leviathan*, 65, 86.

9. See Fiske, *Social Beings*, and Benkler, *The Penguin and the Leviathan*; also, David Brooks, in *The Social Animal*, notes that "Decision making is an inherently emotional business" (17).

10. Fiske, *Social Beings*, notes, "The actual, imagined, or implied presence of others influences the thoughts, feelings, and behaviors of individuals" (34), and "The self is not a fixed entity but depends on the situation" (185).

11. Ibid., 386, 378–385.

12. From a methodological perspective, network theory brings these two worlds together: network structures and dynamics are at least hypothetically the same regardless of whether individuals, corporations, or states constitute the nodes. Social network analysis can work with millions or indeed billions of actors just as well as with 194 states or thousands of parts of states. Indeed, network theory as taught by computer scientists and economists is half graph theory and half game theory, tools that are used equally to study states and people. Still, for purposes of exposition, understanding, and application, it is more helpful to think of two interlinked worlds of states and people. That does not mean, however, that what goes for people automatically goes for states. As Miles Kahler, Emilie Hafner-Burton, and Alexander Montgomery point out, "casual transfer of findings from social networks of individuals must be scrutinized thoroughly. The level of analysis problem in international relations does not disappear in a networked world: are networks of individuals, governments, or other units the subject of investigation?" Hafner-Burton, Kahler, and Montgomery, "Network Analysis for International Relations," *International Organization* 63, no. 3 (2009): 559–592, 586.

13. Some of these dichotomies resemble the split between rationalism and constructivism, in which the modal human thought process is identified as calculation versus socialization. Constructivists are still largely writing about states, however. See Martha Finnemore and Kathryn Sikkink, "Taking Stock: The Constructivist Research Program in International Relations and Comparative Politics," *Annual Review of Political Science* 4 (June 2001): 391–416.

14. Dennis Ross, *Statecraft: And How to Restore America's Standing in the World* (New York: Farrar, Straus and Giroux, 2007), x.

### PART II. STRATEGIES OF CONNECTION

1. Julianne Smith, "Our Overworked Security Bureaucracy," *Democracy Journal* 40 (2016), http://democracyjournal.org/magazine/40/our-overworked-security-bureaucracy/.

2. Donald E. Stokes, *Pasteur's Quadrant: Basic Science and Technological Innovation* (Washington, DC: Brookings Institution Press, 1997).

### CHAPTER 4. RESILIENCE NETWORKS

1. Simon A. Levin and Jane Lubchenco, "Resilience, Robustness, and Marine Ecosystem-based Management," *Bioscience* 58, no. 1 (2008): 28; for a deeper examination of ecological resilience and complexity see Levin's book *Fragile Dominion: Complexity and the Commons* (New York: Basic, 2000); Levin and coauthors Robert M. May and George Sugihara also analyze financial system stability through an ecosystem framework in "Complex Ecosystems: Ecology for Bankers," *Nature* 451, no. 7181 (2008): 893–895.

2. Andrew Zolli and Ann Marie Healy, *Resilience: Why Things Bounce Back* (New York: Simon and Schuster, 2012), 7.

3. Judith Rodin, *The Resilience Dividend: Being Strong in a World Where Things Go Wrong* (New York: PublicAffairs, 2014).

4. Zolli and Healy, *Resilience*, 9.

5. Albert-Laszlo Barabasi, *Linked: How Everything Is Connected to Everything Else and What It Means for Business, Science, and Everyday Life* (New York: Plume, 2003), 145.

6. Paul Baran, "On Distributed Communications: I. Introduction to Distributed Communications Networks," RAND Corporation (1964), http://www.rand.org/content/dam/rand/pubs/research_memoranda/2006/RM3420.pdf.

7. Zolli and Healy, *Resilience*, 100.

8. Ibid., 14–15.

9. See Robert Axelrod, *The Evolution of Cooperation* (New York: Basic, 1984).

10. See Robert D. Putnam, *Making Democracy Work: Civic Traditions in Modern Italy* (Princeton: Princeton University Press, 1993); and

*Bowling Alone: The Collapse and Revival of American Community* (New York: Simon and Schuster, 2000). See also Francis Fukuyama, *Trust: The Social Virtues and the Creation of Prosperity* (New York: Free Press, 1995), who calls the entrepreneurial or associational subset of social capital "spontaneous sociability," creating and carrying vital channels of trust throughout a healthy economy and society.

11. See Barabasi, *Linked*, 112–113, 71.

12. Ibid., 109–122.

13. The United Nations predicts that up to 70 percent of the world's population will live in cities by 2050, an addition of 2.5 billion people; United Nations, "World Urbanization Prospects," UN DESA Population Division, 2015. Most of this urban growth will occur in Africa and Asia: China's urban population was 527 million in 2005; it is on track to hit 1 billion by 2030; McKinsey and Company, "Preparing for China's Urban Billion," McKinsey Global Institute, March 2009.

14. "Zebra" is U.S. medical community slang for a rare or unlikely diagnosis. When a medical professional hears hoofbeats, she is trained to think horses—but in rare instances, the sound actually indicates a zebra.

15. Duncan Watts notes that epidemics follow a logarithmic path of growth, from slow-phase to explosive to burnout. Stopping an epidemic depends not on limiting the size of the initial outbreak but on limiting its rate of growth such that it can't reach the explosive phase. Treating early infecteds in a parallel distributed health system would thus confine and slow the spread of a disease; Duncan J. Watts, *Six Degrees: The Science of a Connected Age* (New York: Norton, 2003), 173.

16. Department of Homeland Security, "Written Testimony of NPPD Under Secretary Suzanne Spaulding and NPPD Deputy Under Secretary for Cybersecurity Communications Phyllis Schneck for a House Committee on Homeland Security Hearing Titled 'Examining the President's Cybersecurity Information Sharing Proposal," February 25, 2015, https://www.dhs.gov/news/2015/02/25/written-testimony-nppd-under-secretary-and-deputy-under-secretary-cybersecurity.

17. See the National Cybersecurity Communications Integration Center webpage on the U.S. Department of Homeland Security site, https://www.dhs.gov/national-cybersecurity-and-communications-integration-center.

18. DHS, "Written Testimony."

19. John Kelly and Bruce Etling, "Mapping Iran's Online Public: Politics and Culture in the Persian Blogosphere," Internet and Democracy Case Study Series, Berkman Center for Internet and Society, April 2008, http://cyber.law.harvard.edu/sites/cyber.law.harvard.edu/ files/Kelly%26Etling_Mapping_Irans_Online_Public_2008.pdf.

20. See Manuel Castells, *Networks of Outrage and Hope* (Cambridge: Polity, 2012), 63–66, 106.

21. A note on terminology here. The type of response networks identified in this section could equally be described as "task networks," networks created for the purpose of executing the task of responding to a disaster. However, the creation of these networks after or preferably before disaster strikes builds resilience of the community or society in critical ways; hence I have included this subcategory of network in the overall category of resilience networks.

22. See testimony from Shona Brown, senior vice president of Google.org, to the U.S. Senate Committee on Homeland Security and Governmental Affairs, "Understanding the Power of Social Media as a Communication Tool in the Aftermath of Disasters," May 5, 2011, https://www.hsdl.org/?view&did=5896.

23. For an account of how Palantir Gotham was used to facilitate response and recovery operations after the Haiti earthquake see Ari Gesher's post on the Palantir Blog, "Haiti: Effective Recovery Through Analysis," April 5, 2010, https://www.palantir.com/2010/04/haiti-effective-recovery-through-analysis/. For how Google's Person Finder was used in the aftermath of the Japanese earthquake and tsunami see "Google Aids Japan Quake Victims," *BBC News*, March 11, 2011, http://www.bbc.com/news/ technology-12711244.

24. Zolli and Healy, *Resilience*, 186–189. For another account of Mission 4636, see Anne Nelson, Ivan Sigal, and Dean Zambrano, "Media, Information Systems, and Communities: Lessons from Haiti," Knight Foundation, January 10, 2011, http://www.knightfoundation. org/media/uploads/publication_pdfs/KF_Haiti_Report_English.pdf. See also Eric Schmidt and Jared Cohen, *The Digital Age: Reshaping the Future of People, Nations, and Business* (New York: Knopf, 2013), 240.

25. Keri K. Stephens and Patty Malone, "New Media for Crisis Communication: Opportunities for Technical Translation, Dialogue,

and Stakeholder Responses," in *The Handbook of Crisis Communication*, ed. W. Timothy Coombs and Sherry J. Holladay (Malden, MA: Wiley-Blackwell, 2010), 381–395, 383.

26. Ben Ramalingam, *Aid on the Edge of Chaos* (Oxford: Oxford University Press, 2013), 306.

27. See "Informal Disaster Governance Systems," City Leadership Initiative, http://www.cityleadership.net/informal-governance-systems/.

28. Social psychologist Susan Fiske in *Social Beings: Core Motives in Social Psychology* (Hoboken, NJ: Wiley, 2010) notes that the need to belong, to form "strong, stable relationships" with others, is the core human social motivation (18). And conflict resolution expert Donna Hicks in *Dignity: Its Essential Role in Resolving Conflict* (New Haven: Yale University Press, 2011) identifies dignity—having one's self-worth and value recognized by others—as a crucial precondition for human connection. Francis Fukuyama in *The End of History and the Last Man* (New York: Avon, 1992) ties this notion to governance, writing that the state's recognition of the essential dignity of its population is necessary for long-term stability.

29. Ruti Teitel, *Humanity's Law* (New York: Oxford University Press, 2011), 217.

30. For example, Brooks notes that when people achieve a sense of close affinity with one another their brain is flooded with contentment-inducing oxytocin, "nature's way of weaving people together"; David Brooks, *The Social Animal: The Hidden Sources of Love, Character, and Achievement* (New York: Random House, 2011), 64.

31. Yochai Benkler, *The Penguin and the Leviathan: How Cooperation Triumphs over Self-Interest* (New York: Crown, 2011), 103.

32. Fiske, *Social Beings*, 282.

33. Tina Rosenberg, *Join the Club: How Peer Pressure Can Transform the World* (New York: Norton, 2011).

34. See, e.g., Jonah Lehrer, "Do Parents Matter?" *Scientific American*, April 9, 2009, http://www.scientificamerican.com/article/parents-peers-children/.

35. Using game theory and repeated experiments, scholars and researchers have shown that the expectation of future interaction—what Robert Axelrod in *The Evolution of Cooperation* calls "the shadow of the future"—is necessary to sustain cooperation.

36. Alex Pentland, *Social Physics: How Social Networks Can Make Us Smarter* (New York: Penguin, 2014), 69.

37. Ibid., 77.

38. See "Global Entrepreneurship Program," U.S. State Department, http://www.state.gov/e/eb/cba/entrepreneurship/gep/.

39. Watts, *Six Degrees*, 241.

40. For example, Matthew Haag and Richard Lagunoff show that in a local setting where player discount factors are unknown, a maximally connected neighborhood design can increase sustained cooperation; Haag and Lagunoff, "Social Norms, Local Interaction, and Neighborhood Planning," *International Economic Review* 47 no. 1 (2006): 265–296.

41. Sean Safford, *Why the Garden Club Couldn't Save Youngstown* (Cambridge: Harvard University Press, 2009), 9.

42. Ibid., 93, 7.

43. Again, see Mark S. Granovetter, "The Strength of Weak Ties," *American Journal of Sociology* 78, no. 6 (1973): 1360–1380.

44. Watts, *Six Degrees*, 118, 146–156.

45. See M. E. J. Newman, *Networks: An Introduction* (New York: Oxford University Press, 2010), 207.

46. Zeev Maoz et al., "What Is the Enemy of My Enemy? Causes and Consequences of Imbalanced International Relations, 1816–2001," *Journal of Politics* 69, no. 1 (2007): 100–115.

47. Moises Naim, *Illicit: How Smugglers, Traffickers, and Copycats Are Hijacking the Global Economy* (New York: Anchor, 2006).

48. Lisa Gansky, *The Mesh: Why the Future of Business Is Sharing* (New York: Portfolio Penguin, 2010), 5, 16.

49. NYU Stern School of Business professor Arun Sundararajan, in *The Sharing Economy: The End of Employment and the Rise of Crowd-Based Capitalism* (Cambridge: MIT Press, 2016), writes that a key characteristic of the sharing economy is "crowd-based networks rather than centralized institutions or hierarchies" (27).

50. Gansky, *The Mesh*, 16; emphasis in the original.

51. Sundararajan writes that the sharing economy "hints at the shift away from faceless, impersonal 20th-century capitalism and toward exchange that is somehow more connected, more embedded in community, more reflective of a shared purpose"; *The Sharing Economy*, 35.

52. Sundararajan again: before the Industrial Revolution, economic exchange was mostly peer-to-peer embedded in communities where trust was based on social ties; today, because of online platforms that create the possibility of trust without a history of personal interaction, the sharing economy is "scaling behaviors and forms of exchange" that used to exist only in tightly knit communities to a "broader, loosely knit digital community of semi-anonymous peers"; ibid., 38.

53. Fukuyama, *Trust*.

54. See part 2 of the UN Framework Convention on Climate Change, "Report of the Conference of the Parties on its Twenty-first Session, Held in Paris from 30 November to 13 December 2015," January 29, 2016, 18.

## CHAPTER 5. TASK NETWORKS

1. Stanley McChrystal et al., *Team of Teams: New Rules of Engagement for a Complex World* (New York: Portfolio/Penguin, 2015).

2. This is a central idea motivating the discipline of social physics. See Alex Pentland, *Social Physics: How Social Networks Can Make Us Smarter* (New York: Penguin, 2014), 6–8.

3. Some of the work on these types of networks in economic theory uses the classic game theory that is the basis of *A Strategy of Conflict* and chessboard approaches to international relations generally. The economics of networks relies heavily on two bodies of theory: graph theory describes network structure, and game theory is used to model and predict individual behavior in networked settings.

4. Axelrod invited notable game theorists to submit strategies for a round-robin tournament of two hundred–round prisoner's dilemma games run on computers. In each game, a player had to commit to a strategy in advance that dictated whether to cooperate with her opponent or defect in each round. The winner, Anatol Rapoport, used the tit-for-tat strategy, which was to cooperate on the first move and then on each subsequent move repeat the opponent's previous move. Axelrod repeated the tournament with a larger group and Rapoport again won using the same strategy. Tit-for-tat was not a new strategy, but after its success in the tournaments, Axelrod popularized it in several prominent papers on cooperation; see three papers from Robert Axelrod: "Effective Choice in the Prisoner's Dilemma," *Journal of Conflict Resolution* 24,

no. 1 (1980): 3–25; "More Effective Choice in the Prisoner's Dilemma," *Journal of Conflict Resolution* 24, no. 3 (1980): 379–403; and, with William D. Hamilton, "The Evolution of Cooperation," *Science* 211, no. 4489 (1981): 1390–1396.

5. See Elinor Ostrom, "Beyond Markets and States: Polycentric Governance of Complex Economic Systems," *American Economic Review* 100 (2010): 1–33.

6. Chess players do understand that governments have a variety of interests and can cooperate with one another on some issues while taking adversarial positions on others. But as Keohane and Nye argue in *Power and Interdependence*, they privilege military security as "the dominant goal," meaning that adversary states on military issues are seen primarily as adversaries, even if they are cooperators on nonmilitary issues; Joseph S. Nye, Jr., and Robert O. Keohane, *Power and Interdependence* (Boston: Little, Brown, 1977).

7. The literature of games on networks is dense, and many researchers have studied the core-periphery structure in various settings. For an experimental finding of this result see the research paper by Yunkyu Sohn et al., "Core-Periphery Segregation in Evolving Prisoner's Dilemma Networks," *arXiv*, 2011, https://arxiv.org/ftp/arxiv/papers/1105/1105.0515.pdf. For theoretical evidence of the stability of the core-periphery network structure see Matthew Haag and Roger Lagunoff, "Social Norms, Local Interaction, and Neighborhood Planning," *International Economic Review* 47, no. 1 (2006), http://faculty.georgetown.edu/lagunofr/sn9.pdf.

8. Gabriella Blum, *Islands of Agreement: Managing Enduring Armed Rivalries* (Cambridge: Harvard University Press, 2007).

9. Robert Keohane, *After Hegemony: Cooperation and Discord in the World Political Economy* (Princeton: Princeton University Press, 1984).

10. The cheapest and most efficient way to provide public goods is through a star network, in which one central actor provides the good, as the United States provided the lion's share of global security and economic prosperity for at least the Western world after World War II. As network theory tells us, however, the star network is highly vulnerable to an attack on the center. Another weakness is that many citizens of the "star" in the network, otherwise described as the "hegemon" in the international system (i.e., the United States), may come to see the disproportionate share of burden as unfair and potentially untenable; see Matthew

O. Jackson, *Social and Economic Networks* (Princeton: Princeton University Press, 2008), 277.

11. Phillip M. Hannam et al., "Incomplete Cooperation and Co-benefits: Deepening Climate Cooperation with a Proliferation of Small Agreements," *Climatic Change*, 2015, doi:10.1007/s10584-015-1511-2; quotations at 5, 1. See also Sander Chan et al., "Reinvigorating International Climate Policy: A Comprehensive Framework for Effective Nonstate Action," *Global Policy* 6, no. 4 (2015): 466–473, which explains how the new climate regime created at Paris can link to the "groundswell" of climate actions from cities, civil society groups, and other nonstate actors; for an overview of how the Paris Agreement creates a new paradigm of international agreement precisely due to its catalyzing and facilitating elements regarding web actors, see Thomas Hale, "All Hands on Deck: The Paris Agreement and Nonstate Climate Action," *Global Environmental Politics* 16, no. 3 (2016): 12–22.

12. Liliana Andonova, Thomas Hale, and Charles Roger, "National Policy and Transnational Governance of Climate Change: Substitutes or Complements?" *International Studies Quarterly*, forthcoming.

13. Phillip M. Hannam et al., "Incomplete Cooperation and Co-benefits," 5, 7, 8.

14. See, e.g., Elinor Ostrom, "Beyond Markets and States: Polycentric Governance of Complex Economic Systems," *American Economic Review* 100, no. 3 (2010): 1–33. Vincent Ostrom, Charles Tiebout, and Robert Warren introduced the idea of polycentricity in 1961 to characterize the provision of public services in cities.

15. Elinor Ostrom, "Nested Externalities and Polycentric Institutions: Must We Wait for Global Solutions to Climate Change Before Taking Actions at Other Scales?" *Economic Theory* 49, no. 2 (2012): 353–369.

16. An exception to the trend is economist Samuel Bowles, who in *The Moral Economy: Why Good Incentives Are No Substitute for Good Citizens* (New Haven: Yale University Press, 2016) makes an economic case for how rewards and punishments crowd out cooperative behavior.

17. For a formalization of this result, see the 2015 research paper draft "Whom Can You Trust? Reputation and Cooperation in Networks" by Maia King, University of London, http://www.fas.harvard.edu/~histecon/informationtransmission/papers/Trust_MK_Draft.pdf.

18. Homophily, "the conscious or unconscious tendency to associate with people who resemble us," has been researched extensively; for an overview see Nicholas Christakis and James Fowler, *Connected* (New York: Little, Brown, 2009), 17. Tina Rosenberg, in *Join the Club: How Peer Pressure Can Transform the World* (New York: Norton, 2011), writes about individuals and movements motivated by preferential association. Alex Pentland discusses the power and limitations of social pressure in *Social Physics*, especially in chapter 4 (62–84). And in both experimental and natural human settings, people will pay cooperative behavior forward even when reputations are unknown and direct reciprocity is impossible, Nicholas Christakis and James Fowler, "Cooperative Behavior Cascades in Human Social Networks," *PNAS* 107, no. 12 (2010), http://www.pnas.org/content/107/12/5334.abstract.

19. Ben Ramalingam, *Aid on the Edge of Chaos* (Oxford: Oxford University Press, 2013), 205.

20. McChrystal et al., *Team of Teams*, 100, 105.

21. In his examination of team intelligence in *Social Physics*, Alex Pentland notes that a group's collective intelligence is an emergent property—different from and greater than the sum individual intelligence of the team's participants (87–91).

22. Humans form close bonds with a limited number of people: Most people have five people in their "inner circle" and up to fifteen they're very close to; Paul Adams, *Grouped: How Small Groups of Friends Are the Key to Influence on the Social Web* (Berkeley, CA: New Riders, 2012). MIT's Alex Peatland notes that the atmosphere and performance of an organization depends on how closely connected teams of people are to one another.

23. McChrystal et al., *Team of Teams*, 127.

24. Ibid., 104, 105. The authors refer to Steven Johnson's book *Emergence: The Connected Lives of Ants, Brains, Cities, and Software* (New York: Scribner, 2001).

25. McChrystal et al., *Team of Teams*, 105.

26. Good idea flow improves the productivity and decision making of a team; Pentland, *Social Physics*, 103. A study of team intelligence and performance published in *Science* found that teams essentially operate as "idea-processing machines in which the pattern of idea flow is the driving factor in performance." Surprisingly, the data showed that the "pattern of idea flow by itself was more important to group performance"

than every other factor combined, including cohesion, motivation, and satisfaction; see Anita W. Wooley et al., "Evidence for a Collective Intelligence Factor in the Performance of Human Groups," *Science* 330, no. 6004 (2010): 686–688.

27. McChrystal et al., *Team of Teams*, 164–169.

28. Sanjeev Goyal, *Connections: An Introduction to the Economics of Networks* (Princeton: Princeton University Press, 2007), 100. This is a formal way of describing "the wisdom of crowds," which is examined by James Surowiecki in *The Wisdom of Crowds: Why the Many Are Smarter Than the Few and How Collective Wisdom Shapes Business, Economies, Societies, and Nations* (New York: Anchor, 2005). Also, the O&I demonstrated that whereas strong ties are important for output, weak ties are important for input, as they carry valuable information across groups and "play a vital role in sustaining technological change and dynamism" in an organization or society; Goyal, *Connections*, 99. The O&I also showcased small world properties—that distant clusters (agencies, units, and so on) could be connected via a shortcut link.

29. McChrystal et al., *Team of Teams*, 213–214, 168; emphasis in the original.

30. Marshall Van Alstyne, "The State of Network Organization: A Survey in Three Frameworks," *Journal of Organizational Computing* 7, no. 3 (1997): 88–151; emphasis in the original.

31. Lisa Gansky, *The Mesh: Why the Future of Business Is Sharing* (New York: Portfolio Penguin, 2010), 118.

32. A "multi-scale network" features horizontal and vertical links across all levels of an organization to optimize information flow. Teams form and connect with one another to work on projects in a "continual swirl of problem-solving activity and ever shifting interactions between the problem solvers, each of whom has information relevant to the solution of a particular problem but none of whom knows enough to act in isolation"; Duncan J. Watts, *Six Degrees: The Science of a Connected Age* (New York: Norton, 2003), 269.

33. Walter W. Powell, "The Capitalist Firm in the Twenty-First Century: Emerging Patterns in Western Enterprise," in *The Twenty-First Century Firm: Changing Economic Organization in International Perspective*, ed. Paul DiMaggio (Princeton: Princeton University Press, 2001), 33–68, 68.

34. Henry Chesbrough, *Open Innovation: The New Imperative for Creating and Profiting from Technology* (Boston: Harvard Business School Press, 2003), xxiv. Also see Chesbrough's Open Innovation Community website, http://openinnovation.net/category/open-innovation/.

35. See Innocentive website About page, http://www.innocentive.com/about-innocentive.

36. Yochai Benkler, *The Penguin and the Leviathan: How Cooperation Triumphs over Self-Interest* (New York: Crown, 2011), 109.

37. See In-Q-Tel website About page, https://www.iqt.org/about-iqt/.

38. See Aaron Metha, "At Silicon Valley Outpost, Carter Hears Pitches from Small Firms," *Defense News*, March 3, 2016, http://www.defensenews.com/story/defense/innovation/2016/03/03/diux-shark-tank-silicon-valley-as-carter-small-firms/81244834/.

39. See Ash Carter, "The 'X' is for Experimental," *Medium*, May 11, 2016, https://medium.com/@SecDef/the-x-is-for-experimental-3c9438e76214#.ebu7ci9qo.

40. Jeff Jarvis, *What Would Google Do? Reverse-Engineering the Fastest Growing Company in the History of the World* (New York: HarperCollins, 2009), 26.

41. See Ilkka Tuomi, *Networks of Innovation: Change and Meaning in the Age of the Internet* (New York: Oxford University Press, 2002), 219. Writing about open-source innovations, Tuomi explores two different models of Internet-enabled innovation, one based on "increasing specialization and the other on combination of existing resources," 6 and chapter 7.

42. Van Alstyne, "The State of Network Organization." Van Alstyne bases this conclusion on his own research as well as that of other information, organizational, and management theorists. There is a large and growing body of research on teams, which finds that the most productive teams have four to twelve members. See, e.g., http://knowledge.wharton.upenn.edu/article/is-your-team-too-big-too-small-whats-the-right-number-2/.

43. Chesbrough, *Open Innovation*, 295.

CHAPTER 6. SCALE NETWORKS

1. Ori Brafman and Rod Beckstrom, *The Starfish and the Spider: The Unstoppable Power of Leaderless Organizations* (New York: Penguin, 2006), 36–37, 46–49.

2. Ibid., 37.

3. Anonymous, *Alcoholics Anonymous: The Big Book* (New York: A.A. World Services, 1939).

4. See the homepage for Team Rubicon Global, http://teamrubiconglobal.org.

5. Tina Rosenberg, *Join the Club: How Peer Pressure Can Transform the World* (New York: Norton, 2011), xx.

6. Ibid., xviii.

7. See the homepage for "A Force More Powerful," http://www.aforcemorepowerful.org/index.php.

8. Alex Pentland, *Social Physics: How Social Networks Can Make Us Smarter* (New York: Penguin, 2014), 41.

9. Malcolm Gladwell, *The Tipping Point: How Little Things Can Make a Big Difference* (New York: Little, Brown, 2000).

10. As Duncan J. Watts writes, "The more people whose actions or opinions you take into account before making a decision, the less influence any *one* of them will have over you. So when *everyone* is paying attention to many others, no single innovator, acting alone, can activate any one of them"; *Six Degrees: The Science of a Connected Age* (New York: Norton, 2003), 240; emphasis in the original.

11. Paul Adams, *Grouped: How Small Groups of Friends Are the Key to Influence on the Social Web* (Berkeley, CA: New Riders 2012), 151, 147, 77–81.

12. Watts, *Six Degrees*, 231.

13. In 2011, Pentland, along with MIT postdoc Yaniv Altshuler and Ph.D. student Wei Pan, analyzed nearly ten million financial transactions on the eToro platform and mapped a distribution with users who made their own isolated trades at one end and those who always copied someone else at the other. They found that those in the middle, who relied on a diversity of ideas, had an average rate of return 30 percent higher than the isolateds and the herd. See Alex Pentland, "Beyond the Echo Chamber," *Harvard Business Review*, November 2013, https://hbr.org/2013/11/beyond-the-echo-chamber.

14. Alex Pentland, *Social Physics: How Social Networks Can Make Us Smarter* (New York: Penguin, 2014), 34, 52.

15. Watts's insight is that a person's critical threshold—the point at which she changes from A to B—can be thought of in terms of degree,

the fraction of a person's neighbors that have adopted the change. If a person's critical threshold is one-third it means she will change from A to B once one-third of the people she is connected to are choosing B. She has a "critical upper degree" of three. If she is connected to four individuals and one chooses B, it will have no effect on her. It's the fraction that matters. *Six Degrees*, 233–234.

16. In Watts's global cascade model, if one or more initial innovators are connected to enough early adopters (nodes with low critical thresholds) then a "percolating vulnerable cluster" exists. For an innovation to jump the cluster and go global, the structure of a network matters as much as the characteristics of the innovation itself. The cluster can't be too sparse—but it also can't be too dense. *Six Degrees*, 235–237.

17. Google Flu "predicts outbreaks by counting the number of Internet searches using the word 'flu' that occur in each state or region"; Pentland, *Social Physics*, 145. Research by Anmol Madan, Wen Dong, and colleagues at MIT found that people change their mobile phone behavior when they are ill; crowd-sourcing this information plus locational data can yield a map to track a pandemic and identify effective places to intervene; cited ibid., 145–149.

18. See, e.g., David Ignatius, "The Antidote to Mideast Violence," *Washington Post*, May 12, 2015, https://www.washingtonpost.com/opinions/an-islamic-state-antidote/2015/05/12/68ae72ce-f8dc-11e4-a13c-193b124d151a_story.html?utm_term=.47a713fcf655&wpmk—K0000203.

19. See Andy Greenberg, "Google's Clever Plan to Stop Aspiring ISIS Recruits," *Wired*, September 7, 2016, https://www.wired.com/2016/09/googles-clever-plan-stop-aspiring-isis-recruits/.

20. Pentland, *Social Physics*, 38–39.

21. See Sarah Chayes, "The Structure of Corruption: A Systemic Analysis Using Eurasian Cases," Carnegie Endowment for International Peace, June 30, 2016, http://carnegieendowment.org/2016/06/30/structure-of-corruption-systemic-analysis-using-eurasian-cases-pub-63991.

22. Walter W. Powell, "The Capitalist Firm in the Twenty-First Century: Emerging Patterns in Western Enterprise," in *The Twenty-First Century Firm: Changing Economic Organization in International Perspective*, ed. Paul DiMaggio (Princeton: Princeton University Press, 2001), 33–68, 61.

23. For an example, see Watts's account of how Toyota's suppliers quickly restored production after a fire wiped out the company's lone P-valve producer; *Six Degrees*, 254–260.

24. See the GAVI website About page, http://www.gavi.org/about/.

25. Similarly, the nascent International Solar Alliance attempts to aggregate demand for solar energy projects to facilitate the flow of financing from developed countries to developing ones; see Arunabha Ghosh and Kanika Chawla, "Can the International Solar Alliance Change the Game?" *Hindu*, August 26, 2016, http://www.thehindu. com/opinion/columns/can-the-international-solar-alliance-change-the-game/article9032508.ece.

26. See David A. Kaye, "Justice Beyond The Hague: Supporting the Prosecution of International Crimes in National Courts," Council on Foreign Relations, Council Special Report no. 61, June 2011, http:// www.cfr.org/courts-and-tribunals/justice-beyond-hague/p25119.

27. See the Global Covenant of Mayors for Climate and Energy homepage, http://www.compactofmayors.org/globalcovenantofmayors/.

28. John Hagel III, John Seely Brown, and Lang Davison, *The Power of Pull: How Small Moves, Smartly Made, Can Set Big Things in Motion* (New York: Basic, 2010); see also David Siegel, *Pull: The Power of the Semantic Web to Transform Your Business* (New York: Portfolio, 2009).

29. Steven Rosenbaum, *Curation Nation: How to Win in a World Where Consumers Are Creators* (New York: McGraw Hill, 2011), 5; emphasis in the original.

30. Google Jigsaw was formerly Google Ideas, the company's think tank. See Jigsaw's website, https://jigsaw.google.com.

31. Nannerl O. Keohane, *Thinking About Leadership* (Princeton: Princeton University Press, 2010), 58.

32. See Nicholas Kristof's piece on how the DIY approach is being applied to foreign aid and development, "D.I.Y. Foreign-Aid Revolution," *New York Times Magazine*, October 20, 2010, http://www. nytimes.com/2010/10/24/magazine/24volunteerism-t.html.

33. See Samasource's website, http://www.samasource.org.

34. Yochai Benkler, *The Penguin and the Leviathan: How Cooperation Triumphs over Self-Interest* (New York: Crown, 2011), 173.

35. Thomas Goetz, "Open Source Everywhere," *Wired*, November 1, 2003, http://www.wired.com/2003/11/opensource/.

36. Tim O'Reilly, "The Architecture of Participation," *O'Reilly Media*, June 2004, http://archive.oreilly.com/pub/a/oreilly/tim/articles/architecture_of_participation.html.

37. Quoted in Goetz, "Open Source Everywhere."

38. Started in 1991 by Linus Torvalds, Linux marked a radical new mode of software development. Rather than taking the characteristic centralized approach, which views large, important software as "cathedrals, carefully crafted by individual wizards or small bands of mages," Torvalds was freewheeling and "open to the point of promiscuity": "the Linux community seemed to resemble a great babbling bazaar of differing agendas and approaches ... out of which a coherent and stable system" emerged and developed "at a speed barely imaginable to cathedral-builders"; Ilkka Tuomi, *Networks of Innovation: Change and Meaning in the Age of the Internet* (New York: Oxford University Press, 2002), 164. By 2000, many major software companies began making their products available for Linux, which had become a viable alternative to Microsoft. More than eighty-five million people now use Linux; see the Linux Counter website, https://www.linuxcounter.net/statistics.

39. Linux was developed collectively without any apparent concern for profit or any other economic factor. The economic impact of Linux—as a cost-cutting, interoperable, nonproprietary alternative to Microsoft or Apple operating systems—is merely a "*side effect* of a long period of technology creation"; Tuomi, *Networks of Innovation*, 3; emphasis added.

40. Clay Shirky, TED Talk, "How the Internet Will (One Day) Transform Government," June 2012, https://www.ted.com/talks/clay_shirky_how_the_internet_will_one_day_transform_government#t-634081.

41. A similar network, the Global Water Partnership, already exists, though it lacks the cumulation piece; see the Global Water Partnership About page, http://www.gwp.org/en/About-GWP/.

42. A defining feature of many network organizations is a powerful central hierarchy of concentrated authority and power. See Geoff Mulgan, "Convexity Revisited," in *Network Logic*, ed. Helen McCarthy et al., *Demos* 20 (2004): 49–62, 53.

43. See the Wikimedia Foundation "Staff and contractors" page, https://wikimediafoundation.org/wiki/Staff_and_contractors.

44. Ash Carter, "Remarks on 'Asia-Pacific's Principled Security Network' at 2016 IISS Shangri-La Dialogue," June 4, 2016, http://www.defense.gov/News/Speeches/Speech-View/Article/791213/remarks-on-asia-pacifics-principled-security-network-at-2016-iiss-shangri-la-di.

CHAPTER 7. NETWORK POWER

1. Anne-Marie Slaughter, "America's Edge: Power in the Networked Century," *Foreign Affairs*, January–February 2009, https://www.foreignaffairs.com/articles/united-states/2009-01-01/americas-edge.

2. Joshua Cooper Ramo, *The Seventh Sense: Power, Fortune, and Survival in the Age of Networks* (New York: Little, Brown, 2016), 34.

3. Steven Lukes, *Power: A Radical View*, 2nd ed. (London: Palgrave Macmillan, 2005).

4. Joseph S. Nye Jr., *Soft Power: The Means to Success in World Politics* (New York: Public Affairs, 2004).

5. Suzanne Nossel, "Smart Power," *Foreign Affairs*, March–April 2004, https://www.foreignaffairs.com/articles/united-states/2004-03-01/smart-power. Nye first used the term nonspecifically in his 2004 book *Soft Power:* "Smart power means learning better how to combine our hard and soft power" (32). In 2006, Nye cochaired the CSIS Commission on Smart Power to develop a comprehensive U.S. smart power strategy; see the commission's report, Richard Armitage and Joseph Nye, co-chairs, "A Smarter, More Secure America" (Washington, DC: CSIS, 2007).

6. Ramo, *Seventh Sense*, 78, 116; emphasis in the original.

7. Walter Powell, "Neither Market nor Hierarchy: Network Forms of Organization," *Research in Organizational Behavior* 12 (1990): 295–336, 304.

8. Ibid., 295; also, corporate anthropologist Karen Stephenson notes that repeated reciprocity solidifies into a "golden trust," which is the key to the power of networks. See Stephenson, "Towards a Theory of Government," in *Network Logic*, ed. Helen McCarthy et al., *Demos* 20 (2004): 35–48, 40.

9. See Michael Kenney, "Turning to the 'Dark Side': Coordination, Exchange, and Learning in Criminal Networks," in *Networked Politics: Agency, Power, and Governance*, ed. Miles Kahler (Ithaca, NY: Cornell University Press, 2009), 79–99, 87.

10. See Miles Kahler, "Networked Politics: Agency, Power, and Governance," in Kahler, *Networked Politics*, 1–20, 15.

11. David A. Lake and Wendy H. Wong, "The Politics of Networks: Interest, Power, and Human Rights Norms," in Kahler, *Networked Politics*, 127–150.

12. Kahler, "Networked Politics," 15. David Singh Grewal, in *Network Power: The Social Dynamics of Globalization* (New Haven: Yale University Press, 2008), calls this feature "availability," the "ease with which a network accepts new entrants" (176).

13. In their book on transnational advocacy networks *Activists Beyond Borders* (Ithaca, NY: Cornell University Press, 1998), Margaret Keck and Kathryn Sikkink write that the "construction of cognitive frames" is an essential component of strategy and power for activist networks (17). Manuel Castells, in *Networks of Outrage and Hope* (Cambridge: Polity, 2012), goes a step farther, asserting that "the construction of meaning in people's minds is a more decisive and more stable source of power" than coercion or intimidation (5).

14. Helen Yanacopulos, "Cutting the Diamond: Networking Economic Justice," in Kahler, *Networked Politics*, 67–78, 72–73.

15. Ramo, *Seventh Sense*, 104.

16. See Kahler, "Networked Politics," 14.

17. See ibid., 12.

18. See the Lowy Institute's interactive Global Diplomacy Index, http://www.lowyinstitute.org/global-diplomacy-index/.

19. Kahler, "Networked Politics," 14.

20. See Singh, *Network Power*, 228–229.

21. Castells, *Networks of Outrage and Hope*, 8–9.

22. Kahler, "Networked Politics," 13.

23. Lake and Wong, "Politics of Networks," 133.

24. The Composite Index of National Capability (CINC) was created in 1963 for the Correlates of War Project as a measure of state power based on economic, military, and demographic strength. The six components are each expressed as a ratio of the world's total, added up, and divided by six to yield that country's CINC score. See the Wikipedia entry on the CINC, https://en.wikipedia.org/wiki/Composite_Index_of_National_Capability.

25. In international relations speak, "Network structure inverts the neorealist view of international structure as a distribution of capabilities; capabilities in the networked view rely on connections to other members of the network"; Kahler, "Networked Politics," 12.

26. This language comes from a piece I wrote for the *Atlantic* called "A New Theory for the Foreign-Policy Frontier: Collaborative Power," November 30, 2011, http://www.theatlantic.com/international/archive/2011/11/a-new-theory-for-the-foreign-policy-frontier-collaborative-power/249260/.

27. Mary Parker Follett, *Creative Experience* (London: Longmans, Green, 1930), xiii.

28. Hannah Arendt, *The Human Condition* (Chicago: University of Chicago Press, 1958), 180.

29. Hannah Arendt, *On Violence* (Orlando: Harcourt, Brace, 1970), 143.

30. Arendt, *The Human Condition*, 200.

31. Remi Peeters, "Against Violence, but Not at Any Price: Hannah Arendt's Concept of Power," *Ethical Perspectives: Journal of the European Ethics Network* 15, no. 2 (2008): 169–192, 174.

32. See Howard Rheingold, *Smart Mobs: The Next Social Revolution* (New York: Basic, 2002).

33. Deanna Zandt, *Share This! How You Will Change the World with Social Networking* (San Francisco: Berrett-Koehler, 2010), ix.

34. Lisa Gansky, *The Mesh: Why the Future of Business Is Sharing* (New York: Portfolio Penguin, 2010).

35. Manuel Castells, *Communication Power* (New York: Oxford University Press, 2009), 43.

36. Ramo, *The Seventh Sense*, 205, 206.

37. Ibid., 235, 236.

38. See the Purpose website, https://www.purpose.com.

39. See the #GivingTuesday website, http://www.givingtuesday.org.

40. Jeremy Heimans and Henry Timms, "Understanding 'New Power,'" *Harvard Business Review*, December 2014, https://hbr.org/2014/12/understanding-new-power.

41. Ibid.

42. Ibid.

43. Google Ideas, the tech giant's former think tank, held a summit in June 2011 that brought together more than eighty former extremists ranging from white supremacists to jihadists to urban gang members. As Eric Schmidt and Jared Cohen recount it in *The New Digital Age: Reshaping the Future of People, Nations and Business* (New York: Knopf, 2013), the participants revealed strikingly similar motivations for joining their respective extremist organization—most driven by the desire to belong to a group and to gain a support network.

44. Tim O'Reilly, "The Architecture of Participation," *O'Reilly Media*, June 2004, http://archive.oreilly.com/pub/a/oreilly/tim/articles/architecture_of_participation.html.

45. See the U.S. Navy, U.S. Marine Corps, and U.S. Coast Guard joint report *A Cooperative Strategy for 21st Century Seapower*, October 2007, https://www.ise.gov/sites/default/files/Maritime_Strategy.pdf.

46. See the 2016 Global Trends Report from the Office of the Director of National Intelligence's National Intelligence Council.

47. Anne-Marie Slaughter, "America's Edge: Power in the Networked Century," *Foreign Affairs*, January–February 2009, https://www.foreignaffairs.com/articles/united-states/2009-01-01/americas-edge; for an excellent analysis of orchestration in networked organizations, see Kenneth W. Abbot and Thomas Hale, "Orchestrating Global Solution Networks: A Guide for Organizational Entrepreneurs," *Innovations Technology Governance Globalization* 9, nos. 1–2 (2014): 195–212.

CHAPTER 8. A DIFFERENT WAY TO LEAD

1. Nannerl O. Keohane, *Thinking About Leadership* (Princeton: Princeton University Press, 2010), 23.

2. Ibid., 1.

3. Scholars of social movements and transnational networks assert the importance of clarified direction for sustaining a movement or organization. See Miles Kahler's edited volume *Networked Politics: Agency, Power, and Governance* (Ithaca, NY: Cornell University Press, 2009), and Margaret Keck and Kathryn Sikkink, *Activists Beyond Borders* (Ithaca, NY: Cornell University Press, 1998).

4. "Orchestrate" is a favorite term of open-innovation scholars. For example, Wim Vanhaverbeke and Myriam Cloodt, in "Open Innovation in Value Markets," in *Open Innovation: Researching a New Paradigm*, ed.

Henry Chesbrough, Wim Vanhaverbeke, and Joel West (Oxford: Oxford University Press, 2006), 258–284, write, "Key players in Open Innovation have to orchestrate the network of partners that are crucial to develop or to exploit particular innovations" (277).

5. See, for example, Yimei Hu and Olav Jull Sorensen's 2012 research paper "Open Innovation in Networks: Specifying Orchestration Capability for SMEs," https://www.djoef-forlag.dk/services/djm/ledelsedocs/2012/2012_2/le_2012_2_2.pdf.

6. See Keohane, *Thinking About Leadership*; Manuel Castells, *Communication Power* (New York: Oxford University Press, 2009); and Jon R. Katzenbach and Zia Khan, *Leading Outside the Lines: How to Mobilize the Informal Organization, Energize Your Team, and Get Better Results* (San Francisco: Jossey-Bass, 2010).

7. See the Partnership Brokers Association website, http://www.partnershipbrokers.org; Satish Nambisan and Mohanbir Sawhney, *The Global Brain* (Upper Saddle River, NJ: Wharton School Publishing, 2008); Jeffrey Walker, "Solving the World's Biggest Problems Takes Ensembles, Not Soloists," *Huffington Post*, October 3, 2014, http://www.huffingtonpost.com/jeffrey-walker/solving-the-worlds-bigges_b_5925092.html; and Vanessa Kirsch et al., "Why Social Ventures Need Systems Thinking," *Harvard Business Review*, July 25, 2016, https://hbr.org/2016/07/why-social-ventures-need-systems-thinking.

8. As this book went to press I was made aware of Network Weavers, a consulting organization led by June Holley that has developed a network leadership checklist with seven "Cs": Connect, Catalyze, Convene, Communicate, Cultivate, Curate, Collaborate.

9. Keohane, *Thinking About Leadership*, 19.

10. Stanley McChrystal et al., *Team of Teams: New Rules of Engagement for a Complex World* (New York: Portfolio/Penguin, 2015), 225.

11. George P. Shultz, interview with Richard Haass, "A Conversation with George P. Shultz," *Council on Foreign Relations*, January 29, 2013, http://www.cfr.org/world/conversation-george-p-shultz/p35380.

12. "Breaking into the Business World with 'Woman-Friendly' Model," Sunday Conversation transcript, NPR, June 23, 2013, available at http://www.npr.org/templates/transcript/transcript.php?storyId=194683800.

13. Private conversation. We were at a party Byrne threw at her house for her husband's sixtieth birthday. A number of us were admiring

her garden, particularly an arbor full of flowers that would make a picture-perfect setting for a wedding.

14. Henry Chesbrough, Wim Vanhaverbeke, and Joel West, "Open Innovation: A Research Agenda," in Chesbrough et al., *Open Innovation*, 285–308, 295.

15. Caroline Simard and Joel West, "Knowledge Networks and the Geographic Locus of Innovation," in Chesbrough et al., *Open Innovation*, 220–240, 229. Similarly, John Hagel and John Seely Brown advise leaders constructing "creation nets," a type of organization based on the open innovation model, to concentrate on "techniques that can accelerate the building of trust and deepening of relationships"; John Hagel III and John Seely Brown, "Creation Nets: Harnessing the Potential of Open Innovation," *Journal of Service Science* 1, no. 2 (2008): 27–40, 39.

16. Jeffrey Walker, "Solving the World's Biggest Problems Takes Ensembles, Not Soloists," *Huffington Post*, October 3, 2014, http://www.huffingtonpost.com/jeffrey-walker/solving-the-worlds-bigges_b_5925092.html.

17. Ibid.

18. Sir Michael Barber, "The Origins and Practice of Delivery," *Stanford Social Innovation Review*, April 16, 2013, available at http://ssir.org/articles/entry/the_origins_and_practice_of_delivery.

19. Wim Vanhaverbeke, "The Interorganizational Context of Open Innovation," in Chesbrough et al., *Open Innovation*, 205–219, 213, 214.

20. Eventually, McChrystal says there were seven thousand participants almost daily; *Team of Teams*, 168.

21. See Nambisan and Sawhney, *The Global Brain*, 69.

22. See Wellcome Trust Sanger Institute Press Office, "Wellcome Trust Announces Major Increase in Human Genome Sequencing," May 13, 1998, http://www.sanger.ac.uk/news/view/1998-05-13-wellcome-trust-announces-major-increase-in-human-genome-sequencing.

23. See Wellcome Trust Sanger Institute Press Office, "The Finished Human Genome—Wellcome to the Genomic Age," April 14, 2003, http://www.sanger.ac.uk/news/view/2003-04-14-the-finished-human-genome-wellcome-to-the-genomic-age.

24. "A Quest for an Opposition Leader," *New York Times*, February 9, 2011, http://www.nytimes.com/interactive/2011/02/09/world/middleeast/20110209-egypt-opposition-leaders.html.

25. Mike Giglio, "How Wael Ghonim Sparked Egypt's Uprising," *Newsweek*, February 13, 2011, http://www.newsweek.com/how-wael-ghonim-sparked-egypts-uprising-68727.

26. For an examination of why it has failed, see Beth Simone Noveck, *Wiki Government: How Technology Can Make Government Better, Democracy Stronger, and Citizens More Powerful* (Washington, DC: Brookings Institution Press, 2009). For examples of civic engagement platforms and initiatives of varying success and promise, see Micah L. Sifry and Jessica McKenzie, eds., *A Lever and a Place to Stand: How Civic Tech Can Move the World* (New York: Personal Democracy Media, 2015).

27. See the DemocracyOS homepage, http://democracyos.org/; also, Michael Scaturro, "Designing an Operating System for Democracy," *Atlantic*, July 19, 2014, http://www.theatlantic.com/international/archive/2014/07/designing-an-operating-system-for-democracy/374526/.

28. See Roger L. Martin and Sally R. Osberg, *Getting Beyond Better: How Social Entrepreneurship Works* (Boston: Harvard Business Review Press, 2015), 125–130.

## CHAPTER 9. A GRAND STRATEGY

1. Terry L. Deibel, *Foreign Affairs Strategy: Logic for American Statecraft* (New York: Cambridge University Press, 2007).

2. Kennan renounced aspects of this strategy in the 1957 Reith Lectures, transcripts of which are available at http://www.bbc.co.uk/radio4/features/the-reith-lectures/transcripts/1948/#y1957; nonetheless, Kennan and containment are inextricably linked.

3. These characterizations are taken from diplomat Dennis Ross, *Statecraft and How to Restore America's Standing in the World* (New York: Farrar, Straus and Giroux, 2007), 4.

4. Alec Ross made this point in a closed White House meeting in August 2011. I used it as the point of departure for the Richard S. Salant Lecture on Freedom of the Press at the Harvard Kennedy School in 2012, transcript available at http://shorensteincenter.org/wp-content/uploads/2012/02/Salant-2012-Transcript-REV.pdf.

5. Alec Ross, *The Industries of the Future* (New York: Simon and Schuster, 2016), 215, 239. The *Economist*, in July 2016, declared that open vs. closed had supplanted right vs. left as the new political fault line in Europe and the United States.

6. See Helen McCarthy et al., "Introduction: Network Logic," in *Network Logic*, ed. Helen McCarthy et al., *Demos* 20 (2004): 11–21.

7. See Geoff Mulgan, *Connexity: How to Live in a Connected World* (Boston: Harvard Business School Press, 1997).

8. Open does not necessarily mean anarchic; all networks need some element of hierarchy, just as hierarchies inevitably contain networks. Each form must be tempered by the other. An "open" trade regime, for instance, must embrace the principle of equitable distribution of the resulting benefits.

9. Eric Schmidt and Jared Cohen, *The New Digital Age: Reshaping the Future of People, Nations, and Business* (New York: Knopf, 2013), 85.

10. As the former dean of the Woodrow Wilson School of Public and International Affairs at Princeton, I am acutely sensitive to the debate swirling around the characterization of Woodrow Wilson as a racist president who resegregated the federal government. Celebrating Wilson's legacy is hurtful to many African-Americans, a sentiment that other Americans should recognize and respect. However, in international affairs, the Wilsonian legacy, while also flawed, is inextricably intertwined with the championing of universal values against power politics, harking back to Immanuel Kant; see my chapter "Wilsonianism in the Twenty-first Century," in *The Crisis of American Foreign Policy: Wilsonianism in the Twenty-first Century* (Princeton: Princeton University Press, 2009), 89–118. Perhaps in time this tradition too will be renamed, but for present purposes, I will use the nomenclature familiar to international relations scholars and practitioners.

11. See Anne-Marie Slaughter, *A New World Order* (Princeton: Princeton University Press, 2004).

12. Joshua Cooper Ramo, *The Seventh Sense: Power, Fortune, and Survival in the Age of Networks* (New York: Little, Brown, 2016), 255, 257, 258, 265; emphasis in the original.

13. Ibid., 266–267.

14. Schmidt and Cohen, *New Digital Age*, 110.

15. Ramo, *Seventh Sense*, 267.

16. Ibid.

17. Hillary Rodham Clinton, "Remarks on Internet Freedom," U.S. Department of State, January 21, 2010, transcript available at http://www.state.gov/secretary/20092013clinton/rm/2010/01/135519.htm.

NOTES TO PAGES 207-211

18. In this sense I am building on the Liberal theory of international relations, developed by Andrew Moravcsik and others, which holds that states engage in international behavior because of "demands from individuals and groups" in society that define "state preferences—the substantive social purposes that give states an underlying stake in the international issues they face." Indeed, without such "social concerns that transcend borders, states would have no rational incentive to engage in world politics"; see Andrew Moravcsik, "The New Liberalism," in *The Oxford Handbook of International Relations*, ed. Christian Reus-Smit and Duncan Snidal (Oxford: Oxford University Press, 2008), 234–254.

19. Ramo, *Seventh Sense*, 266.

20. See Chris Fussell and Charles Goodyear, forthcoming, 2017.

21. As *Wired* founder Kevin Kelly writes about new technology, attempts to "stop it, prohibit, deny it, or at least make it hard to use" inevitably "backfire"; harnessing and managing it successfully requires "deep engagement, firsthand experience, and a vigilant acceptance"; Kevin Kelly, *The Inevitable: Understanding the 12 Technological Forces That Will Shape Our Future* (New York: Viking, 2016), 5. What goes for our technology goes for ourselves.

22. Juliette Kayyem, *Security Mom: An Unclassified Gide to Protecting Our Homeland and Your Home* (New York: Simon and Schuster, 2016), 9.

23. See Stephen Flynn, *The Edge of Disaster: Rebuilding a Resilient Nation* (New York: Random House, 2007), 14–16.

24. Ramo describes the "new caste" as comprising the immensely powerful designers and controllers of the networks of technology, finance, biotech, or "any discipline in which connection marks a change" and "on which we all depend"; *Seventh Sense*, 177, 179.

25. Ibid., 246–247.

26. Schmidt and Cohen, in *New Digital Age*, suggest that nations will intensify filtering and censorship to keep their citizens within their version of the Internet, even going so far as to require "virtual visas" to access it (93).

27. Senator Elizabeth Warren, in a speech titled "Reigniting Competition in the American Economy," Washington, DC, June 29, 2016, described as grave threats to the American economy and democracy the extreme consolidation of American industry and the concentration of economic power under a few oligopolistic corporations; transcript available at http://washingtonmonthly.com/2016/06/30/elizabeth-warrens-

consolidation-speech-could-change-the-election/. Barry Lynn and Philip Longman, in "Populism with a Brain," *Washington Monthly*, June–August 2016, http://washingtonmonthly.com/magazine/junejulyaug-2016/populism-with-a-brain/, describe how late-nineteenth- and early-twentieth-century Populism drove the U.S. government to adopt antimonopoly legislation and other pieces of an agenda aimed at reducing concentrated power and curtailing corruption; they suggest that populists today ought to revive this tradition by, among other things, fighting for localized banking, the break-up of tech monopolies, and common carrier principles in all big data realms.

28. See Ross, *Industries of the Future*, who calls data the "raw material of the digital age" and says owning it is as important as "who owned the land during the agricultural age and who owned the factory during the industrial age" (182).

29. For an examination of concentrations of corporate power over the past several decades, see Barry Lynn, *Cornered: The New Monopoly Capitalism and the Economics of Destruction* (Hoboken, NJ: Wiley, 2010).

30. Arun Sundararajan, *The Sharing Economy: The End of Employment and the Rise of Crowd-Based Capitalism* (Cambridge: MIT Press, 2016), 119, 125.

31. Scott Malcomson, in *Splinternet: How Geopolitics and Commerce Are Fragmenting the World Wide Web* (New York: OR Books, 2016), warns of the fracturing of the Internet along traditional lines of states, laws, and cultures; Schmidt and Cohen in *New Digital Age* predict the "balkanization" of the Internet (83).

32. Additionally, a global Internet, with its multiple, interoperable platforms, means a more resilient system.

33. See John G. Ruggie, "International Regimes, Transactions, and Change: Embedded Liberalism in the Postwar Economic Order," *International Organization* 36, no. 2 (1982): 379–415.

34. See the Open Government Partnership website, http://www.opengovpartnership.org/.

35. See the Open Government Declaration, http://www.opengov-partnership.org/about/open-government-declaration.

36. See Clay Shirky's 2012 Ted Talk, https://www.ted.com/talks/clay_shirky_how_the_internet_will_one_day_transform_government?language=en.

37. Open Government Declaration.

38. See New America DC director Laurenellen McCann's work developing models of civic engagement whereby public institutions work with, not for, communities in defining and pursuing priorities, at "Build with, Not For," http://buildwith.org.

39. Mulgan, *Connexity*, 14.

40. John D. Donahue and Richard J. Zeckhauser call this "collaborative governance," and in *Collaborative Governance: Private Roles for Public Goals in Turbulent Times* (Princeton: Princeton University Press, 2011) define the concept as "carefully structured arrangements that interweave public and private capabilities on terms of shared discretion" (4). The "shared discretion" piece is key to distinguish collaboration from traditional private-public partnerships, which tend to strictly bind contractors; see also Beth Simone Noveck, *Wiki Government: How Technology Can Make Government Better, Democracy Stronger, and Citizens More Powerful* (Washington, DC: Brookings Institution Press, 2009), who considers coproduction a component of "wiki government."

41. See Noveck, *Wiki Government*, xiv; she argues that coproduction is a unique form of democratic participation that combines "open-source volunteer participation with government's central coordination, issue framing, and bully pulpit" (18).

42. Quoted at the MacArthur Foundation Research Network on Open Governance website, http://www.opening-governance.org/#the-context. The Network, operated by the NYU GovLab, is developing and testing collaborative governance projects of three types: "Smarter governance," whereby government bodies gather the input of outside citizens to inform decision making; "open data governance," where government bodies share data that citizens and private entities can use and analyze to solve problems; and "shared governance," by which agencies and legislatures delegate responsibility for certain government functions such as budgeting to citizens.

43. The NYU GovLab, website available at http://www.thegovlab.org/, is coordinating many of these initiatives and several others: The Open Data 500 Study surveys a wide range of companies around the globe to understand how they use, value, and could use open government data; see the study's one-pager at http://www.thegovlab.org/static/files/od500-onepager-cropped.pdf. A network of sixty-five international ex-

perts joined online coaching sessions to help the city of Quito, Ecuador, tackle disaster management problems such as communication coordination, evacuation planning, and gathering data in real-time from citizens; see project details at http://www.thegovlab.org/project-crowdsourcing-innovations-in-disaster-management.html. Chile, the Kurdish region of Iraq, and other governments are crowd-sourcing laws via the online platform LegislationLab, which was first used to crowd-source a draft of the new Moroccan constitution in 2011; of the ten thousand comments received, 40 percent were incorporated into the final version of the country's new constitution—see this account and others at http://thegovlab.org/a-growing-community-of-global-crowdlaw-practitioners/.

44. See Robert O. Keohane and Joseph S. Nye, *Power and Interdependence: World Politics in Transition* (Boston: Little, Brown, 1977).

45. See Anders Fogh Rasmussen's speech at the 2010 Munich Security Conference, "NATO in the 21st Century: Towards Global Connectivity," February 7, 2010, transcript available at http://www.nato.int/cps/en/natolive/opinions_61395.htm. In addition to the twenty-eight Allies, NATO now has structured partnerships with forty-one countries, plus the United Nations, the European Union, and the Organization for Security and Co-operation in Europe; at the 2016 NATO Summit in Warsaw, the alliance affirmed that these partnerships were essential to NATO's "broad cooperative security network" and that the alliance would continue "to expand political dialogue and practical cooperation with any nation that shares the Alliance's values and interest in international peace and security"; see "Warsaw Summit Communiqué," NATO, Press Release 100, July 9, 2016, http://www.nato.int/cps/en/natohq/official_texts_133169.htm.

46. This strategy entails "moving beyond the hub-and-spoke alliance framework" with the United States at the center by "encouraging spoke-to-spoke linkages," especially between core U.S. allies such as Japan and Australia and peripheral partner nations such as Vietnam and India; see Elsina Wainwright, "ANZUS and the US Asian Alliance Network," Australian Strategic Policy Institute, March 29, 2016, http://www.aspistrategist.org.au/anzus-and-the-us-asian-alliance-network/. The United States is also strengthening the Asian-Pacific's "institutional architecture to reinforce a rules-based order, including through joining the East Asia Summit and sending the first resident U.S. Ambassador to

ASEAN"; see White House press release "FACT SHEET: Advancing the Rebalance to the Asia and the Pacific," November 16, 2015, https://www.whitehouse.gov/the-press-office/2015/11/16/fact-sheet-advancing-rebalance-asia-and-pacific. It's possible to understand this network as a "gateland," in the sense that it is a network that anyone can join who follows the rules. Ramo is not specific enough about his definition of gatelands to be sure. But he emphasizes the closed nature of gatelands, with the United States as the single gatekeeper. The Asian security network will be governed by all its members, even if the United States has a particularly large say. And its goal is to spread and build connections, not to seal members off in a protected space.

47. Systems theorists call this "negative entropy"; see David S. Walonick, "General Systems Theory," 1993, http://www.statpac.org/walonick/systems-theory.htm.

48. For an example of how the U.N.-regional organization relationship works in security affairs, see Stewart M. Patrick, "The UN Versus Regional Organizations: Who Keeps the Peace?" *Council on Foreign Relations Blogs*, March 23, 2012, http://blogs.cfr.org/patrick/2012/03/23/the-un-versus-regional-organizations-who-keeps-the-peace/.

49. See Jessica T. Matthews, "Power Shift," *Foreign Affairs*, January–February 1997, https://www.foreignaffairs.com/articles/1997-01-01/power-shift.

50. See the Financial Stability Board's website, http://www.fsb.org/.

51. See the highlights of the U.N. Department of Economic and Social Affairs report, "World Urbanization Prospects: The 2014 Revision," 2014, available at https://esa.un.org/unpd/wup/Publications/Files/WUP2014-Highlights.pdf.

52. See Benjamin R. Barber, *If Mayors Ruled the World: Dysfunctional Nations, Rising Cities* (New Haven: Yale University Press, 2013).

53. See the UNHCR website, http://www.unhcr.org/en-us/.

54. See GAVI's website, http://www.gavi.org/about/partners/developing-country-governments/.

55. See, e.g., Michele Kelemen, "U.N. Panel Blocks Accreditation Bid by Committee to Protect Journalists," National Public Radio, May 27, 2016, http://www.npr.org/sections/parallels/2016/05/27/479740466/u-n-panel-blocks-accreditation-bid-by-committee-to-protect-journalists.

56. See my Project Syndicate article on the negotiations, "The Paris Approach to Global Governance," December 28, 2015, https://www.project-syndicate.org/commentary/paris-agreement-model-for-global-governance-by-anne-marie-slaughter-2015-12.

57. International lawyers have debated for centuries about the "monist" or dualist nature of that system, an intellectual detour that need not detain us now.

58. See William W. Burke-White and Anne-Marie Slaughter, "An International Constitutional Moment," *Harvard International Law Journal* 43, no. 1 (2002): 1–22.

59. This is not to say that important human rights advances did not take place during the Cold War. Margaret Keck and Kathryn Sikkink, in *Activists Beyond Borders* (Ithaca, NY: Cornell University Press, 1998), note that in the 1970s the U.N. Commission on Human Rights became much more active and the U.N. Human Rights Committee began to function; and in 1984, the General Assembly adopted the U.N. Convention Against Torture. But in Latin America, Africa, and elsewhere, questions of whose rights to protect against which government were continually colored and distorted by overarching ideological struggles between capitalism and communism.

60. See Gary J. Bass, *Stay the Hand of Vengeance: The Politics of War Crimes Tribunals* (Princeton: Princeton University Press, 2000).

61. See the report "The Responsibility to Protect," the International Commission on Intervention and State Sovereignty (December 2001), vii, available at http://responsibilitytoprotect.org/ICISS%20Report.pdf.

62. Ibid., 13, 8; emphasis in the original.

63. Report from the Commission on Human Security, *Human Security Now* (New York, 2003), 2, 4, available at http://www.un.org/humansecurity/sites/www.un.org.humansecurity/files/chs_final_report_-_english.pdf. Ogata herself helped situate human security in the wider web world: "The Commission focuses on people as the main stake holders of ensuring security," she wrote. "By people, we refer particularly to communities that bind individuals along ethnic, religious, social links and values. Public opinion and civil society organizations play an increasingly important role in the prevention of violent conflicts as well as the eradication of poverty"; Sadako Ogata, "Empowering People for Human Security," Payne Lecture, Stanford University, May

28, 2003, available at http://www.sarpn.org/documents/d0001513/documents/4_Empowering_People_Ogata.pdf.

64. United Nations General Assembly, "Resolution Adopted by the General Assembly 60/1. 2005 World Summit Outcome," October 24, 2005, 30, available at http://www.un.org/en/preventgenocide/adviser/pdf/World%20Summit%20Outcome%20Document.pdf#page=30.

65. As of August 25, 2016. For the list of these resolutions, see http://www.globalr2p.org/resources/335.

66. Henry Kissinger, *World Order* (New York: Penguin, 2014), 30, 26.

## CONCLUSION

1. See Helen McCarthy et al., "Introduction: Network Logic," in *Network Logic*, ed. Helen McCarthy et al., *Demos* 20 (2004): 11–21, 11–12.

# Acknowledgments

I have been working on networks for more than two decades and have wanted to write this book since 2009, when I became director of policy planning in the State Department under Secretary Hillary Clinton. When I came out of government in January 2011, I immediately returned to teaching at Princeton's Woodrow Wilson School. That spring, and again in the spring of 2012, I taught a seminar called Making Networks Work. The students joined me in exploring the academic literature on networks from multiple disciplines, looking for ways to turn description into prescription. When I began assembling research materials for this book, I started with their final papers. I am grateful to Alex Bollfrass, Ani Akinbiyi, Will Tucker, Derek Kilner, Sarita Vanka, Melissa Lan, Eugen Yazdani, Nate Adler, Nat Myers, Chloe Poynton, Jordan Lee, Karen Grissette, Rebecca Cousins, Christopher Deutsch, Rebekah Grindlay, Andrew Hyslop, Heidi Jovanovic, Brian Kelly, Eung Ji Kim, Benjamin Naimark-Rouse, Laura Noonan, Nicole Ruder, Kevin Smith, Mary Svenstrup,

# ACKNOWLEDGMENTS

Kathleen Uribe, Baligh Yehia, Farah Ahmad, and Christopher Domencic. Elizabeth Sully and Joshua Haecker also provided valuable research assistance during this period.

I planned to start writing this book in the summer of 2012, but found myself heading in a quite different direction for the next three years as a result of an article I published in the *Atlantic* in June 2012 entitled "Why Women Still Can't Have It All." I embarked on a different book, *Unfinished Business: Women, Men, Work, Family*, which was published by Random House in 2015. I worked very closely during that period with a talented editing team, publisher Susan Kamil and editor Sam Nicholson. They made me a better writer, which in turn made this book easier to write, and I hope easier to read.

In 2013 I received a welcome invitation from the distinguished political theorist Ian Shapiro, director of the MacMillan Center at Yale, to deliver the Stimson Lectures. I agreed not only owing to the prestige of the Lectures themselves, but also because of the chance to tie myself to the mast and ensure that this book would get written. I ultimately gave the lectures in November 2015 and am grateful to Ian, the staff of the MacMillan Center, and the excellent audiences for all three lectures; several audience members suggested specific things I should read or add. Even when I was not able to follow your advice, you helped my thinking. My indispensable former assistant, Hana Passen, also prepared the slides for those lectures and ran down various sources.

I could not have made it through the final stretch of turning those lectures into the present book without Gordon LaForge, who began as my research assistant and became an invaluable thought and writing partner. He read sources on his own and made suggestions and improvements through many successive drafts. My Yale University Press editor, Bill Frucht, has been excited about this book from the beginning; his enthusiasm and input sustained me throughout the writing process. Simon Levin, George M. Moffett Professor of Biology and Professor of Ecology and Evolutionary Biology at Princeton, took an interest in this book from the beginning and generously pointed me to work that I might never have otherwise encountered. Simon's own work on complexity and resilience won him the National Medal of Science in 2015. My longtime friend, mentor, and colleague Robert Keohane gave me his special brand of tough love, reading the final manuscript and improving it even in areas where we continue to disagree. Allison Stanger, a friend and supporter in so many ways, read the entire manuscript twice and made it better.

Chris Fussell, Charles Goodyear, David Zaring, and Tom Hale all provided valuable research leads; Peter Bergen, Nadia Oweidat, Rabia Chaudry, and two anonymous reviewers contributed useful comments on all or parts of the final manuscript. Dan Heaton was a terrific copy editor; I am also grateful to the rest of my Yale University Press team, particularly Karen Olson. And I have never yet succeeded in writing a book without my longtime assistant Terry Murphy, who is an editor in her own right and an indispensable partner in getting things done! Isabel Bonnyman has also managed to keep my office running through the final throes of turning a manuscript into a book.

I stand on the shoulders of many scholars and thinkers in writing this book, some of whom I know personally from twenty-five years in the academy. I have that tried to make my debts clear in the text and will refrain from repeating them here.

Will Lippincott is the best agent anyone could ask for: a combination of friend, advocate, confidante, and gentle but effective noodge. Those of us who have been privileged to work with him count ourselves lucky.

Finally, as always, my greatest debt is to my family. As I wrote at length in *Unfinished Business*, everything that I do rests on that foundation: my brothers, my sisters-in-law, my uncles, aunts, cousins, nieces, nephews, and biologically unrelated people who have become family members over the years. I owe special thanks to my parents, to whom I dedicate this book; my sons, who have pursued their own remarkable journeys over the past two years; and above all my beloved husband, Andrew Moravcsik, who can be irascible and frustrating, but is so often right.

# *Illustration Credits*

Figure 1. Matthew A. Russell, *Mining the Social Web: Data Mining Facebook, Twitter, LinkedIn, Google+, GitHub, and More*, 2nd ed. (Sebastopol, CA: O'Reilly, 2013). Copyright © 2014 Matthew A. Russell. All rights reserved. Used with permission.

Figure 3. Paul Baran, "On Distributed Communications: I. Introduction to Distributed Communications Networks," RAND Corporation (1964). Reprinted with permission.

Figures 4, 5. Albert-Laszlo Barabasi, *Linked: How Everything Is Connected and What It Means for Business, Science, and Everyday Life* (New York: Plume, 2003). Copyright © 2003, reprinted by permission of Penguin Group Inc.

Figure 6. Zeev Maoz et al., "What Is the Enemy of My Enemy? Causes and Consequences of Imbalanced International Relations, 1816–2001," *Journal of Politics* 69, no. 1 (2007): 100–115. Published by the University of Chicago Press. Reprinted with permission.

Figures 10, 11. Stanley McChrystal et al., *Team of Teams: New Rules of Engagement for a Complex World* (New York: Portfolio/Penguin, 2015), copyright © 2015 McChrystal Group LLC, used by permission of Portfolio, an imprint of Penguin Publishing Group, a division of Penguin Random House LLC.

Figures 12, 13. Henry Chesbrough, *Open Innovation: The New Imperative for Creating and Profiting from Technology* (Boston: Harvard Business School Press, 2003). Copyright © 2003 Harvard Business Publishing Corporation; all rights reserved; reprinted by permission of Harvard Business Review Press.

Figure 14. Jeremy Heimans and Henry Timms, "Understanding 'New Power,'" *Harvard Business Review*, December 2014. Copyright © 2014 Harvard Business Publishing Corporation; all rights reserved; reprinted by permission of *Harvard Business Review*.

# Index